LOVING LINCOLN

Loving Lincoln

A Personal History of the Women Who Shaped Lincoln's Life and Legacy

STACY LYNN

Southern Illinois University Press
Carbondale

Southern Illinois University Press
siupress.com

Printed in the United States of America

First printed April 2025.

Jacket and cover illustration: Cover illustration by Steve Kress, based on a photo of the author by Levi Shand.

Frontispiece: Photograph of Abraham Lincoln, circa 1846, by Nicholas Shepherd, Springfield, Illinois. Library of Congress, Prints and Photographs, https://www.loc.gov/pictures/item/2004664400/

ISBN 978-0-8093-3966-2 (cloth)
ISBN 978-0-8093-3967-9 (paperback)
ISBN 978-0-8093-3968-6 (ebook)
This book has been catalogued with the Library of Congress.

Printed on recycled paper ♻

SIU
Southern Illinois University System

For Savannah, to the memory of Mackenzie,
and in honor of all the women who never had
a chance to tell their own stories.

I want in all cases to do right, and most particularly so, in all cases with women.

—Abraham Lincoln, August 16, 1837

CONTENTS

PART IV: WOMEN, THE LAW, AND LAWYER LINCOLN

PART V: WOMEN AND PRESIDENT LINCOLN

PART VI: WOMEN AND LINCOLN'S LEGACY

ILLUSTRATIONS

PREFACE

I TOOK MY SEAT on the platform in a motel ballroom in Springfield, Illinois. My legs were wobbly. My stomach was rumbling because I had not eaten all day, my body too nervous for food in those early days of public speaking. It was one of my first historical conferences as a participant. My inexperience had set fire to my nerves, and my master's degree in history from a small, public university was a thump of inadequacy in my head. I was an interloper, a young woman in heavy eyeliner among silver-haired scholars with PhDs and blazers with elbow patches. It was a month before I gained admission to the doctoral program in history at the University of Illinois. I lacked scholarly pedigree and confidence, and Lincoln studies was unwelcoming to women.

I was, however, fast accumulating historical knowledge about the law and Abraham Lincoln as an assistant editor at the Lincoln Legal Papers Project. Founded in 1985 in Springfield to document Lincoln's law practice, the Project had the imprimatur of the Abraham Lincoln Association, the Illinois Historic Preservation Agency, and the University of Illinois Springfield (UIS), which employed me and other staff editors. Our modest offices were in the Old State Capitol's basement, but we were on the verge of becoming the Papers of Abraham Lincoln, a step that would increase not only the scope of our work but also our national exposure, staff, and grant funding from the National Endowment for the Humanities, the National Historical Publications and Records Commission, the State of Illinois, UIS, and private donors.

Despite the Project's rising fortunes, my position was soft funded and precarious. In fact, I was an accidental editor of Lincoln's papers, having fallen into an internship in 1992, which led to short-term contracts and then to a full-time position in 1996. When you only have a master's degree in history, you cling to any employment in the field you can find, and my job at the Lincoln Papers provided a paycheck and health care for my young family. My salary reflected my status at the bottom of the Project's hierarchy, and I did not expect to remain long term. I had two colleagues who encouraged me to stay the Lincoln course, but the director discouraged my application to doctoral programs and asked me to consider whether it was fair to my husband and two young daughters to take on such a challenge. He thought I was a mom with a history hobby. Fortunately, my husband and daughters cheered me on, and I possessed just enough audacity to apply to the University of Illinois, to which I was accepted. Doctoral work would prove to the doubters—and to myself—that I was serious about history and serious, too, about Lincoln. I planned to keep clinging to Abraham Lincoln as long as possible, but in March 2000 I was a nobody presenting a Lincoln paper far from groundbreaking at an obscure public history conference.

On the platform, I shuffled my notes. I picked at my bloody cuticles. I watched people arrive, the chattering hum in the room growing louder as they met friends and found seats.

And then Abraham Lincoln arrived, doffing his stovepipe hat.

The tension in my jaw released into a smile.

A second Abraham Lincoln entered the room. Then a third. Then a fourth. Four bearded men dressed in black dusters, deliberately disheveled cravats, and versions of Lincoln's iconic hat were taking their seats in my audience. Four Abraham Lincolns. At a small history conference in Lincoln's hometown. Attending a session on the topic of Abraham Lincoln's law practice.

Nearly eighty years after Lincoln settled in Springfield, the wistful poet and fellow Springfieldian Vachel Lindsay wrote: "Abraham Lincoln walks at midnight . . . a bronzed, lank man!"[1] There I was, eighty-six years after Lindsay's poem, also aware of Lincoln's presence—although not an ethereal one mourning the tragedy of world war but a corporeal one in the form of grown men in costumes.

I had lived in Springfield long enough to understand that Abraham Lincoln was more than a favorite son and famous tether to the past, more engrained in the city's identity than the imposing state capitol building and its role as the seat of Illinois government. I often saw these living Lincolns. They were part of the cityscape, ubiquitous in restaurants and shops and on the plaza surrounding the Old State Capitol during fall festivals, art fairs, and conventions. They were frequent participants of popular public events at the Lincoln Home, the Lincoln Tomb, and the Lincoln and Herndon Law Office.

Unlike the real Lincoln when he walked Springfield's clapboard sidewalks, these Lincoln presenters always have beards, and they rarely stand six feet and four inches. I smiled at those four Lincolns in my audience as I evaluated their relative Lincoln-ness. One of the four Lincolns looked taller than the real Lincoln and one much shorter. One looked nothing at all like Lincoln beyond his costume. And one I recognized as a locally famous Mr. Lincoln. Seeing Lincoln on the streets was normal but seeing four Lincolns in the audience at a history-conference felt ridiculous. The absurdity, however, eased the tension in my muscles, calmed my public-speaking anxiety, and made me fall in love with my professional life.

Oh, no. I have caught the Lincoln bug and there is no cure for it.

I had tried to resist the lure of Mr. Lincoln in the face of my tentative position at the Lincoln Papers, but just like Mary Todd I succumbed to Lincoln's charms. I had fallen into Lincoln studies like Alice down the rabbit hole. What a wonderful world I found there. I could no longer deny the glorious coincidence of my historical circumstances either: I was a budding historian living in an 1860s house on Lincoln Avenue in Lincoln's Springfield, with one daughter attending Lincoln School and the other attending a school named for Lincoln's friend Jesse K. Dubois. I was working for a project collecting and editing Lincoln's legal papers in the building where Lincoln delivered his House Divided speech. And so, therefore and to wit, with four Abraham Lincolns as my witnesses, I hitched my scholarly wagon to Abraham Lincoln and never looked back.

Five months later, I was a doctoral student at the University of Illinois in the history department made famous by Lincoln scholar James G. Randall. I wrote a dissertation in legal history with Lincoln's law practice at its center, and I, too, became a Lincoln scholar. My plan to stay the Lincoln course, which I reaffirmed with the completion of my PhD in 2007 and my rise to associate editor and assistant director of the Lincoln Papers in 2009, offered intellectual rewards. I was a coeditor of the groundbreaking digital edition *The Law Practice of Abraham Lincoln* and the award-winning, four-volume letterpress edition of *The Papers of Abraham Lincoln: Legal Documents and Cases.* I was a founding editor of the Papers of Abraham Lincoln, a project to digitize and transcribe Lincoln's documents from the Illinois legislature to the presidency.

Studying Lincoln, editing his papers, engaged in innovative work in digital humanities was a dream profession, providing a bevy of research topics and affording opportunities for writing, travel, and engagements I could never have imagined. During my tenure as a Lincoln editor, I published a book based on my dissertation and a Mary Lincoln biography. I wrote dozens of essays and book reviews, spoke on the stage at Ford's Theatre, appeared in two Lincoln documentaries, and joined the board of the prestigious Abraham Lincoln Institute. Along my Lincoln path, I also assembled a brilliant collection of Lincoln folk, people who possess a ceaseless intellectual curiosity about Lincoln but who also find joy in the absurdities dancing around the edges of scholarship, people who, like me, have Lincoln bobbleheads on their bookcases next to full sets of *The Collected Works of Abraham Lincoln.*

I was one lucky Lincoln duck, privileged to be engaged not only in the niche field of historical editing but also in digitizing Lincoln documents at the Copley Library in La Jolla, California, the University of Maine in Bangor, and in more than one hundred repositories and private collections in between. I conducted research at institutions famous for their Lincoln collections, including the Abraham Lincoln Presidential Library, the Library of Congress, the National Archives, the Illinois State Archives, and special collections libraries at Harvard, Yale, and Indiana University. I scanned one of the five copies of the Gettysburg Address, identified letter fragments found in the walls of the Lincoln Home, oversaw the complicated digitization of a twenty-five-foot-long petition to President Lincoln at the New-York Historical Society, and scanned the Lincoln legal documents owned by former Illinois governor Jim Thompson while chatting with Big Jim in his Chicago law office overlooking Lake Michigan. At the time I left the Papers of Abraham Lincoln in November 2016, my colleagues and I in Springfield and Washington had digitized 102,000 Lincoln documents, in addition to the more than 90,000 legal documents we had already published.

Despite thrilling discoveries, fulfilling work, and gratitude for earning a salary with benefits to study Abraham Lincoln, there was a dark side to my Lincoln journey. Like Lincoln's own melancholy, there was pain below the surface of my joy and good fortune. My struggle was, in part, rooted in my own insecurities. Unattached to an academic department, I always felt outranked by tenured professors who published books and appeared on television. I felt trapped between academic and public history. Even though I was suited to editing work, I pined for a professorship, a job far easier to explain than scholarly editing. I knew editing Lincoln's papers made me a Lincoln scholar. But would Lincoln studies ever accept me as one?

Not long after making Abraham Lincoln my historical muse, I traveled to St. Louis for the Organization of American Historians annual meeting to give a paper on digital historical editing. At an evening reception, a colleague introduced me to a prominent scholar. The man did not say hello or extend his hand in greeting. Instead, he leaned back, his chin resting on his chest, and ogled me, up and down, avoiding my eyes. Then, in a booming voice, he said: "You must be the new Lincoln Legal eye candy." I should not have been shocked, because his reputation preceded him. In fact, I had prepared myself to endure something gross. Yet nothing could have prepared me for the crestfallen slump of my ego and the humiliation burning on my cheeks. His comment was not half of the offense, however. While I stood there pursing my lips to contain my scream, three male colleagues standing with me in that god-awful cocktail circle, sipped their drinks in awkward silence.

I was silent, too. I was having a conversation in my head with Abraham Lincoln. He was horrified on my behalf. He was on my side, even if no one, not even me, would offer a defense. Lincoln was worth this little indigestion, I said to myself, and I believed it. I was heartbroken but not broken, because I believed in Abraham Lincoln.

I am the scholar I am today because of my determination in the face of disrespect and rejection, but the indignities were painful. Another formative affront came a few years after the wretched cocktail party from an older man I liked despite his arrogance and abrasive personality. He was brilliant and funny, and I enjoyed talking with him. In a convention center hallway between sessions of a history conference, we were talking when he stopped short, looked at me with a furrowed brow, and asked: "Do you think anyone takes you seriously in such heavy eye makeup?"

My mind raced to the bathroom mirror, to the morning hours when I had painted on my eyeliner, the only makeup I have ever applied with care.

No. Same as always. Less, in fact, now,
because it is hot, and I am sweating.

I looked back at this man, standing there in his tweed blazer with elbow patches. I was in my mid-thirties, a mother, a grown-up professional woman with four semesters of cutthroat doctoral seminars under my belt, but I was shocked, once again, into silence. I did not respond, channeling not Lincoln this time but my mother.

If you don't have anything nice to say, keep your mouth shut.

In my head, I had my own questions.

Do you wonder if the curated stubble or combovers of my male
colleagues make them suspect? Do you say such things aloud to men?

His question stung me because while he was speaking for himself, I suspected his question was on the tips of other male tongues. His question was a harbinger of all the times a man would take credit for my ideas, talk over me, or tell me I talked too much and should listen more. His question was a classic riff on a tired old power dynamic at play. He was an older, respected scholar, a man with a prestigious doctoral degree. I was a young woman, still a doctoral student with only one publication to my name. That distance between us had falsely given him license to ask me such a question, the same as it had silenced my defense.

Yet I did not abandon my eyeliner after that embarrassing conversation. Instead, every morning afterward, its application became a putting on of armor, my preparation for all the battles I would fight in the contentious field of Lincoln studies. Years later, with the personal confidence earning a PhD provides and with the experience that comes from living long as a woman in a sexist society, I broached the eyeliner comment with that curmudgeon. Oddly, perhaps, I still liked him; and I liked him even more when he apologized. He was embarrassed, he said. He admitted he was wrong, and he wished I would have called him out all those years ago. But I was in no place to call him out back then and he was in no place to hear it. We all live, and we learn. Hopefully, we grow, including scholars in eyeliner as well as in tweed.

These painful experiences compelled me to a civil voice in the dissonance of Lincoln studies. They helped me better understand women's historical experiences. They also made me a defender of the most important woman in Lincoln's life. The vitriol toward Mary Lincoln in the field is as strong as the love for her husband, and fighting hard against it, for her and for me, gave me purpose. By the time I published my Mary Lincoln biography in 2015, my heart was beyond the reach of the uncivil. I was too brave to be rattled by the doubters. I outgrew the need for acceptance from those who would not give it.

During my year of Mary Lincoln book talks, I gracefully fielded hostile questions from men in my audiences who prefaced their questions with negative comments about Mary Lincoln. They dismissed her as crazy and accused me of wrongly protecting her. One prominent Lincoln scholar publicly accused me of peddling "lies" about Mary Lincoln. I did not dignify his comment with a response. I did not need to. By then I had the wisdom to know his words reflected his character, not mine.

It makes me sad that Lincoln studies is rife with such hostility; it seems to me anathema to the qualities we admire in Abraham Lincoln.

But Lincoln studies does not have the sexist market cornered. I have heard dozens of stories from women across academia and in other fields who have felt marginalized, talked over, talked down to, and dismissed as irrelevant. I have listened to too many women tell me their stories about sexual assault or harassment in the classroom, in the workplace, and at professional conferences. I do not share my experiences to be provocative, to seek sympathy, or to defame Lincoln studies, from which I have experienced far more civility and collegiality than disrespect. I share them because they are at the root of my becoming. They are the wounds and the lessons I collected on my journey to this book about Abraham Lincoln. I honor those wounds and lessons because they fueled me in the way struggle inspires the determined.

I am grateful for these experiences because they trained my eyes on the women. They made me look for the unheralded stories around every Lincoln corner. Stories about Lincoln's pioneer mothers. Stories about Mary Lincoln, the smart, sassy woman who nurtured her husband's ambitions. Stories about the female friends with whom Lincoln could confide his failings and his grief. Stories about the women who hired Lincoln to help them divorce their husbands, secure their dowers, defend them in criminal court, collect debts owed them, and sue men who slandered them, calling into question the most important thing they owned: their character. Stories of women who appealed to President Lincoln during the Civil War, seeking remedy for their suffering: women like Juliette

Kinzie, who sought permission from Lincoln to send supplies to her daughter and grandchildren trapped in Savannah; Matilda Ivers, who was seeking a job in the Treasury Department; and Fanny Ames, who asked Lincoln to discharge her son who was too young to be in the army.

Focusing on the shadows of the Lincoln story, gazing on the periphery, gave me distance from the discouraging experiences. I believed working in the margins of Lincoln studies, editing his papers and writing about the women, would keep me safe. It was false security. It did not protect me. However, it gave me something far more valuable: my voice. What began as an unconscious method of survival and then a coping strategy became a beautiful, breathing entity all its own, informing and shaping my perspective.

Loving Lincoln is a biography of a man through the collective biography of women, but it is also a memoir of my personal relationship with Abraham Lincoln and with history. My personal and professional experiences, my spirit, and my wistful, joyful engagement with the historical figures I study inform my understanding of the past.

Loving Lincoln is my scholarly goodbye to the man I have loved so long. It is my emergence as Stacy Lynn, the historian formerly known as Stacy Pratt McDermott. I claim both women as myself, but all the love, the

The author in reproduction stovepipe hat, 2009. Author's Photo

loss, and the history I have experienced as a human and as a scholar are now vested in a new life, a new journey, and a new name. As a scholar I have now returned to the Progressive Era, back where I started before that fateful internship at the Lincoln Legal Papers. Before I move on, I want to tell my collected tales of women and Abraham Lincoln to paint a picture of women's historical experiences across the ages. In shining the light on women, I am doing right by Lincoln and doing right by myself.

Abraham Lincoln's compassionate heart steered a young, timid female scholar through the rough waters of Lincoln studies and made her an industrious, honest, and successful editor and historian. It took me half a lifetime to earn the pluck necessary to tackle such a personal book as this one. Time and distance have made me bold. Love and loss and history gave me courage.

I have earned my tweed blazer with elbow patches.

But I still rock the eyeliner.

Stacy Lynn
October 2024

ACKNOWLEDGMENTS

I CANNOT DO ANY creative or intellectual work without the emotional support of my family, which is small but mighty. My daughter Savannah McDermott and her husband Levi Shand are my reason for being. My sister Tracy Pratt Wavering and her husband Jason Wavering feed me and keep me safe. My ever-optimistic niece Zoe Wavering gives me hope. My sweet mother Marie Pollard and her husband Mike Pollard offer unconditional love. My closest female friends lift me up and make me brave, stretching my brain, keeping my heart open, and offering wisdom and encouragement. I am grateful for my Springfield Sallies: Sandra Mutman Doyle, Alicia Erickson, Maureen McKinney, and Christi Parsons; my childhood friend Bridgett Jensen, who has seen the best and worst of me at every age; the Writer Babes: Mary Maddox, Daiva Markelis, and Angela Vietto; my three college roommates who are always on Team Stacy: Julie Feigl, Michelle Kauble, and Diane Opperman; and Marilyn Mueller, who will drive miles and miles with me to see sunflowers and bakes the best damn cookies in the world. I want to thank Paul Beals, Pam Brown, Ann Brownson, Will Cooley, James Cornelius, StaLynn Davis, David Gerleman, Patrick Doyle, Charlotte England, Kurt Erickson, Dan Hagen, Jennifer Halperin, Kathryn Harris, Callie Hawkins, Cynthia Larsen, Ann Liston, John Lupton, Carol Manning, Kevin McDermott, Dave McKinney, Cody Moser, Terry Mutchler, Boyd Murphree, Ronda Schappaugh, Glenna Schroeder-Lein, Carol Stevens, and Jay Vlahon. At various times since my daughter's death, each has offered a kindness or two or three or more that kept me from losing my mind and giving up on living.

I am indebted to my earliest academic mentors Robert Kuhn McGregor and the late Deborah Kuhn McGregor who saw a scholar in me long before I saw one in myself. Vernon Burton was *the* best PhD mentor I could have ever imagined. He taught me so much about life and history, allowing me the freedom to embrace my unique perspective and to be a brave historian on an unusual path. I was fortunate to study constitutional history with the great Lincoln scholar Phillip Paludan and legal history with Christopher Waldrep; and Professors Jim Barrett, Fred Hoxie, and Dave Roediger at the University of Illinois supported my unconventional journey through my doctoral program. I am also grateful to David Racine and the University of Illinois Springfield, whose support of me never wavered when the Lincoln Papers fell apart.

I also want to thank my Lincoln friends: Ed Doadt, Geoff Elliott, Mary Fincher, David Kent, Jen Price, Laura Rowland, and John Winterbauer. They cheered me on from afar. Their love of history and Abraham Lincoln gives me perspective, reminding me that studying Lincoln has been more than an occupation. It has been a joy.

I want to acknowledge Sylvia Frank Rodrigue, executive editor at Southern Illinois University Press. A decade or so ago, she asked me to call her first when I was ready to write my book on Abraham Lincoln. I am glad I called her, because she has been a cheerful stalwart of my quirky book through the entire process. I am ever grateful for her faith.

Finally, I want to sing the praises of my colleagues at the Jane Addams Papers Project: Cathy Moran Hajo and Tori Sciancalepore. These two smart and gentle women assisted me during a difficult transition in my life. To work in a healthy, nurturing environment with such good women is a privilege; to document the life of the incomparable Jane Addams with them is an honor.

It has been a pleasure to be on this earth with all these good people. They have shared my joy, witnessed my sorrow, supported me, taught me, checked in on me, and laughed with me, and some have read drafts of this book. I am alive and well because of them. Every human life is a collection of stories made up of the overlapping stories of all the people who accompany us on our journey. We are all connected, made better and made whole by one another. I have been fortunate with the companions who have traveled this life with me. This book reflects what has been for me a sentimental journey. Those with hardened hearts need not venture forth.

NOTE ON TRANSCRIPTIONS

THE ESSAYS IN THIS volume are replete with the words of Abraham Lincoln, the women who knew him, and the women who have written about him and contributed to his legacy. Most transcriptions from letters and documents I present within are from the *Collected Works of Abraham Lincoln*, *Mary Todd Lincoln: Her Life and Letters*, and the Abraham Lincoln Papers at the Library of Congress. However, in some instances I have standardized punctuation and capitalization and corrected misspellings for easier reading. Any [bracketed] text is editorial content I have added to provide ready clarity for the reader.

LOVING LINCOLN

Introduction

> To this place, and the kindness of these people, I owe everything.
>
> —Abraham Lincoln, Springfield, Illinois, February 11, 1861

In 1860, CAMPAIGN BIOGRAPHERS crafted an image of Abraham Lincoln as a self-made man. Coined by Lincoln's political hero Henry Clay in an 1832 speech, the phrase had woven its way into the fabric of an American ideal. In America, there was a grand belief that any white man could rise on his own hard work and merits. Abraham Lincoln was a poor boy, born into what he defined as "undistinguished families."[1] He had risen from son of a dirt farmer to middle-class lawyer. Despite having no family wealth and no formal education, he found a profession and parlayed his passion for politics into the Illinois House of Representatives and the United States Congress and then onto his party's ticket for the presidency.

He had done it.

All by himself.

Or so people thought, and so people have said.

It was a political choreography writ large in a historic presidential campaign. Lincoln, the rail-splitting common man, would become the sixteenth U.S. president. The rags-to-riches, up-by-his-bootstraps image is an intoxicating one, as much now as it was in 1860. Lincoln's rise from log cabin to White House is carved into the granite of his legacy and is legend in Lincoln biography, despite the fact that four U.S. presidents before him and untold numbers of successful people in Lincoln's generation were born in log cabins.[2] Lincoln embraced the image of a man in shirtsleeves splitting rails, despite his friend Eliza Browning's fears that the rail-splitter image overshadowed Lincoln's intellectual gifts. Yet the self-made ideal was, indeed, a motivator for men of Lincoln's generation, and voters responded to the image of their leaders as self-made.[3]

I might say I am a self-made Lincoln historian. I earned my degrees at public universities and did not benefit from family legacy or elite academic pedigree. For twenty-five years I quietly toiled, editing Lincoln's papers. Despite my place on the periphery of academia, I made a Lincoln career for myself and wrote this book all by myself. But I did not make a career in Lincoln studies all by myself. All my experiences, good and bad, and all my professional and human relationships, great and awful, played a role in my making. All my disappointments as well as my triumphs paved the path I journeyed, and over every cobblestone on the road there were people all around me.

This road is the way every life unfolds. I am no more a self-made woman than Abraham Lincoln was a self-made man. Lincoln played the role for the campaign, but he knew he did not rise alone. When he stood on the platform in Springfield, Illinois, on February 11, 1861, just before departing on the train for Washington, he said: "To this place, and the kindness of these people, I owe everything."[4]

The American legend of Lincoln's rise is a myth. It subdues historical realities and denies the familial, social, and professional connections that make a man. It denies the role of economic and political contexts, professional opportunities, and the people who help and hinder a person along the way. It ignores a man's humanity, and it is a gross denial of women. There is no man without a woman who labored to bring him into the world. All the stories of all the great men throughout history are tangled up with the stories of sisters and wives and female cousins, women friends and the wives of male friends, female professional acquaintances, and even the women dreamed about and read about across a lifetime. Just as my life is filled, fulfilled, hindered, inspired, engaged, enraged, nurtured, neglected, heckled, or cheered on by men, so was every man's life filled, fulfilled, hindered, inspired, engaged, enraged, nurtured, neglected, heckled, or cheered on by women. Men do not become men or legends on their own. No lawyer ever built a law practice without clients. No politician wins an election without voters. Leaders are unnecessary if there is no one to follow.

Women surrounded Abraham Lincoln. Nancy Lincoln gave birth to him. His sister Sarah played with him at their mother's knee, where he learned his first lessons of family, community, and life. Stepmother Sarah Lincoln finished raising him, and stepsisters Betsy and Matilda loved their new brother the rest of their lives. Ann Rutledge touched his tender, young man's heart, and Elizabeth Abell and Hannah Armstrong befriended him when he was young and poor and had no idea who he was. Nancy Dorman, Hannah Goode, Emma Stark, Mary Shelby, and dozens of other women hired Lincoln to be their attorney, trusting him with their cases and often with the intimate details of their personal and financial lives. They paid him fees, contributing to his livelihood as well as to his developing legal expertise, to say nothing of what exposure to their economic and social circumstances as women taught him about America, inequality, society, and the human spirit. And then there was Mary Lincoln, the woman who was his life partner for twenty-three years, helped him build a middle-class life, nurtured his political ambitions, and brought into his life four children and a bevy of sisters, a beloved cousin, and a maiden aunt who became his family.[5]

Lincoln was a man made in beautiful combination with a family, a wife, male colleagues, friends of both sexes, antebellum American society, his chosen profession of the law, historical circumstances, the emergence of the Middle West, the growing economic and political importance of Illinois, and the integrity and compassion born in his own heart and bloomed in great measure by the love and tending of women. Lincoln was a man among men, but he was also a man among women.

Historian and Lincoln biographer Jean Baker argues that biography is social history, that through historical biography "minor figures become vehicles through which themes, cultures, and even ideas can be revealed."[6] But what if we focus on the minor figures in great lives? What if for a heroic figure like Abraham Lincoln, we train our eyes on the lesser-known lives intersecting his own? As the sociologist Anna Malaika Tubbs argues, the lives of the mothers of great men give us illustrative perspectives on history. The life experiences of great men and the history they lived are always informed by women who walked through those life experiences with them.[7]

Abraham Lincoln was infinitely curious about the world, eager to learn from every experience. It would be absurd to argue he learned nothing from women.

I have spent years wondering what Abraham Lincoln, a humble and serious man, would make of the mythology surrounding his life and his legacy. What would he say about the Lincoln bobblehead in my cabinet of Lincoln curiosities or the price his faded signature on a document from a forgotten Illinois legal case fetches today in a manuscript auction?

What would he make of Mount Rushmore or his profile on a shiny new penny? He certainly could not have dreamed that editing his dusty old papers would make a career for a woman who was born 101 years after he died. These are ahistorical wonderings, I know, but if I could summon Abraham Lincoln, I think he would tell me I am right about the women. He would tell me stories about his mothers and his sisters. He would remember Elizabeth Abell's early encouragement. He would describe his concern for the women in his divorce cases. He would confirm that he loved Ann Rutledge *and* Mary Lincoln.

Historians train to evaluate historical evidence objectively. As a former colleague of mine used to say, objectivity is a worthy goal. But historians are as human as the historical figures they study. We often look for what we see, or want to see, in ourselves. We view our subjects wearing our unique colored glasses, no matter the effort we exert bending toward objectivity. We tell the stories we want to tell, and we look in the direction of our own truth. It is wise to admit this human subjectivity, and I believe embracing it opens me up to a wider understanding of the past.

Personal writing in the humanities has gained ground recently, and a genre that blends the personal and the historical is inspiration here. I am also turning biography a little sideways by viewing Lincoln's life not as a singular, spectacular story of one human's greatness but rather by understanding one man's story as the overlapping stories of the women within it. I am bending conventions of historical writing to invite emotional as well as intellectual connections with Lincoln and his American context. Narrative history can constrain the writer and impoverish the reader. My goal, by blurring the lines between history and personal history, biography and memoir, is for readers to feel the past as well as read it.[8]

Women's stories offer evidence of Abraham Lincoln's kindness and sensitivity, his patience, his moral center, his social and political virtues, the breadth of his compassion, and his inspirational legacy. They illustrate how the well-being of women was central to Lincoln's personal, professional, and political ethos. They also reveal the ways in which emotion and human connection defy the rigid boundaries of historical context and show how historical empathy opens the door to richer historical understanding. Wherever it is possible to do so, I let the women and Abraham Lincoln do the talking. Hearing their voices helps us to see ourselves in their experiences. If we view the past as a foreign country, as a place we can never visit, populated by people we can never fully understand, why should we care about history at all? History matters most if it engages our minds *and* our hearts.

Loving Lincoln is a collection of thirty historical and personal essays in honor of my thirty-year relationship with Abraham Lincoln. The Lincoln sources I use are the same ones all biographers use to tell Lincoln's story. All I do here is shift my gaze. I always saw Lincoln through a woman's eyes, but in writing this book I now see Lincoln's story as a breathtaking collection of stories of all the women who knew him, loved him, hired him as their lawyer, appealed to him when he was president, and contributed their female voices to his beautiful legacy. It is a humble refocusing, but the fresh new picture it paints is glorious.

Loving Lincoln is my love letter to all the women who loved a great man into being. It is an homage to the women who gave me and the world Abraham Lincoln.

PART I

Mothers, Sisters, and the Bosom of Family

1. *Earthly and Angel Mothers*

He was the best boy I ever saw.
—Sarah Lincoln, interview with William Herndon, September 8, 1865

THE TINY COMMUNITY AT Little Pigeon Creek in southern Indiana was primitive and remote but populated with brave, hopeful, hardworking women. These women understood what it meant to pick up everything you owned, load it into a wagon, and start over in a new place, often relocating and rebuilding with young children on the breast and at the knee. The backbone of extended families, isolated and huddled together in the trees, these women relied upon their inner strength and leaned on one another in this unsettled wilderness. While their husbands carved farms out of the rugged terrain, the women had little choice but to work until their bones ached and to pray their efforts would be good enough to make a better life for themselves and their children.

Indiana was brand new when Nancy Lincoln and her family arrived, and all the state could yet offer poor pioneers like her was affordable land, backbreaking work, and dreams. Although she had traveled just one state north and well understood the labor expected of farm women, she must have looked around that wild place in late 1816 and wondered if her husband Thomas had brought her and her two children to end of the earth. The unsettled Indiana landscape in winter was likely a shock to Nancy Lincoln, who had believed she would raise her children in Kentucky, marry them off there, and then die in the community that raised her. She had been born on the Virginia frontier on February 5, 1784, to Lucy Hanks, but she grew up in Kentucky in the bosom of extended family. On June 10, 1806, in Washington County, Kentucky, she married Thomas Lincoln. He was six years older than her, a child of a family, like hers, who came west from Virginia on the Wilderness Trail.

Thomas was a hardworking and literate man well known to Nancy's family, of similar stock and with shared community ties.[1]

In Kentucky, the Lincolns were not wealthy, but they were better situated than other families. Thomas Lincoln owned land, raised livestock, and built a farm on Knob Creek, northeast of Hodgenville, on a challenging piece of land full of clay and stones called Sinking Spring Farm. Lexington was eighty miles to the northeast, and Nashville 140 miles to the southeast, but Elizabethtown, the Hardin County seat, where the Lincolns had friends and family, was just fifteen miles north. Nancy Lincoln's children were born in the gorgeous, rural Kentucky landscape into a hardscrabble but respectable existence. Sarah, or Sally as she may have been called, came first on February 10, 1807, then Abraham on February 12, 1809, and later another boy who did not survive. The deliveries of Nancy's children were attended by female family members or perhaps a midwife well known to her, and she was surrounded by family to help her with her babies. Thomas Lincoln provided for the family by hunting and raising corn, clover, and alfalfa; and in 1816 he became a road surveyor. As they grew, Nancy's children did simple domestic chores and attended a country school at brief intervals. Sarah helped her mother cook, clean, and wash and mend clothes. Abraham ran errands and filled the wood bin. Both children helped their mother forage for berries and nuts.[2]

Life in Kentucky was hard, but it was familiar. It was home. Unfortunately, however, the Lincoln family would not write the rest of their story there. Two years after purchasing their farm, a large tract of the land came into dispute, and the outcome of litigation cost Thomas Lincoln his land title, which the law declared faulty. The family fell victim to the imperfect system of land titles in the state, and Thomas Lincoln decided to pack up and move north to the free state of Indiana. Indiana was the second state formed out of the Old Northwest Territory and was a land of opportunity, but Nancy Lincoln knew no dreams could come true in pioneer Indiana, or anywhere else, without women's hard work. She was thirty-two years old when she started all over again in frontier Indiana, with no towns and only about twenty families in the surrounding area. Gentryville, the nearest town more than a mile from where the Lincoln family settled, was not much of a town at all. Yet Thomas Lincoln had hope in the prospects of this fresh start, and he loaded the wagon with his wife, his children, and all their possessions. Beds and dishes and livestock dragged across the countryside, where there were no roads, Nancy Lincoln's husband cutting paths out of the brush as they traveled.[3]

During the first Indiana winter, Nancy did the best she could to keep her family warm, fed, and comfortable in the primitive lean-to cabin Thomas built upon their arrival. The family lived on what they hunted and foraged through the first winter and spring until Thomas could plant and harvest the first crops. One difficult task was clearing the land for farming, and in addition to her household duties, Nancy probably helped remove rocks from the soil, her children joining in and her son splitting logs and helping his father with the plowing. All farm children worked, contributing in whatever way their growing bodies allowed. No family could afford able-bodied members to sit idle.[4]

In the second year, in a more solid cabin, small and simple with a dirt floor, Nancy made a cozy home for her growing children. Eight-year-old Abraham was a sensitive, lanky child with dark hair, and ten-year-old Sarah was dark complected and dark haired but heavier built than her little brother. Nancy Lincoln hugged her children close, put her faith in her god, and relied on her stern but hardworking husband and her maternal relations to provide companionship and support. Nancy's twenty-year-old cousin Dennis Hanks had come with the Lincolns to Indiana, along with Betsy and Thomas Sparrow, an aunt and uncle with whom Nancy was raised in Kentucky. The migration of family groups was common, reducing risk and allowing for the pooling of work and resources as well as providing a ready community.[5]

Indiana soil was rich, and the forested areas were thick with game. But life in Indiana was far less settled than it had been in Kentucky, the clearance of land for agriculture just underway and towns springing up into tentative existence. We do not know many specific details about Nancy Lincoln's life in Indiana, but as one Lincoln scholar noted, "her brief story was that of the American pioneer woman."[6] We can assume there was great hardship, as there always was in a land where the soil was unbroken. Pioneers wagered all the body's energy on a gamble, and even middling success required great mettle. In 1859, Abraham Lincoln would describe his family heritage for a campaign biography as undistinguished, yet nothing could be more distinguished than a mother who is strong enough and brave enough to settle a wilderness, to face great hardship and scarcity, and to raise children to be productive adults and good human beings.[7]

Nancy Lincoln spent her brief time upon this earth in service to her home and family, and she dared not dream about riches for herself. She wore simple, homespun clothing, slept on a straw-filled mattress, grew vegetables, and cooked, cleaned, and cared for children. Frontier cabins during Nancy's lifetime were small, typically fifteen to eighteen feet in length and twelve to fourteen feet wide, divided into two rooms, space extended into the eaves to create sleeping lofts for children. Women cooked over open fires and conducted domestic tasks like sewing and churning butter, most chores performed in the same rooms where people (and sometimes animals) slept and where the family ate and greeted guests. Life was difficult on the frontier, but it was not without beauty and refuge. The Indiana landscape Nancy Lincoln knew was breathtaking, human bonds were forged there in shared purpose and struggle, and social activities like dances and harvest festivals smoothed the harsh edges of the frontier. Many historians have made a great fuss over the hardships of Abraham Lincoln's childhood, but it is important to remember his childhood was a typical pioneer childhood for children in Kentucky, Indiana, and Illinois, and it was not without grace and dignity. The Lincolns were typical Hoosiers, a "hardy, fearless and generally honest" bunch of settlers, rough and maybe a little reckless, but also hardworking, courageous, and general good folk.[8]

In 1818, just as the Lincoln family was making a home Nancy Lincoln might have recognized as permanent, the settlement at Little Pigeon Creek suffered an episode of "milk sick," an intestinal ailment caused by drinking the milk of a cow who had consumed poisonous white snakeroot. The tainted milk caused trembling, vomiting, and horrific abdominal pain. The condition was often fatal, a dreadful illness for which there was no remedy. Thomas and Betsy Sparrow fell ill first, and Nancy Lincoln nursed them. When they died, Thomas Lincoln made their coffins, perhaps with the assistance of his son. Nancy soon fell ill, too, succumbing to the illness on October 5, 1818. She was thirty-four years old. There were no doctors to tend to her. There was no medicine to soothe her. Hopefully, her children's faces at her bedside in the cabin she had made into a home gave her solace as she slipped away from the living.[9]

Nancy Lincoln missed raising her children to adulthood, but she made her mark upon them. Her death was a bitter loss for her son, who in a condolence letter to another grieving child in 1862 would write: "In this sad world of ours, sorrow comes to all; and, to the young, it comes with bitterest agony, because it takes them unawares."[10] Many children lost a parent in the early nineteenth century, but this truth was no solace to any child. His mother's death was a grief, but her life was the bigger influence on Abraham Lincoln. There are no portraits of Nancy Lincoln, and all descriptions of her come from reminiscences recorded long after her death. Abraham bore little resemblance to his father and looked somewhat like Dennis Hanks, so perhaps he favored his mother in appearance. People who knew Nancy described her as having brown hair and gray eyes; and Dennis Hanks remembered her as tall for the era with a thin frame like her son. Hanks also remembered it was Nancy who taught Lincoln his alphabet, charity, and kindness, and that she enjoyed her son's teasing. Sending her children to school, Nancy was the first person in the world to encourage Abraham's intellectual curiosity. From overlapping accounts, we know Nancy was intelligent, industrious, and kind, the qualities we admire in her son. As one friend who had known Lincoln and the Hanks families in Kentucky believed, Lincoln "inherited his good sense from the old stock of his Mother's relations."[11]

Although grief introduced itself early to Abraham Lincoln, he was lucky. A second mother stepped into his life to complete his journey to adulthood, to contribute to his wise understanding that although life has its sorrows, sorrow does not destroy a man's capacity to be useful and to find joy along the way. Sarah Bush Johnston was a blue-eyed, curly-haired widow with three children. Thomas Lincoln married her in December 1819 in Elizabethtown, Kentucky, and brought her and her children to Indiana. Sarah Lincoln was thirty-one when she arrived in Indiana to blend the motherless Lincoln family with her fatherless one.[12]

The new Mrs. Lincoln was resourceful and conscientious, a woman "of great energy" and "remarkable good sense."[13] She loved Nancy Lincoln's children like her own. "Abe was a good boy," she once said, "never gave me a cross word or look and never refused in fact, or even in appearance, to do anything I requested him."[14] In turn, Abraham loved his handsome new parent and called her Mother. She was a gentle counterbalance to his father who was stern and demanding and against whom Abraham, "a modest and sensitive lad," always chafed.[15] She improved the Lincoln

Wood engraving of Sarah Lincoln, n.d. Courtesy of Library of Congress, Prints and Photographs, https://www.loc.gov/pictures/item/2021792094/

cabin by adding her finer furniture and demanding a finished floor, and facilitated a loving blending of the five Lincoln-Johnston children. She made the Lincoln family cabin bright and cheerful again. Although not always easy, such blending of families was common in the early nineteenth century when many men and women died young and widows and widowers with young children remarried.[16]

Abraham Lincoln's childhood was not something he had to overcome. It gave him everything he needed to be a good man. Hard work and strong family relationships informed his childhood, the harsh realities of his humble upbringing softened by two nurturing mothers. When he left Indiana for Illinois with his family in March 1830, he was a twenty-one-year-old man, ready to make his way in the world, thanks to the unconditional love of two women. As he faced his future in Illinois, his pockets were packed with good memories and good grounding. When Sarah Lincoln kissed her stepson goodbye and sent him out on his own to find his life, she trusted he would do well in that life. The self-described "friendless, uneducated, penniless boy, working on a flat boat—at ten dollars per month" was ready to launch himself into the world.[17]

In 1837, Lincoln's parents settled permanently in rural Coles County in south-central Illinois, moving onto a farm in the Goosenest Prairie area, south of Charleston. Lincoln moved to Springfield the same year to start practicing law. Over the distance between them, Sarah Lincoln kept loving her stepson, as mothers are wont to do, and Lincoln made visits when his work took him to Charleston. In 1841, Lincoln purchased forty acres from his parents and gave them use of the land for their natural lives, a gesture to provide his mother financial security. After Thomas Lincoln died in January 1851, Sarah had a particular advocate in her stepson, who often ran interference from her biological son's attempts to take unfair advantage of their mother. Lincoln wanted his mother to suffer no "want of any comfort," and he always spoke of her with great affection.[18]

In 1842, when he eulogized his friend Benjamin Ferguson, Abraham Lincoln said: "After an illness of only six days, he closed his mortal existence . . . in the bosom of his family."[19] Abraham Lincoln often wrote about family, because when he took his first steps into the world on his own, he had the backbone of family in his body. He had two mothers to go in spirit with him. One mother was on the earth to keep him in her heart, and another "angel mother" was tucked deep into his own.[20]

2. *Sisters and Girls*

Is little Siss Eliza Davis at your house yet? If she is kiss her 'o'er and o'er again' for me.

—Abraham Lincoln to Mary Speed, asking after a young niece in the family, September 27, 1841

SARAH LINCOLN WAS TWO years older than her baby brother Abraham, but the family stories say he was the protective one. The Lincoln siblings were friends and happy playmates, and for short periods during their shared childhood in Kentucky and Indiana, they attended school together. Yet no experience would bind them together more closely than sitting beside the deathbed of their mother. When Nancy Lincoln died in October 1818, the household chores fell to Sarah. She was twelve, but the absence of a woman made her the home's keeper for her father, her brother, and cousin Dennis Hanks, who lived with the Lincolns. Sarah, a kind and amiable girl, fed the family and did her best to keep the house tidy, but these responsibilities sometimes overwhelmed her. She would sit by the fire and cry; and then Abraham and Dennis would fetch a baby animal—a racoon or a turtle—to cheer her up.[1]

When Thomas Lincoln married Sarah Johnston in 1819, little Sarah Lincoln's burdens lifted, and the wild, motherless months in the Lincoln cabin ended. Sarah and Abraham welcomed a kind stepmother and three Johnston siblings—twelve-year-old Betsy, nine-year-old John, and eight-year-old Matilda. It was a fast-blended Lincoln family full of playmates. "Tilda" Johnston, who remembered Abraham as "truthful, good to me—good to all," kept wonderful childhood memories of Lincoln-Johnston shenanigans. When their parents were away, Abraham would keep his siblings in line by reading aloud, telling stories, or delivering speeches with moral lessons. Once when John threw a turtle against a tree, Abraham admonished him and lectured the others to be kind to animals. Matilda remembered one story of Abraham's maturity, when he was on his way out to the field to work: "I ran—jumped on his back—cut my foot on the axe," she remembered. "We said—'What will we tell Mother as to how this happened': I said I would tell her 'I cut my foot on the axe that will be no lie'—said Lincoln, 'but it won't be all the truth—the whole truth—will it Tilda—Tell the whole truth and risk your Mother.'"[2]

Life in the enlarged Lincoln family had its struggles and the cabin was crowded, but the childhood experiences within it were typical of the era. There was work and laughter, love, and mischief. Childhood in Indiana for the Lincoln children meant farm labor and household chores, reliance on seasonal foods and wild game, and frosty winter nights spent shivering under quilts. There was also joy and learning in the household. It is something of legend that Abraham Lincoln suffered under his stern, uncompromising father. Lincoln's father was indeed a somber, serious man, but he was not an ogre. And Abraham Lincoln had three sisters, kind and precious. Childhood was warm and companionable. As Lincoln himself later remembered it in verse: "My childhood-home I see again, / And gladden with the view; / And still, as mem'ries crowds my brain, / There's pleasure in it too. . . . Now twenty years have passed away, / Since here I bid farewell / To woods, and fields, and scenes of play / And school-mates loved so well. . . ."[3]

It is not great poetry, but the sentiment is human and lovely and true. And sisters were part of the stories in Lincoln's fond childhood memories.

From an early age, Abraham Lincoln eschewed organized religion, but his sister Sarah became religious in her teens. In 1823, she joined the Little Pigeon Creek Baptist Church with her father and stepmother. There she met Aaron Grigsby, a fellow congregant. The young couple married in August 1826 when Sarah was nineteen, and they settled close to her family home. About her married life we know little, although there is one questionable reminiscence suggesting that Aaron Grigsby was a disagreeable young man. We can assume Sarah's domestic life mirrored that of both her mothers, that she was occupied with domestic tasks. Proximity to her Lincoln family soothed her; but while Abraham, Betsy, John, and Matilda would grow up to raise children of their own, Sarah Grigsby was not so lucky. On January 20, 1828, she delivered a stillborn child and died from complications of childbirth. Few mortality statistics or studies exist for the early nineteenth century, but childbirth deaths were common, a majority caused by puerperal fever (postpartum infection). That many mothers and newborns died, however, was no solace for Sarah's family. Sorrows go deep when one is young, but Abraham Lincoln's childhood in Indiana included a bevy of women to both soften life's harsh realities and to model strength.[4]

Abraham Lincoln had two mothers, and he had three sisters to watch over. He had Sophia Hanks, another cousin who lived with the Lincolns, and there were other female members of his extended Hanks family nearby. These kinships enriched Abraham Lincoln's sense of family. In 1821, Dennis Hanks married Abraham's stepsister Betsy, and the couple remained in Indiana, where they had three daughters, Sarah in 1822, Nancy in 1824, and Harriet in 1826. Lincoln was a happy young uncle. Harriet would become particularly precious to him, and he would host her in his Springfield home and befriend her husband years away in the misty future. As Lincoln protected and teased his sisters, he did so with those little nieces, part of the family that nurtured him. When Lincoln left Indiana for Illinois in 1830, it must have been difficult to leave behind loved ones, dead and buried. But the childhood Lincoln left there, for all its loss, had also been filled with love.[5]

The first thing Abraham Lincoln learned was to be a brother. This childhood experience either made him a kind and protective brother to sisters or it nurtured what was already in his heart. The girls in his childhood were his practice for all the girls and young women who would be lucky enough to make his acquaintance. When Lincoln wed Mary Todd in 1842, he married into a family bursting with sisters, and Lincoln adopted four of them as his own. Elizabeth, Frances, and Ann in Springfield and Emilie in Kentucky became dear to him. Family connections mattered, as evidenced in the names of Abraham and Mary Lincoln's sons: Robert for Mary's father, William for sister Frances's husband William Wallace, Edward for a close Todd and Lincoln family friend, and Thomas for Abraham's father. Lincoln adored all the little ones, especially the girls. Frances Wallace remembered her brother-in-law as being as much attached to her little daughter Mary as he was to his own sons.[6]

Sister-in-law Elizabeth Edwards was slower to warm to Lincoln. In time, however, she cared for Lincoln like a brother. When Willie Lincoln died in 1862, it was Elizabeth Edwards who offered the most important emotional support for Mr. and Mrs. Lincoln. She tended Mary like a surrogate mother, and she offered her brokenhearted brother-in-law solace by providing brief distractions from duty and from grief. One day Elizabeth led Lincoln on a stroll through the White House Conservatory, "where the world is represented by flowers that speak," she later remembered. At one point during their walk, Elizabeth said to Lincoln, "O—how beautiful this is—these roses," and Lincoln answered, "I never was in here before: how Spring like it looks."[7]

Accepting the support from his sister-in-law was easy for Lincoln, and he was grateful she was in Washington where they needed her most. Whenever it was in his power for him to support female family members, he did so, like hosting Harriet Hanks when she was attending school in Springfield and giving Frances's struggling husband a paymaster post in the army. Mary Lincoln later took credit for the Wallace appointment, but there is more evidence suggesting Lincoln liked Frances better than his wife did. Abraham Lincoln often bestowed favors upon his wife's relatives, but it is important to remember that these relatives were Lincoln's family, too. While Lincoln's relationships with his father and stepbrother John Johnston were strained, he remained close throughout his life with his stepmother, stepsisters, and cousin Dennis Hanks. He cared about his nieces and nephews, recording their births in his family record, corresponded with them, and, though they lived far from Springfield, saw them occasionally.[8]

Abraham Lincoln once wrote: "I regret the necessity of saying I have no daughters."[9] If Lincoln had had the good fortune of a daughter, he would have doted on his little girl. He might have even named her Nancy or Sarah, after one of his mothers or his sister. Lincoln's kindnesses to his friends' daughters are further evidence of his open heart for girls. When his law partner John Stuart was serving in Congress, Lincoln would check in on Stuart's family. In December 1839, he wrote Stuart: "Whenever a letter comes from you to Mrs. Stuart, I carry it to her, and then I see [Bettie]. She is a tolerably nice *fellow* now."[10]

His correspondence with Grace Bedell, the little girl who wrote him a letter urging him to grow a beard, is famous evidence of Lincoln's heart. "All the ladies like whiskers and they would tease their husbands to vote for you and then you would be President," eleven-year-old Grace wrote. "If I was a man I would vote for you," she added. Lincoln replied to her letter, and he sought her out in her hometown on his inaugural train trip to Washington. Taking his place on the platform in Westfield, New York, he called into the crowd: "Some three months ago, I received a letter from a young lady here; it was a very pretty letter, and she advised me to let my whiskers grow, as it would improve my personal appearance; acting partly upon her suggestion, I have done so; and now, if she is here, I would like to see her." Grace Bedell was, indeed, in the crowd, and Lincoln stepped down from the car and "gave her several hearty kisses," scratchy with his new beard.[11]

Lincoln's relationship with his sister-in-law Emilie Todd was another tender example of his capacity for paternal instincts toward female family members. Emilie was the beloved, baby sister of the Todd family, beautiful and precocious. Born in 1836, the last child of Mary Lincoln's father Robert Todd and stepmother Betsey Todd, Emilie was the charming family pet. Emilie first met her brother-in-law in November 1847 when the Lincoln family visited Lexington. Emilie, who was eleven at the time, remembered being scared by her brother-in-law's height. When Lincoln entered the Todd home, he put down his son Bobby, picked up Emilie, and said: "So this is little sister." In 1854, Emilie made a six-month visit to her Springfield sisters and stayed with the Lincoln family, further endearing herself to Lincoln. Once when Emilie delivered a sharp retort to an insolent gentleman visitor, Lincoln smiled and said, "The child has a tongue like the rest of the Todds."[12]

After Lincoln's inauguration as president, he offered a commission to Emilie's new husband Benjamin Helm, a West Point graduate who was pursuing a career in the law. He had hoped to keep the Helms in the Union and in the family, but Benjamin Helm accepted a commission in the Confederate Army instead. Emilie then pledged her love to her husband and her loyalty to the South. When Captain Helm died from wounds suffered at the battle of Chickamauga in September 1863, Emilie was trapped in Madison, Georgia, and needed Lincoln's help to get home. Lincoln ordered a pass for Betsey Todd to bring Emilie and her children back to Kentucky. In December, authorities stopped Emilie at Fortress Monroe, where she refused to take an oath of allegiance and was, thus, denied passage. The officer who detained her sent word to Lincoln, who ordered that Emilie be sent to him in Washington. She arrived pregnant at the White House with her elder daughter Katherine. About the family reunion there, Emilie later recalled: "Mr. Lincoln and my sister met me with the warmest affection, we were all too grief-stricken at first for speech . . . We could only embrace each other in silence and tears."[13]

Emilie Helm's happy reunion could not last. A Confederate officer's widow living in the White House would raise suspicion, and Lincoln confided to his friend Senator Orville Hickman Browning that he hoped to keep his sister-in-law's visit quiet. But the White House was too busy with people to keep secrets. Lincoln's secretary John Hay noted in his diary; "I visited with Mrs. L. Her sister, Mrs Gen. Helm is with her just arrived from Secessia."[14]

General Daniel Sickles was shocked to learn of Helm's presence and scolded: "You should not have that rebel in your house," to which Lincoln responded: "My wife and I are in the habit of choosing our own guests."[15]

But Mr. and Mrs. Lincoln both understood the political problem "Litter Sister" posed, and President Lincoln tried to solve it by compelling Emilie to abandon her Southern sympathies. He demanded she sign the amnesty document he penned for her on December 14, telling her she must profess her allegiance to the U.S. government if she wished to remain in Washington. She refused to sign it, and Lincoln issued her a pass to go home. "It is my wish that Mrs. Emily T. Helm . . . now returning to Kentucky, may have protection of person and property, except as to slaves, of which I say nothing," he wrote. Emilie wrote to Lincoln on December 20 to announce her safe arrival in Lexington. "Love to Sister Mary," she closed the letter, "& kind regards to yourself and Tad."[16]

Emilie Helm never saw her brother-in-law again. In October 1864, when she was struggling to support herself and her fatherless children, she blamed Lincoln. "I also would remind you that your *Minié* bullets have made us what we are," she wrote.[17] The splintering of the Lincolns and the Kentucky Todds was a common story of fractured families during the American Civil War. In this instance, even Abraham Lincoln's love and compassion for his sister-in-law could not overcome the war's terrible realities. Mary Lincoln never forgave her sister for taking up the Confederate cause against her husband. After Lincoln's death, however, Emilie's own harsh feelings softened. When the historical dust had settled, she held tight to her personal connection to Abraham Lincoln. She maintained a fondness for the tall brother-in-law who had loved her like a sister. In 1887, when someone asked her for a signed letter from Abraham Lincoln, she said she could not consent to part with it. Across the political divide, through personal sorrow and a nation's grief, it was the goodness in Lincoln that Emilie Helm remembered.[18]

3. *A Mother's Fear*

> [S]omething told me that something would befall Abe and that I should see him no more.
>
> —Sarah Lincoln, interview with William Herndon, September 8, 1865

SARAH LINCOLN WAS RESTLESS. Since her son's election as president of the United States in November 1860, she worried about his health, his safety, and the challenge ahead of him. Family concern for her emotional health prompted a letter to Abraham Lincoln. "She is getting somewhat childish and is very uneasy about you fearing some of your political opponents will kill you," his nephew-in-law Augustus Chapman wrote on January 3 from Charleston, Illinois. "She is very anxious to see you once more and could you pay us a visit before your departure for Washington it would be a great comfort to her and we would all be highly pleased to see you."[1]

On Wednesday, January 30, 1861, Abraham Lincoln answered his mother's distress call. He boarded a train on the Great Western Railroad at Springfield and traveled ninety-five miles to Charleston. He knew his seventy-two-year-old stepmother might die before his presidency ended. He wished to give her comfort, to let her see him one last time. But he may have made that trip to quiet his own anxieties as well, perhaps needing to see himself reflected through his mother's loving eyes before facing the biggest challenge of his life. Maybe Lincoln's three-day, round-trip journey, just twelve days before he was scheduled to depart for Washington, was as much for himself as it was for his mother.[2]

Lincoln arrived in Charleston in the evening and made his way from the train depot to the nearby home of Illinois state senator Thomas Marshall, his friend and a fellow attorney. I live just ten blocks from the Marshall home, an elegant, whitewashed Italianate mansion. Built in 1855, it was one of the grandest homes off Charleston's town square. The house's glamour has long faded since Lincoln's visit 163 years ago, and although that block of Jackson Avenue is still brick, the streetscape bears little resemblance to what Lincoln would have seen in 1861. Still, architecture and place are powerful tethers, reminding us we are not far away from history. I sometimes go past the house on daily walks, and it is easy for me to imagine Lincoln standing on the wide front porch or up on the gracious balcony above, surveying a large assembly of well-wishers. On that shivery night, Lincoln declined to deliver remarks to the crowd made up of citizens, including women who could not vote, in the town in which I am now a resident and a registered voter. It was not those well-wishers, his soon-to-be constituency, that Lincoln had come to Charleston to see. Lincoln was thinking about his mother, who was anticipating his visit, tucked in by the fire in a house not far away from where he stood bracing himself from the cold.[3]

In the morning after breakfast with his stepsister Elizabeth Hanks and her husband Dennis Hanks, Lincoln climbed into Augustus Chapman's buggy. They drove south from Charleston toward the home of Matilda Moore, Lincoln's other stepsister, where Sarah Lincoln was waiting for her son. When Lincoln arrived, Sarah saw the lanky boy she had raised, the Lincoln child who always had his nose buried in a book. To her he was not the president-elect of a nation facing a possible war. He was just her son, and she and her daughter and all their neighbors were happy to welcome him. He was one of their own.[4]

Matilda's home was located on Main Street in the little community of Campbell. She and her friends had prepared a feast, with chicken and turkey and "the nicest cakes and pies." The modest home is still standing, a sleepy, wayside tourist stop on the old Lincoln Highway. If you stand at the front door, you can almost hear the buzz inside the house, crammed with tables and chairs for Lincoln's dinner and ringing with chatter and laughter spilling through the cracks in the clapboard siding.[5]

During their last hours together, mother and son rode out to the old Lincoln farm. They visited Thomas Lincoln's humble grave in a cemetery north of the farm, and Sarah accompanied her son back to Charleston for a public reception. They likely shared family memories, like the time Abe preached to the Pigeon Creek children against cruelty to animals, arguing "that an ants' life was to it, as sweet as ours to us."[6] Lincoln probably teased his mother, an effort to keep the mood light, and they laughed and remembered lost loved ones. Overwhelmed by memories, Sarah shed the bittersweet tears of an old woman who has known all the joys and sorrows of being human, Lincoln resting a large hand on his mother's shoulder and lifting her spirit with stories of his rambunctious sons. Augustus Chapman later remembered that before Lincoln left, Sarah embraced him, lingering in the folds of his wrinkled travel duster. She whispered into his ear her fears for his life, and Lincoln wrapped his mother up in his long arms and begged her not to worry, likely whispering back that all would be well.[7]

Sarah Lincoln was right to feel the cold fingers of dread. She would never see her son again. She had a mother's intuition, the universe signaling its alarm in a mother's bones. I have felt this intuition myself, and my heart knows something of Sarah Lincoln's weeping heart and her next four years of worry. When Sarah Lincoln heard about her son's assassination, she covered her face with her apron and wept. In an interview five months later, she said: "I did not want Abe to run for Presdt—did not want him elected—was afraid somehow or other—felt it in my heart that something would happen [to] him . . . Abe & his father are in Heaven I have no doubt, and I want to go there—go where they are—God bless Abm."[8]

Sarah Lincoln would have four years to endure her worry, and then four more to endure the death of Abraham Lincoln. Having suffered the loss of two husbands and two sons, grief would be her constant companion as she lived out her days, surrounded by a doting extended family. She had to bury two children, John in 1854 and Abraham in 1865, but by all family accounts it was the death of her "best boy" Abe that broke her spirit forever. One family member remembered: "She had no heart after that to be chirp and peart like she used to be."[9]

Sarah Lincoln died on April 12, 1869, with a lifetime of loves and losses etched upon her heart. The knowledge of her son's place in history must have been a bittersweet solace.

Today when you walk through the grass and the clover among the graves in what is now known as the Thomas Lincoln Cemetery, old trees sway in the prairie breeze. The stone marker etched "SARAH BUSH LINCOLN 1788–1869" is low to the ground and lies inside a rusty iron fence. A large, modern monument, erected in gratitude for the good people who raised Abraham Lincoln, shades Sarah's and her husband's matching stones. Two towering cedar trees lean into the sleepy cemetery like sentinels keeping watch over the dead. A modest entry gateway beckons visitors from the parking lot of the adjacent Shiloh Presbyterian Church, built and abandoned long after the Lincolns passed. The cemetery sits off a country road in the middle of cornfields and nowhere, yet every year visitors find their way to it, navigating rural Coles County to pay respects. Visitors from the nearby Lincoln farm, which is now a museum and living history center, visit the cemetery, as well as other old history souls like me who come only to sit with the ghosts of Lincoln's parents. All these visitors are pilgrims, compelled to honor the path of human existence.[10]

Gravesite of Sarah Lincoln, Coles County, Illinois, 2023. Author's Photo

The Lincoln cemetery and the Lincoln farm offer snippets of history in the form of stories told for local tourism in the Land of Lincoln. But they are so much more than tourism for the visitors who take the time and the trouble to find them. They are markers of the place where Lincoln was a frequent visitor, practiced law in the Coles County Courthouse, and debated Stephen Douglas in 1858. There are museums, statues, murals, and historical markers preserving these Lincoln footsteps. If you follow Lincoln Avenue, the main commercial strip running through Charleston, after it becomes Illinois Route 16, you will pass the county's hospital. Sarah Bush Lincoln Health Center is named in her honor, a gesture acknowledging a mother's nurturing purpose, a woman's work to raise up a child and give him over to the world. The hospital name, as well as the maintenance of the Lincoln Cemetery and the preservation of Sarah Lincoln's gravesite and Matilda Moore's home, are part of a human imperative. They mark in time our precious human footprints and provide places for us to stand between the past and the present. These historic sites, these hallowed spaces, are not only about Abraham Lincoln. This kind of remembering is about something larger than one human man. It is an acknowledgment of the ties that bind us together. Each one of us. Mothers to sons. Beating hearts to historical memory. Past and present and posterity.

4. *My Lincoln Family*

Lincoln is dead, Mom. You know that, right?
—Mackenzie Kathleen McDermott, c. 2011

On July 30, 2000, I flew to Philadelphia with my political reporter husband and the Illinois delegation attending the Republican National Convention. We took our girls with us. Savannah was twelve and Mackenzie six, and I was determined to give them a week-long, immersive history lesson while their father worked. My father Jim was flying in to meet us, and he planned to join us to tour the Liberty Bell, Independence Hall, and the U.S. Mint. But first things first: Abraham Lincoln and Gettysburg. At dawn on July 31, I packed my girls into a rental SUV and made the two-and-a-half-hour drive west to Gettysburg National Military Park. My daughters napped, ate snacks, and complained about how early it was and how long it was taking us to get there. Their whining did not dampen my spirits, however. We were a history family, dammit. I turned on the *Gettysburg* movie soundtrack for historical ambiance and to muffle the grumbles of my disgruntled daughters.

"Listen to the music," I said, raising the volume. "We're almost there," I lied.

The girls had watched *Gettysburg* twice. Not of their own volition, of course. I made them watch it, hoping it would help them understand what we would see in Gettysburg. I lectured them about Lincoln's Gettysburg Address and had them read it. They were not thrilled about any of it. They were annoyed. They were sorry they did not have a normal mother. They complained that the movie was too long and too boring. They deemed the music old-fashioned, like something their two fifty-something grandmothers would like.

"War movies are dumb," said Savannah. "War is dumb, and men are stupid to fight."

"Mulan's not stupid," Mack replied. Both girls then agreed *Mulan* was a way better war movie than *Gettysburg* and Mulan way cooler than Lincoln. What blasphemous children I was raising.

We started our tour of Gettysburg at the visitor center with the exhibits and introductory movie. I bribed the girls with souvenirs, and I purchased the guide booklet for our self-guided driving tour of the park. We set off, Savannah riding shotgun and in charge of the guide, and Mack in the backseat eating the rock candy she had selected instead of her close-second choice, a book about Harriet Tubman. As we pulled into the first designated stop and Savannah finished reading the appropriate paragraph from the guidebook, Mack chirped from the back seat: "When are we going to get to Little Round Top?"

"That's not until the second day, so shut up," answered her sister.

I did not shut down Savannah's shut up because I was too impressed with my daughters' spongy brains. They had paid attention. They knew about Joshua Lawrence Chamberlain's famous flanking maneuver at Little Round Top. They had learned it from Jeff Daniels, but they knew it. I was thrilled. This was going to be an amazing day. We got out of the car and looked at the monuments while Savannah recited descriptions from the guidebook. She began to enjoy her role as history tour guide, and Mack was running around the monuments while Savannah and I read all the plaques. We returned to the car to head to the second tour stop, and Savannah started reading to us about it. But then, from the back seat, there was a chirpy little voice.

"When are we going to get to Little Round Top?"

"When are we going to get to Little Round Top?"

"When are we going to get to Little Round Top?"

Over the next two hours, Mack repeated this question at least a thousand times more. She was relentless until Savannah and I lost patience and agreed to drive straight to Little Round Top.

"This is it," I said, looking at Savannah, who was rolling her eyes.

Mack jumped out of the car and headed for those big rocks. That was the end for her. It was the end for all of us. After seeing those disappointing rocks, we agreed battlefields were not our thing. War is not a subject on which this mother and her daughters could hang a vacation, so we skipped the remaining stops of the self-driving tour and made our own flanking maneuver toward the Abraham Lincoln statue, the sun still high in the sky.

We stood by the Lincoln statue on the spot where he delivered the Gettysburg Address, and I handed Savannah the copy of the speech I had printed for her to read aloud. It was a transcription of the Everett copy of the address, of course, the version belonging to our State of Illinois. It is the copy Lincoln gave to Edward Everett, the minister who was the principal speaker at the Gettysburg dedication ceremony on November 19, 1863. One of five known copies, it is the one Illinois schoolchildren collected pennies to purchase, supplemented with a handsome donation by Marshall Field, and presented to the Illinois Historical Library in March 1944. It is located in Springfield, Illinois, and both my girls had seen it up close.[1]

In my daughter's sweet voice, Lincoln's speech was a wondrous thing. I got the goosebumps I always get when history's ghosts walk through me. I was misty watching Savannah reading Lincoln's words through her round, wire-framed spectacles, so earnest and serious in her delivery. Mack was not so moved, or so serious. She pointed at her sister and laughed and laughed through the entire reading. Blessed is the brevity of a 272-word speech when a six-year-old girl, hopped up on sugar and way past Little Round Top, is heckling you.

The poetry of the Gettysburg Address never loses its luster, and Savannah's reading where he stood is a cherished memory for me. The speech anchors Lincoln to our American family, and our family trip to Gettysburg tethers me and my girls to one another and to history. I felt Lincoln's spirit that day. Savannah felt it, too, although the tears in her mother's eyes embarrassed her. It would take more time to fully bring Mack into my Lincoln family fold.

My girls often teased me for being in love with Abraham Lincoln, a dead dude. However, they knew Lincoln helped pay the family bills, and they thought he was likable as far as dead presidents go. My family embraced the woman in their house who talked about Mr. Lincoln in the present tense, and they adopted Lincoln as a man in the present as well as in the past. They still smirked, but they were good sports. They came to enjoy visits to Lincoln historic sites, and the girls often chose Lincoln as a topic for school papers. In one college essay, Mack wrote: "The weight of Lincoln's legacy is a heavy burden to bear." But Mack bore her strange burden with good humor. They all did. They indulged my random recitations and frequent history lectures at the dining table, and they posed with every Lincoln statue we ever saw. Even when my husband went to Cuba on a journalism assignment, he made the effort to have his picture taken in front of the Abraham Lincoln school in Havana.

Abraham Lincoln was family. And I have the pictures to prove it.

*The author's daughters Mackenzie (*left*) and Savannah with prototype figure for Abraham Lincoln Presidential Museum, Springfield, Illinois, January 2001.* Author's Photo

PART II
Friends and Lovers

5. *A Good Man among Good Women*

> He was always social and lively and had great aspirations for his friends.
> —Elizabeth Abell telling William Herndon about Abraham Lincoln, February 15, 1867

STRONG KENTUCKY WOMEN RAISED Abraham Lincoln, and it was another strong Kentucky woman who greeted him when he arrived in New Salem as a young man. Elizabeth Abell was a fast friend to Lincoln and a formative inspiration for his earliest ambitions. Abell was part of a community of kind women who welcomed Lincoln into their homes. Understanding these women and the lives they lived brings into sharper focus the person Abraham Lincoln became: a kind, honest, compassionate human being.

The story of Abraham Lincoln wrestling Jack Armstrong when he was a newcomer to New Salem is a popular one in the Lincoln narrative. It illustrates Lincoln's successful effort to prove his masculinity and gain acceptance into the village's world of men. This story is true, but I do not care that Abraham Lincoln was athletic enough to best a man in a wrestling match. I prefer to think about Lincoln swapping stories with Jack's wife Hannah while she sewed his britches by the fire. I admire Lincoln for being kind and honest and a deep thinker. Most people do not admire Lincoln because he whipped Jack Armstrong in wrestling. They, too, admire him because he was kind and honest and a deep thinker. The women of New Salem did not accept Lincoln because he could wrestle the neighborhood bully. They accepted him because they were generous and compassionate and interested in a smart newcomer who could tell them a funny story. They liked Lincoln because he was friendly and humble. The men of New Salem might have put Lincoln to the test, but the good women who opened their homes and offered friendship to a poor, friendless new arrival required no proof of his worthiness. It is a curious thing to idolize a man for his softer virtues but venerate his masculinity; and I'll take the Hannah story over the Jack story any day.[1]

One lovable quality of Abraham Lincoln was his talent for conversation and storytelling. Elizabeth Abell and Abraham Lincoln liked each other immediately, partly because she enjoyed a good debate. Everybody in New Salem knew she was a great talker. Elizabeth and her husband Bennett Abell, formally educated with a home filled with books, were what passed for local literati in the hamlet. Born in 1804 and raised in Richmond, Kentucky, Elizabeth attended the Brush Creek Academy in Green County, a school established by her father Nathaniel Owens, a wealthy Kentucky landowner. She later attended Nazareth Academy near Bardstown, where she met Bennett Abell, a learned but poor man who was eight years her senior and a student at nearby St. Thomas Seminary. Elizabeth's father disapproved of the match, but she followed her heart when she married Bennett in January 1822. She was a woman who knew her own mind.[2]

When Lincoln arrived in New Salem, the Abell household was buzzing with growing children, domestic activities, and arduous farm work. The family was comfortable but not wealthy, and they were generous, always opening their door to guests and wayward newcomers. Elizabeth was twenty-seven when she met Abraham Lincoln. He was twenty-two. She was a settled woman, married with three sons and two daughters, the youngest child an infant. He was an untethered, determined yet uncertain young man. However, these two great talkers were contemporaries, both born in the nineteenth century's first decade, upland southerners replanted in the fertile new state of Illinois. They shared Kentucky roots, the northern migration of families, and a love of books and learning. They had a great deal to talk about, perhaps even sharing stories of strained relationships with fathers, not so much born from difficult childhood experiences but from a generational conflict as they looked beyond the old-world, traditional perspectives of their parents.[3]

The first thing Elizabeth Abell would have noticed about Abraham Lincoln was his poverty. During this westward-pushing period of American history, many poor young men stumbled into infant towns holding all they owned in a rucksack, looking for first starts or second chances. Abell first met Lincoln in the New Salem general store or at the home of Bowling and Nancy Green, who also befriended the newcomer. It was summer 1831. Lincoln was young and restless and all limbs in ill-fitting clothes. His hair and attire were disheveled because, as his stepmother put it, "fashion cut no figure with him."[4]

Yet Abraham Lincoln's poverty and unfashionable attire did not matter to Elizabeth, or to most folks in New Salem in the 1830s. It was a lively little village, but it was not a fashionable place, and even if Lincoln had not been so gangly and so shabbily dressed, he would have stood out to the villagers. All fresh faces are interesting to residents of plain, rural hamlets, especially to people like Elizabeth, scanning the horizon for anything or anyone out of the ordinary. There was a quick and comfortable kinship between Elizabeth and Abraham. He called her his "great friend." To her, "Friend Abe" was a welcomed guest in the Abell cabin.[5]

New Salem was a typical town blooming in the emerging Midwest, with a majority of young single men yet grounded as well with a strong collection of families. It was a relatively self-sufficient village with a mill, general stores, a blacksmith shop, and a tavern, among other basic amenities. The homes and businesses in town were simple, sturdy structures, and log cabins dotted the surrounding landscape. It was a village of industrious, optimistic people, but most residents were poor to middling folk. New Salem, as an outpost of the Upland South, also had a reputation as rough-and-tumble. Lincoln navigated well both its gentle and rough-hewn elements. Hard-working and garrulous, he endeared himself to the men in the hamlet, while his kindness and honesty endeared him to the women. New Salem women befriended Lincoln because hugging in the needy was natural to those whose lives required cooperation with others. Mostly, however, they seemed to have liked Lincoln at the very sight of him.[6]

Elizabeth Abell appreciated Lincoln's integrity and humility, and she defined him as too "honest a man for this world." Abell, Hannah Armstrong, and Nancy Green were drawn to the young man who established a reputation in the village as a person who loved children, cared for animals, and went out of his way to help people. Hannah Armstrong remembered that at social gatherings Lincoln "would tell stories—joke people. . . . He would nurse babies—do any thing to accommodate any body." Likewise, Nancy Green, who was fifteen years older than Lincoln, admired his character, and her husband, a local justice of the peace, was a willing mentor. The Greens viewed Lincoln more as a son than a friend, but Elizabeth Abell and Hannah Armstrong claimed Lincoln as a friend. He was a friend who bounced their babies on his knees while they cooked him a meal and told him their stories. He was a friend they assisted when he was young and in need and upon whom they would later be able to call when they needed legal aid or a presidential favor.[7]

The women of New Salem did not swoop into Lincoln's life to mother him. They had their own kids to raise, and, besides, Lincoln was not an orphan. He was a grown man. He did not float into New Salem looking for a surrogate mother. He was looking for friends. These New Salem women may have fed Abraham meals, but they offered him something far more valuable than a hot supper. They offered him friendships every bit as formative as his friendships with men. New Salem was the setting for Lincoln's entry into politics, his painful failures in business, and the building of his confidence. His woman friends were not peripheral to these experiences.[8]

When he arrived in New Salem, Abraham Lincoln was eager to be part of the community, and there was no better way to build friendships than to spend time with people by the hearth. Lincoln spent so much time in Elizabeth Abell's kitchen, in fact, that people in the village teased that her youngest child was his. Margaret Abell, who was born in September 1833, might have had a striking resemblance to Abe Lincoln because her father Bennett Abell was also a tall and lanky Kentucky man with dark hair and a long, narrow face. Lack of resemblance, however, was no bar for such good-natured teasing among friends. Jack Armstrong also joshed Lincoln about having a son with Mrs. Armstrong. Jason Duncan, a doctor who boarded with Lincoln at Rutledge's Tavern in New Salem, recalled that in Lincoln there was a good deal "of humor in his composition sometimes bordering on innocent mischief especially among his lady acquaintances, though only with those he was well acquainted." Lincoln was, in modern parlance, a people person. He loved personal interactions of all kinds. He liked spending time with his male and female friends, holding his own in the tavern and by the hearth. "He was the best natured man I ever got acquainted with," Elizabeth Abell said.[9]

Based on the New Salem evidence, Lincoln enjoyed women's company, and everyone in the village knew it. Elizabeth Abell's friendship with Lincoln was central, and there were those among their mutual friends who said it was she who inspired Lincoln's "ideas of a higher plane of life—that it was she who gave him the notion that he might improve himself by reading."[10] No doubt, Lincoln's use of the Abells' library led to discussions in Elizabeth's home about literature, history, religion, and the natural world. Their mutual gift of gab clinched their comradery, and she inspired his ambition. After Lincoln's death, however, it was Mentor Graham, a New Salem teacher, who claimed credit for Lincoln's New Salem education. In May 1865, he bragged to William Herndon, Lincoln's first biographer, that he was the one who offered encouragement to the young, unlearned Lincoln. Other biographers perpetuated the story, because, I suppose, they assumed a male schoolteacher, even one with less formal education than Elizabeth Abell, deserved more credit than any woman did. I take a middle ground. Lincoln arrived in New Salem already a voracious reader with an appetite for knowledge. He was a sponge for learning, and he soaked up all the knowledge *any* acquaintances there offered him. Mentor Graham may have loaned Lincoln books and offered encouragement, but Elizabeth Abell has the greater claim, if there is one, although she never boasted about it.[11]

When I think about Abraham Lincoln looking at Elizabeth Abell, surrounded by her children, laughing and talking with him, I wonder if he saw his sister Sarah's face. She might have been sitting at her own hearth had she lived, surrounded by children, joking with him. In befriending Elizabeth and Hannah, Lincoln might have been collecting sisters as much as he was collecting friends. And anyone who has ever had the honor and privilege of knowing a good sister knows that sisters make the best friends. Whether friend or surrogate sister or both, Elizabeth Abell was a strong thread knitting the fabric of Abraham Lincoln's early adulthood during his most formative life experiences. She opened her home and shared her family with him. She lent him books, mended his clothes, spent time with him, and fixed him up with her sister Mary Owens (that wonderful story comes later).[12]

"If we have no friends," Abraham Lincoln wrote in 1842, "we have no pleasure."[13] Friendship was a human joy Lincoln greatly valued, and he counted women among his friends. He was adept at navigating the civic and political friendships with men, rooted in the masculine virtues of courage and strength, and he also possessed the sensitivity and humility that made him a natural friend of women. Elizabeth Abell and the New Salem women were witness to Lincoln's early failures, successes, and all his efforts to find himself and make his way in the world. They saw Lincoln off to the Black Hawk War with the local militia unit; they knew his good service as their postmaster; they watched him become a surveyor, lose his surveying equipment to debt, take proprietorship of a store, fail in business, and begin studying law. These women were there for Lincoln's unsuccessful political bid for a seat in the Illinois House of Representatives in 1832, and they cheered him on when he won a seat two years later. When Lincoln stood for reelection in 1836, I suspect he was thinking about his good friend Elizabeth Abell when he declared in his published campaign statement that he was in favor of "admitting all whites to the right of suffrage, who pay taxes or bear arms, (by no means excluding females)."[14]

What else, no, *who* else could have inspired a twenty-seven-year-old political novice to see the possibility of women as voting citizens in 1836, twelve years before the Seneca Falls Convention and eighty-four years before the adoption of the Nineteenth Amendment granting women the right to vote? What kind of man in 1836 makes such a stunning statement about women's worthiness to be part of the body politic? I will tell you what kind of a man. A man who respected women and called them friends. A good man among good women.

6. Much Ado (or What to Do) about Ann Rutledge?

> He, in the year 1833 & 4 was in love with a young lady in New Salem by the name of Miss Ann Rutledge.
>
> —New Salem resident William Greene to William Herndon, May 30, 1865

Once upon a time, there was a lovely young woman with auburn hair and blue eyes living in a picturesque hamlet on the Sangamon River. The good-natured and kind daughter of the proprietor of the town's tavern, she had promised her hand in marriage to a dashing scoundrel when she made the acquaintance of a new young man in town known for his height and his integrity. The lovely young woman had multiple suiters, for she was handsome and would make a good wife, and the tall and honest man fell in love with her. Sadly, the woman never had a chance to marry anyone at all. One sweltering summer, a fever swept through the village, and death carried her away. The tragedy rained grief upon the hearts of everyone who had known and loved her.

Years later, after the lanky, honest man became a great leader and martyr to his country, the people of that hamlet remembered his story of first love. From foggy, long-ago memories then bloomed the tale of a great romance between the beloved leader and the young woman whose shocking death so broke his heart that he never loved again. For years and years ever after, romantics, poets, and historians spun yarns with the golden hair of the sweet beauty who had stolen a hero's heart.

The Ann Rutledge story in Abraham Lincoln's story is a proper-good fairytale. Like all such tales, it is based on a little truth and embellished with fiction to satisfy a particular agenda. William Herndon, Lincoln's law partner, did not like Mary Lincoln. After Lincoln's death, he made a name for himself giving lectures and writing about Lincoln's New Salem romance. He based his narrative on interviews he conducted with New Salem residents who had known Lincoln and Rutledge, leading them by the nose with his questions and abetting the recovery of their three-decade-old memories. Lincoln's son Robert thought Herndon was making an ass of himself, peddling the Rutledge story for his own gain, but many other people at the time relished the story, and a whole generation of Lincoln biographers believed it. The only "evidence" of Lincoln's love and heartbreak, however, comes from reminiscences Herndon collected, and as we used to say at the Lincoln Papers Project: "Billy must have been drunk at the time."[1]

I am sympathetic toward Herndon. Abraham Lincoln liked his junior law partner and tendered great compassion toward this friend of his who struggled with insecurities and with alcohol. I like Herndon. He was a studious fellow, a capable lawyer who specialized in family law, and he was against slavery and in favor of women's rights. He loved Abraham Lincoln, and I appreciate that he wanted to hitch his wagon to Lincoln's legacy. Although I disagree with Herndon's conclusion that a Lincoln-Rutledge romance proved that Lincoln never loved Mary, I like this Lincoln fairy tale. Lincoln could have loved Ann Rutledge, and from mutual friends' fond memories she sounds like the kind of young woman to whom Lincoln would have been drawn. Elizabeth Abell remembered the terrible shock of Ann's death to the entire village and to Lincoln. "I never seen a man mourn for a companion more than he did for her," she recalled. "He made a remark one day when it was raining that he could not bear the idea of its raining on her Grave."[2] I trust Abell's memory to a good extent, although the last bit sounds too sentimental for the Lincoln I have come to know.

I hope Lincoln experienced love in New Salem when he was a young man and the world for him was new. I hope Ann Rutledge knew Lincoln's sweet affections before she left the earth too soon. Yet if Rutledge promised herself to John McNamar, with whom Lincoln was friendly, I am loathe to believe Lincoln would have courted a woman who had already promised herself to his friend.[3] Lincoln was no rake. Judge David Davis, who traveled the Eighth Judicial Circuit with Lincoln for twelve years, said: "Lincoln was a man of strong passion for woman—his conscience kept him from seduction—this saved many—many a woman."

Many of Lincoln's early male friends chased women while Lincoln, in contrast, was ever respectful. Abner Ellis remembered that Mr. L. had "many opportunities" for being a rogue, while hanging out with Joshua Speed and William Butler, "two old rats in that way."[4] In contrast to the knaves, Lincoln wished to be known as an honorable man, respectful toward women, not a seducer of them. And so, I suppose, it is possible that if Lincoln loved Ann Rutledge, it may have been a love unrequited, which is its own special kind of heartbreak.

The truth is this: the Lincoln-Rutledge story is one of history's mysteries we cannot know for certain. The undisputed details are few. Ann Rutledge was a real New Salem woman, a daughter of the prominent Rutledge family with whom Abraham Lincoln was acquainted. She died, unmarried, at twenty-two in August 1835. There are no extant contemporary love poems or letters mentioning Ann's love for Abraham or his love for her. The Lincoln-Rutledge love affair only exists in romanticized stories told after both parties were dead. The memories are also problematic, because they involve the sparsely documented, early years of a man who became the president of the United States and was assassinated. Mary Owens, the woman Lincoln courted not long after Rutledge died, did not remember ever hearing Rutledge's name.[5]

After Lincoln left New Salem for good, he was too busy building and maintaining his legal career, practicing politics, being married, and raising four sons to pine away on the memory of an old flame. Lincoln was a compassionate man, but he was not sentimental. When Mary Lincoln publicly denied the Lincoln-Rutledge affair in 1868, she was defending her own heart and her husband's legacy. However, I do not think she was lying. Lincoln likely never mentioned Ann Rutledge to his wife because he wasn't pining for the long-dead woman or he loved his wife and did not wish to hurt her. Mary Lincoln was Abraham Lincoln's lover for longer than Ann Rutledge lived, and I am content to let Lincoln's wife have the last words on the subject. In a letter to David Davis in 1867, she wrote: "Ann Rutledge is a myth—for all his confidential communications, such a romantic name, was never breathed. . . . Nor did his life or his joyous laugh, lead one to suppose his heart was in any unfortunate woman's grave."[6]

7. Courting Mary Owens

> This letter is so dry and stupid that I am ashamed to send it, but with my present feelings I cannot do any better.
>
> —Abraham Lincoln to Mary Owens, December 13, 1836

ONE YEAR AFTER ANN Rutledge's death, thirty years before she became a legend, Abraham Lincoln began a relationship with Mary Owens. Although it would fail to be a successful courtship, it is a courtship historians can document. There are surviving letters. There are details. The facts are fascinating. The story is hilarious.

Abraham Lincoln was a good friend to women, but he was not a romantic man. He was awkward and hesitant around eligible women. He was a man of "deep feeling," as Mary Lincoln described him, but he was not "demonstrative" when it came to sharing his emotions.[1] Lincoln's ineptitude in romance may have been what compelled his friend Elizabeth Abell to play cupid for him. Matchmaking in the 1830s was common, and although more couples proceeded without parental consent in this period, men and women still came together through family connections, friendship circles, and community relationships. New Salem was a small town, and there were few eligible young women. Introducing Lincoln to her sister made good sense to Abell. She loved her sister, and she knew Lincoln was a respectable, kind man with a bright future. She knew her friend would make a good husband, so why not bring two lonely people she loved together? When she traveled to Kentucky in 1836, she told Lincoln she would bring back her younger sister for him. Lincoln had met Mary Owens before and could recall no unpleasantness about her. He respected the friend and agreed to see the sister, likely giving it little thought.[2]

Mary Owens had qualities that recommended her to Lincoln. Born in September 1808, she was the same age as Lincoln, educated and cultured like her sister, well read, and intelligent. She stood five feet and five inches and had fair skin, blue eyes, and dark curly hair. One mutual friend compared her to Ann Rutledge, remembering Owens as "a handsome woman—a fine looking woman—was sharp—shrewd and intellectual. . . . Miss Rutledge was a pretty woman—good natured—kind—wasn't as smart as Miss Owens by a heap." Regardless of her merits, Mary Owens did not much impress Abraham Lincoln. Upon seeing her again, his heart did not flutter. Although he believed no woman had a finer face and admitted she had a good mind, there was no love at first sight. Lincoln later told a female friend that Mary Owens looked a little too much like his weathered mother, older than her years.[3]

The Lincoln-Owens courtship commenced in the fall 1836. The couple had compatible interests, like books and reading, and they enjoyed pleasant interactions in the company of Abell family members and other New Salem friends. In December, however, Lincoln the state legislator packed his bags for the Illinois General Assembly session in Vandalia, where the state capitol was then located. The couple made no determined plans for marriage, nor did they sever the relationship. Lincoln's departure left the situation quite up in the air. Mary Owens remembered: "In

Mary Owens, n.d. Courtesy of Library of Congress, Alfred Whital Stern Collection of Lincolniana, https://www.loc.gov/item/scsm000873/

many things we were congenial spirits. In politics we saw eye to eye," but there were no heartfelt confessions of love.[4] Lincoln wrote to Owens from Vandalia. The letter was all political news and pure Lincoln angst:

> I have been sick ever since my arrival here, or I should have written sooner. It is but little difference, however, as I have very little even yet to write. And more, the longer I can avoid the mortification of looking in the Post Office for your letter and not finding it, the better. . . . You recollect I mentioned in the outset of this letter that I had been unwell. That is the fact, though I believe I am about well now; but that, with other things I cannot account for, have conspired and have gotten my spirits so low, that I feel that I would rather be any place in the world than here. I really cannot endure the thought of staying here ten weeks. Write back as soon as you get this, and if possible say something that will please me, for really I have not been pleased since I left you. . . . Your friend Lincoln.[5]

Owens was likely already having doubts about her anxious beau. She was a perceptive woman, already questioning Lincoln's prospects to be "a kind husband." Lincoln was, she later said, "lacking in smaller intentions."[6] Mary Owens was looking for a more romantic fellow than Abraham Lincoln. By 1830, more people expected sparks to fly, intent as they were, more so than their parents' generation, on finding romance. They spent more time evaluating what they wanted in a partner and worried more about making a companionable match. While Owens was thinking about romance, Lincoln was discovering that he was not ready for love. He was a serious young man, serving his second term in the Illinois legislature. He was a novice lawyer just completing the requirements to practice law. Lincoln had a profession to learn and a practice to build, and he did not possess the time or the energy to win a woman's heart.[7]

Lincoln traveled to New Salem the second week in March 1837. During this visit or another, Owens and Lincoln went horseback riding with New Salem friends, setting out from the Abell farm toward the village. Owens took note that while the other men helped the women cross a creek with high waters, Lincoln left her to fend for herself. She remarked to him: "You are a nice fellow; I suppose you did not care whether my neck was broken or not," to which Lincoln laughed and responded that she was "plenty smart to take care" of herself.[8] Mary Owens believed Lincoln was, in his mind, paying her a compliment, but his lack of chivalry appalled her. Lincoln vexed her, yet she let the relationship limp forward, perhaps like her woebegone suitor, going along to get along with her sister.

On April 15, 1837, Lincoln left New Salem for good, relocating to Springfield to live and to become the junior law partner of John Todd Stuart. He bought necessary items on credit at a Springfield general store and moved into a room upstairs with the store's proprietor, Joshua Speed. On May 7, Lincoln wrote to Owens, discussing his loneliness and struggle to settle into life in Springfield. He was missing his New Salem friends, but he wrote nothing about missing her.[9] Instead, the letter was all about Lincoln. Poor Lincoln.

> I am often thinking about what we said of your coming to live at Springfield. I am afraid you would not be satisfied. There is a great deal of flourishing about in carriages here, which it would be your doom to see without sharing in it. You would have to be poor without the means of hiding your poverty. Do you believe you could bear that patiently? Whatever woman may cast her lot with mine, should any ever do so, it is my intention to do all in my power to make her happy and contented; and there is nothing I can imagine, that would make me more unhappy than to fail in the effort. I know I should be much happier with you than the way I am, provided I saw no signs of discontent in you. What you have said to me may have been in jest, or I may have misunderstood it. If so, then let it be forgotten; if otherwise, I much wish you would think seriously before you decide. For my part I have already decided. What I have said I will most positively abide by, provided you wish it. My opinion is that you had better not do it. You have not been accustomed to hardship, and it may be more severe than you now imagine. I know you are capable of thinking correctly on any subject; and if you deliberate maturely upon this, before you decide, then I am willing to abide your decision.[10]

The couple must have been talking about marriage, but there was a misunderstanding between them. Or, at least, Abraham Lincoln was confused. And waffling. On August 16, Owens saw Lincoln in New Salem again, but still the couple resolved nothing. I cannot help but imagine that Mary Owens might have been, by this time, having a little too much fun watching Lincoln wiggle on her hook, content to let the vague promise of marriage hang in the air between them. On the evening Lincoln returned to Springfield, he penned another letter to Owens:

> You will, no doubt, think it rather strange, that I should write you a letter on the same day on which we parted; and I can only account for it by supposing, that seeing you lately makes me think of you more than usual, while at our late meeting we had but few expressions of thoughts. You must know that I cannot see you, or think of you, with entire indifference; and yet it may be that you are mistaken in regard to what my real feelings towards you are. If I knew you were not, I should not trouble you with this letter. Perhaps any other man would know enough without further information; but I consider it *my* peculiar right to plead ignorance, and your bounden duty to allow the plea. I want in all cases to do right, and most particularly so, in all cases with women. I want, at this particular time, more than anything else, to do right with you, and if I *knew* it would be doing right, as I rather suspect it would, to let you alone, I would do it. And for the purpose of making the matter as plain as possible, I now say, that you can now drop the subject, dismiss your thoughts (if you ever had any) from me forever, and leave this letter unanswered, without calling forth one accusing murmur from me. And I will even go further and say that if it will add anything to your comfort, or peace of mind, to do so, it is my sincere wish that you should. . . . If you feel yourself in any degree bound to me, I am now willing to release you, provided you wish it; while, on the other hand, I am willing, and even anxious to bind you faster, if I can be convinced that it will, in any considerable degree, add to your happiness. This, indeed, is the whole question with

> me. Nothing would make me more miserable than to believe you miserable—nothing more happy, than to know you were so. . . . If it suits you best to not answer this—farewell—a long life and a merry one attend you. . . . My respects to your sister. Your friend Lincoln.[11]

Is your head now spinning in a blur of unromantic confusion? Poor Lincoln. And poor Mary Owens to have read such a letter.

Abraham Lincoln was too kind to say it plainly, but he did not love Mary Owens. There was no romantic chemistry between those two good people. Lincoln was not yet ready for marriage, and his courtship with Owens made this fact as plain as the long nose on his face. His letters to Owens reveal his internal conflict and his uncertain place in the universe. He was neither emotionally mature enough for marriage nor financially fit enough to support a wife. And so, Mary Owens let her wiggling suitor off her hook and went home to Kentucky. She summed up the relationship in 1866: "I thought Mr. Lincoln was deficient in those little links which make up the great chain of woman's happiness, at least it was so in my case; not that I believed it proceeded from a lack of goodness of heart."[12]

Mary Owens held no grudges against Lincoln, but her rejection left him smarting. He was embarrassed. In the end, however, Lincoln took the blame and moved past the turmoil. Sometime after the breakup, Elizabeth Abell saw Lincoln in Springfield, and he said to her: "Tell your sister, that I think she was a great fool, because she did not stay here and marry me."[13]

"Characteristic of the man," would be Mary Owens's reply.[14]

Lincoln was teasing, bantering with his good friend. Like Mary Owens, he held no grudges and had no hard feelings for the woman who got away. The courtship had been an education for both parties. Mary Owens entertained other suitors before marrying the brother-in-law of another Owens sister in 1841. Jesse Vineyard was a farmer, two years younger than Mary; and the couple moved to Weston, Missouri, north of Kansas City, where they raised three children and buried another. Jesse Vineyard died in 1863, and Mary Vineyard lived out her life as a widow. In the Pleasant Ridge Cemetery in Weston, next to her original gravestone, stands a modern stone marker: "Here lies Mary Owens Vineyard who rejected Abraham Lincoln's proposal of marriage in 1837."[15]

Such a curious claim to historical fame. I am not sure Mary Owens would appreciate being so reduced, but I also suspect she would hold no grudge against Lincoln and her place in his extraordinary story. As for Abraham Lincoln, his road to marriage and four children would take a little bit longer. As he wrote his friend Eliza Browning in April 1838: "I have now come to the conclusion never again to think of marrying; and for this reason; I can never be satisfied with anyone who would be block-head enough to have me."[16]

One scholar has argued that Lincoln's relationship with Ann Rutledge was passionate but inconvenient and that his relationship with Owens was convenient but loveless. Based on Lincoln's declaration never to marry, that scholar argues that both failed romances left Lincoln "feeling embittered."[17] I disagree. To be bitter was anathema to Abraham Lincoln. He just needed more time to feel ready for marriage. He needed to find the right woman. And, as we all know, he would live to swallow his promise, because he was about to make the acquaintance of the woman who would woo him.

8. *Mary, Molly, Lover, Wife*

My hand will never be given, where my heart is not.
—Mary Todd to Mercy Levering, July 23, 1840

MARY

Mary Todd first visited Springfield, Illinois, in 1837, spending three months with her eldest sister Elizabeth Edwards. During this time, she likely met Abraham Lincoln, who had just settled in Springfield to practice law with Mary's cousin John Stuart. She returned to Kentucky to complete her education, but she was soon homesick for her more independent life in Springfield. She longed to distance herself from her parents—particularly her stepmother, against whom she chafed. She made the permanent move to Illinois in October 1839, happily settling into the Edwards home. Her brother-in-law Ninian W. Edwards was wealthy and well connected, and her sister Elizabeth was famous for her elegant parties.[1]

Mary Todd was "quick, lively, gay—frivolous . . . social and loved glitter, show & pomp & power."[2] She was the life of every party, fending off suitors, and loving her life. In 1840, she was a twenty-two-year-old woman living in a stately home on Aristocracy Hill, the neighborhood of Springfield gentility and fashion. She was charming and spirited, "a bright, lively, plump little woman" and "a good talker." She was the smartest and most politically astute of all the eligible young ladies in Springfield and became the center of attention in a social circle made up of politically engaged women and young politicians.[3]

In December 1840, Mary was missing her dearest friend Mercy Levering, who was visiting relatives out of state, but she was enjoying time with a new friend Matilda Edwards, her brother-in-law's relative. Mary found the eighteen-year-old Matilda "a congenial spirit," and told Mercy "A lovelier girl I never saw." Matilda was drawing "a concourse of beaux & company round us"; Mary was enjoying female friends, social engagements, and partisan politics. As she wrote Mercy:

> I suppose like the rest of us *Whigs*, though you seem rather to doubt my *faith*, you have been rejoicing in the recent election of Gen Harrison, a cause that has excited such deep interest in the nation and one of such vital importance to our prosperity—This fall I became quite a *politician*, rather an unladylike profession . . . Once more, allow me my dear friend to wish you were with us, we have a pleasant jaunt in contemplation, to Jacksonville, next week there to spend a day or two. Mr Hardin & Browning are our leaders the van brought up by Miss E, my humble self, Webb, Lincoln & two or three others whom you know not. We are watching the clouds most anxiously trusting it may snow, so we may have a sleigh ride—Will it not be pleasant?[4]

William Henry Harrison had just won election to the presidency, and the campaign year had been a historic one for women. More politically engaged than ever before, women participated in the presidential campaign by attending barbeques and debates, making banners, and preparing campaign materials. Mary Todd read all the political newspapers, and she even kept track of local and national politics during her summer trip to visit an uncle in Colombia, Missouri. It was in this exciting political context that Mary and Matilda were holding court with a group of Illinois legislators—John J. Hardin, Orville Hickman Browning, Edwin B. Webb, and Abraham Lincoln—all of them Whigs. Hardin and Browning were already married, and Webb was a widower who had unrequited feelings for Miss Todd. As 1840 was ending, Mary Todd was not quite ready for what she called the "crime of matrimony," but she had already found the good man to whom she would promise her heart.[5]

MOLLY

By the time of the trip to Jacksonville, Miss Todd had fallen in love with Abraham Lincoln, who called her Molly. She saw Lincoln's good and noble character, despite her sister's worry that Lincoln was poor and unrefined and beneath her station. Although Mary could not say Abraham was handsome, she found his heart as large as his arms were long. His gray eyes, which reflected an inner sadness, were dreamy windows

Mary Lincoln, circa 1846. Photograph by Nicholas Shepherd, Springfield, Illinois. Courtesy of Library of Congress, Prints and Photographs, https://www.loc.gov/pictures/item/2004664342/

to a compassionate soul, and she was ready to bet on his rising star. In turn, Lincoln was "charmed with Mary's wit and fascinated with her quick sagacity—her will—her nature—and Culture." Keeping a watchful eye on her sister, Elizabeth Edwards was not blind to the affection between the lovebirds. "I have happened in the room where they were sitting often & often Mary led the conversation," she later remembered. "Lincoln would listen & gaze on her as if drawn by some superior power, irresistibly so; he listened—never scarcely said a word."[6]

Abraham Lincoln's Molly loved literature and reading, smart conversation, and sharp-tongued debate. Like other Kentucky women Lincoln knew, Mary Todd was a great talker and knew her own mind. In these qualities, her formal education, and her affluent Kentucky upbringing, she was a similar spirit to Abraham Lincoln's best New Salem friend Elizabeth Abell. Miss Todd and Mr. Lincoln were companionable souls, and there was a sexual spark between them that Lincoln had not enjoyed with Mary Owens. Shared passion for partisan politics kept the spark burning, and Molly's pluck further inspired Abraham's fascination. One story in particular set Mary Todd apart from other Springfield women, revealing the cheerful, determined spirit of the woman with whom Abraham Lincoln was falling in love.[7]

Springfield's muddy streets were a mess in the rainy spring of 1840, but Mary Todd had cabin fever and convinced Mercy Levering to walk with her five blocks up to the courthouse square. To protect their long skirts and shoes from the mud, Mary devised a plan to spread wood shingles as they walked. They made it to the square unsoiled, but walking home would spoil their silk slippers and delicate hems. Spotting a drayman, Mary flagged him down for a ride. A dray is a cart for hauling goods, not young ladies, but Molly took the ride, unphased by what people who saw her might think. Her adventure gave her friends a good laugh. Lincoln retold the story of "the little drayman that hauled Molly," and one of their friends penned a poem about "a pretty lass a riding on a dray" who "popped heads, to see this Lady gay in silken cloak and feathers white a riding on a dray."[8]

Molly had been smart enough to ford a proverbial spring all by herself. Abraham Lincoln knew she could and would take care of herself. She could be self-sufficient, another test Mary Owens had failed. Molly was comfortable with her agency and did not let public perception ever alter her purpose. There was an independent streak in her that Lincoln appreciated, a trait he wanted in a partner. As his eyes fixed on Molly's, he saw a strong-willed woman; and in his eyes she saw his kindness and all the hopes she dreamed for him. "I would rather marry a good man—a man of mind—with a hope and bright prospects ahead for position—fame & power," Mary told her sister, "than to marry all the houses—gold & bones in the world."[9]

LOVER

Mary Todd did not seduce Abraham Lincoln. She was a proper lady. However, what if her passion for partisan politics, her social graces, her pretty dresses, and the sparkle in her eye charmed the high-water pants off the romantically clueless Mr. Lincoln? Might Lincoln, a middling lawyer with a crooked cravat who kept legal documents in his hat, have been happy to succumb to a smart Kentucky woman who was well born and lovely and in love with him? Abraham Lincoln was a brilliant and shrewd man, and we should give him a little credit for choosing a wife who matched his interests, a woman whose intellect he admired with a political ambition resembling his own. After the failed courtship with Mary Owens, we can assume Lincoln would not have married Mary Todd had there been no sexual chemistry between them. It is also important to note that Lincoln understood that marrying well would help him attain his goals and that Mary Todd was a catch, not to mention that she was from a prominent Kentucky family with close ties to Whig legend Henry Clay. Abraham Lincoln would be marrying up, and it is far more curious Miss Todd chose Mr. Lincoln than that Mr. Lincoln selected Miss Todd.[10]

It should surprise no one that Abraham and Mary found their way to each other in political Springfield. I disagree with the notion that Mary and Abraham could not have married for love or sympathetic companionship because they were unmatched in temperament. If we look in on the couple in 1840, it is easy to see their compatibility, well suited as friends and life partners. They complimented each other's interests and balanced each other's deficits. She was the social charmer to his lackadaisical attitude toward the social necessities of middle-class respectability. He was the cool-headed pragmatist to her frivolity. Each confronted emotional struggles—his detachment and melancholia and her insecurities and emotional fits of pique. Mary loved her beloved man's "great tenderness & gentleness of character," and she accepted his inability to express his emotions. They were beautiful, imperfect humans, but they would be far less imperfect together.[11]

Oh, but if only true love was perfect.

In June 1841, Mary Todd lamented to her friend Mercy Levering: "[Lincoln] deems me unworthy of notice, as I have not met *him* in the gay world for months, with the usual comfort of misery, imagine that others were as seldom gladdened by his presence as my humble self, yet I would that the case were different, that he would once more resume his Station in Society, that 'Richard should be himself again,' much, much happiness would it afford me."[12] She wished her King Richard to recover from the winter of his discontent.

On March 27, 1842, Lincoln wrote his best friend Joshua Speed:

> I am not going beyond the truth, when I tell you, that the short space it took me to read your last letter, gave me more pleasure, than the total sum of all I have enjoyed since that fatal first of Jany. '41. Since then, it seems to me, I should have been entirely happy, but for the never-absent idea, that there is *one* still unhappy whom I have contributed to make so. That still kills my soul. I cannot but reproach myself, for even wishing to be happy while she is otherwise. She accompanied a large party on the Rail Road cars, to Jacksonville last Monday; and on her return, spoke, so that I heard of it, of having enjoyed the trip exceedingly. God be praised for that.[13]

Oh, no, what happened?

Well, dear reader, we don't exactly know. The true story is buried in the Lincoln family crypt in Springfield. All we know for certain is that the lovers parted ways on what Lincoln called "that fatal first," and that for months afterward he was depressed. He missed several days of the legislative session due to illness and distress, and when he apologized to John Stuart for his short update from Springfield on January 20 he wrote: "I have not sufficient composure to write a long letter." Three days later in another letter to Stuart, Lincoln was pathetic: "I am now the most miserable man living. If what I feel were equally distributed to the whole human family, there would not be one cheerful face on the earth. Whether I shall ever be better I cannot tell; I awfully forebode I shall not. To remain as I am is impossible; I must die or be better, it appears to me."[14]

Abraham Lincoln was miserable and stayed away from the couple's social circle. Mary Todd was miserable but put on a brave face and maintained her social connections, although an Edwards cousin reported that she was "as lonesome as a gay company loving girl could be so situated." What had transpired between the lovers was fodder for the Springfield gossip mill and for the delusions of William Herndon, Lincoln's first biographer, who told the wild story of Lincoln abandoning Miss Todd at the altar. Another equally creative tale had Lincoln falling in love with Matilda Edwards. Both stories are untrue and thoroughly debunked in an impeccably reasoned chapter entitled "Broken Engagement" in Ruth Painter Randall's 1953 biography of Mary Lincoln.[15]

It is Randall who also put forth the most plausible reason for the breakup: the economic and social divide between Abraham Lincoln and Mary Todd and the argument of Ninian and Elizabeth Edwards that Lincoln was not good enough to marry into their family. In January 1841, Lincoln, with his growing law practice, was more financially settled than he was when he worried that Mary Owens "would have to be poor" if she cast her lot with him. The difference in their stations did not bother Mary Todd, but Lincoln may have harbored doubts that he was secure enough to support any wife, let alone one like his Molly who was accustomed to luxuries he could not afford. I believe Abraham Lincoln loved Mary Todd, but the imposing Ninian Edwards, who was effectively Mary's guardian, could have gotten into his head. Randall's scenario speaks to Lincoln's financial and emotional uncertainty in 1841 and 1842. He was filled with doubts. It also makes sense to the extent that Mary Todd seems to have harbored no resentment toward Lincoln for their parting and long estrangement.[16]

We will likely never know the nature of the breakup, as we are rarely, if ever, privy to the real tempers and truths of other people's romantic relationships. We can mostly trust the story of mutual Springfield friends nudging the couple back together in the late summer of 1842 because they saw the good in Abraham and in Mary and in the improvement of their natures when they were in a room together. It is clear to me that their shared passion for politics rekindled the flames when they teamed up to lambaste a Lincoln political rival in the partisan press in September 1842. Regardless of fact or fiction, it doesn't matter that Abraham Lincoln and Mary Todd broke up at all, and I have already spent too much time writing about it. I don't know why inquiring minds want to know, because what we do know is that Abraham Lincoln and Mary Todd got married. Whatever came between them did not matter on November 4, 1842, nor did it ever matter again.[17]

Because. In the end . . .

There was something special about Mary Todd, radiant in a pleated dress of fine silk arguing about Whig politics at a party. Her eyes twinkled with mischief as her sharp tongue engaged in debate. Poised among Abraham Lincoln's circle of political friends, holding her own, Miss Todd was a unique creature. She was a charming Southern belle whose passions contradicted a typical antebellum lady's character. Her grace, elegance, and formal education, which gave her an open-minded perspective on the world far beyond her Kentucky home, painted a pretty picture for Mr. Lincoln, a smart but informally educated, rough-hewn, uncertain young man.

There was something special about Abraham Lincoln, arguing about Whig politics in a rumpled coat and pants failing to reach the ankles of his long legs. His steely eyes sparkled with intellect as he used his rapier wit like a dagger against his Democratic opponents. A towering figure in a Victorian parlor among Mary Todd's social circle, Mr. Lincoln, who commanded the room with his humorous stories, was a unique creature. He was an uneducated farmer's son, but his intelligence and determination fueled an ambition beyond the dreams of his humble Kentucky and Indiana upbringing. In his smart oratory, his moral and political convictions, and his unruly hair, Mary saw what the world had yet to know. Theirs was not an accidental or an unfortunate union. She was not a great man's greatest mistake. Mary Todd was not an indecisive woman, and Abraham Lincoln was not a half-hearted man. Whether for love or for politics, for both, or for a hundred other reasons we will never know, they chose each other.[18]

WIFE

On November 4, 1842, wearing a white satin gown and a string of pearls, twenty-three-year-old Mary Todd got married. A self-described "ruddy pine knot,"[19] her figure in a fine skirt was a vision. Her groom was the humble, moody, and disheveled Abraham Lincoln. He was gangly and dark complected and had coarse black hair he rarely bothered to smooth into obedience. Mary Todd and Abraham Lincoln may have appeared as a peculiar couple to the wedding guests assembled. Lincoln was an awkward fellow marrying the belle of the ball. There were wedding guests who decades later defined the Lincoln marriage as a political union, but no one in the parlor that day had any inkling of the future rise of the groom's political star, such reminiscences filtered as they were through the lens of historical hindsight. On that winter day in 1842, Mary Todd and Abraham Lincoln were just two ordinary people getting married in an ordinary town, their future, ordinary life together nothing but a hopeful mystery.[20]

9. *Our Friend Mrs. Browning*

Our love to Mrs. Browning and yourself.
—Abraham (and Mary) Lincoln to Orville
Hickman Browning, June 24, 1847

WHEN ELEVEN-YEAR-OLD WILLIE LINCOLN died from typhoid fever on February 20, 1862, Abraham Lincoln, heartbroken and worried about his inconsolable wife, sent a carriage for Senator Orville Hickman Browning and his wife Eliza. Old Illinois friends, beloved faces from the past, would be a balm for the broken hearts of the devastated parents. The Brownings remained in the White House overnight, consoling the Lincolns and sitting with Willie's body while the Lincolns tended to Tad Lincoln, who was gravely ill with the fever. The senator departed for the capitol at noon the next day, but Eliza stayed on because the Lincolns needed her gentle presence. She helped care for Tad and sat with his grief-stricken mother. Eliza Browning was grieving, too. She felt Mary's sorrow layered upon her own. She and her husband, who would arrange for Willie's funeral, had recently lost their twenty-two-year-old foster son William Shipley in the Battle of Belmont in November 1861. Eliza, like Mary, had also buried a baby back in Illinois. There was solace for all the parties in sharing old sorrows, raw grief, and the long friendship between their families, which had begun in Vandalia, Illinois, in 1836.[1]

Abraham Lincoln first met the Brownings when the Tenth Illinois General Assembly convened in the state capital on December 5, 1836. Orville Hickman Browning was a first-term state senator from Quincy and a Whig who would become a friend and important political ally. However, it was Browning's wife who first drew Lincoln's attention. Eliza Caldwell Browning, born in 1807, was a tall, confident, charming Kentucky woman who became known in political and social circles for her intellect, candor, and humor. After a short courtship in February 1836, she had married Browning, a lawyer and fellow Kentuckian, whom she had met through the arrangement of Browning's sister. The couple settled in Quincy, where they would live throughout their marriage, but with Orville's election they decided to go together to Vandalia for the legislative session.[2]

Eliza Browning met Abraham Lincoln at a delicate moment in his life, a time when he was beginning a career in the law and making sense of his personal relationship with Mary Owens. Lincoln was on edge and, it seems, clung to Eliza, another strong Kentucky woman to befriend and admire. Lincoln picked up a friendship with Eliza Browning just where his New Salem friendship with Elizabeth Abell left off, and the two new friends enjoyed conversation and sharpening each other's wit. During that legislative session, Lincoln spent evenings with the Brownings, and Eliza kept Abraham on his toes with her strong opinions. She became a mentor, tutoring Lincoln in the ways of gentility and helping to build up his confidence after a shaky year away from the safety and comfort of New Salem.[3]

In April 1838, Lincoln penned a lengthy, humorous letter to Eliza Browning about his failed courtship with Mary Owens. The personal details he shared, like his emotional confusion in the courting and his mortification over his ultimate rejection, speak to the comfort he had in his friendship with Eliza. The humor and the tone in this remarkable letter make clear that Abraham and Eliza understood much about each other's personalities and perspectives. Lincoln began the letter: "Without apologizing for being egotistical, I shall make the history of so much of my own life, as has elapsed since I saw you, the subject of this letter," ending it with: "When you receive this, write me a long yarn about something to amuse me."[4] The letter is a masterclass in self-deprecation and an example of Lincoln's ability to tell a good story and to humble his own role within it. In explaining the relationship with Owens, Lincoln wrote:

> I was mortified, it seemed to me, in a hundred different ways. My vanity was deeply wounded by the reflection that I had so long been too stupid to discover her intentions, and at the same time never doubting that I understood them perfectly; and also, that she whom I had taught myself to believe nobody else would have, had actually rejected me with all my fancied greatness; and to cap the whole, I then, for the first time, began to suspect that I was really a little in love with her. But let it all go. I'll try and out live

> it. Others have been made fools of by the girls; but this can never be with truth said of me. I most emphatically, in this instance, made a fool of myself.[5]

Lincoln dated his letter April 1, so Eliza wondered whether it was just a story or partly true and embellished for comedic effect. Years later in Washington, she would learn the story was, indeed, true. Old friends could now laugh about their awkward youthful past over a late supper or during a stroll on the White House lawn.[6]

I view this Lincoln letter as evidence of a man figuring himself out while at the same time trusting in a platonic friendship between two like-minded people comfortable in each other's company. It might be a simple matter of perspective, but the proof for me is in the endurance of Lincoln's friendship with Eliza and her husband into his marriage with Mary Lincoln. As well, the social company Lincoln kept with Eliza in Vandalia was based on the same interplay between men and women, with shared political passion and intellectual capacity, that he would enjoy in Springfield. That Vandalia context was the preparation for Lincoln's introduction to the Springfield society in which he would meet his future wife.

Eliza Browning is yet another strong, articulate woman at the center of the Lincoln story. Among political men and women, she held court like a benevolent queen. In 1839, after the state capital moved to Springfield, Lincoln and his fellow legislator Edwin Webb endorsed to Mrs. Browning this request: "There is no doubt if you were here, there would be extensive improvements in the important business, of visiting, conversation & amusement. . . . I have been visiting the ladies this evening, they say it will be quite gay this winter—several ladies from a distance are here, with the intention of spending the winter. . . . Many others besides your humble petitioners are inquiring for your Honoress." Mary Todd was among the ladies mentioned. Eliza Browning was a social bridge of sorts for Abraham Lincoln.[7]

One historian wrote this about Mrs. Browning: "Her force of mind made her a respected adviser of men who ordinarily despised the brains of women."[8] A backhanded compliment, because, actually, men respected Eliza Browning for her *mind*. Her husband, Abraham Lincoln, and other Illinois legislators liked her because she was smart, curious about the world around her, and willing to share her opinions.

Over the years, the friendship between the Lincolns and the Brownings endured. In an 1847 letter to Browning, Lincoln wrote: "I hope this may find you well, and Mrs. Browning recovered from her hurt."[9] Eliza's sorrow is unknown, but the statement is evidence of the intimacy between the couples. The Brownings lived in Quincy, 110 miles west of Springfield, but they were guests in the Lincoln home throughout the 1850s. Mr. Browning was the more frequent visitor, but together the couple attended parties with the Lincolns, enjoyed quiet dinners together, and shared refreshments on warm summer nights. For example, the Brownings were in Springfield on July 22, 1852, to dine at the Lincoln home, and when the Lincolns were in Chicago in July 1859, Mary Lincoln made a point to see Orville Browning, who was also in the city. They took a carriage ride together with Adelia Dubois, a friend and neighbor from Springfield.[10]

Abraham Lincoln and Orville Browning were political allies, and Mary Lincoln and Eliza Browning, although temperamentally different, were friends. Both women were politically engaged, well read, and comfortable sharing their opinions with men. When Lincoln's presidential campaign settled on the rail-splitter image to celebrate Lincoln as the candidate of the common man, Eliza Browning disapproved. She wrote Illinois Republican Ozias Hatch: "I fear fence rails nor the low 'slang name' of Old Abe will not do it; but the Hon Abram Lincoln with the hearty efforts of all good Republican[s], & the blessing of an Over-ruling Providence will do it."[11]

Browning was comfortable with politics on her mind and on her tongue, and after Lincoln became president, she lobbied him to appoint her husband to the U.S. Supreme Court: "Amid your many cares, vexations, & responsibilities; please excuse the intrusion of an old friend for a few moments," she wrote. "If it is possible, my dear Sir, for you to appoint Mr Browning to the Supreme Judgeship without doing violence, to your feelings, or better judgment; you will gratify a sincere friend . . . I know men in Indiana (that horse leech State always crying, give! give!) want the office I know men in Ohio (that have had it for thirty years) want it. Now I ask you Mr Lincoln in view of the whole matter, do you conscientiously do you, think any of them have Stronger claims than Mr Browning? If so, I have not a word to say, I bow submissively. . . . please excuse an anxious wife, May God bless you, and make you the

Savior of our dear, dear, country very respectfully your old & Sincere friend E. H. Browning sub rosa."[12]

In her letter, Browning's apology for being a woman and assertion of her risk in overstepping a political line, her conviction of mind, her staunch support of her husband, and her request for privacy, sub rosa, are identical in character and tone to the many such political letters Mary Lincoln penned to political men. The similarities between these two dynamic women are striking evidence of the type of women Abraham Lincoln appreciated.

In June 1861, Orville Hickman Browning won the appointment to fill the Illinois U.S. Senate seat vacated by Stephen Douglas's death. He first came to Washington alone, but in February 1862, Eliza Browning and their adopted daughter Emma joined him. It was not long after Eliza's arrival when the Lincoln boys fell ill with typhoid fever, her arrival a fortunate coincidence for her grief-stricken old friends. In the year following, Orville Browning attended church with Mary Lincoln and joined her for carriage rides, and Eliza and Emma Browning were often at the White House keeping company with the Lincoln family. On March 9, 1862, for example, President Lincoln sent a carriage for the Brownings—the senator for a meeting with Lincoln, while the women visited with Mrs. Lincoln and Tad.[13]

Eliza Browning loved her friend Lincoln, but she also admired her president. In a letter to her aunt in March 1862, she wrote:

> When I first came to Washington I spent a week at the "White House." I had many conversations with the President about the state of things in our Country; and I do think he is one of the wisest best men of the age. I think we have great reason to thank God that we have <u>such</u> a man at the head of affairs, at <u>such a time</u>. We feel that the south has brought this <u>causeless wicked</u> rebellion on our country and that it is the duty of the government to <u>put</u> it <u>down</u>.[14]

When Orville Browning completed his term in the U.S. Senate, Mary Lincoln was worried the Brownings would return to Quincy. On December 14, 1862, she told Browning that her husband was anxious to have him and Mrs. Browning in Washington permanently. The Lincolns were disappointed when their friends returned to Illinois, and by 1864 distance began to loosen the bond between their families. Orville

Browning's politics also shifted toward a conservativism counter to Lincoln's later policies, there were jealousies on Browning's part, and Mary Lincoln's emotional difficulties after Willie's death caused strain. Yet the connection remained. In the spring of 1864, the Sisters of Good Samaritans in Quincy made Mary Lincoln an honorary member. Eliza Browning had arranged for the First Lady to endorse her local work to support the war effort, and Mary Lincoln obliged her friend. Orville Browning was a pallbearer at Lincoln's funeral, and Mary Lincoln corresponded with him after Lincoln's death.[15] Yet sadly, like so many important female friendships, Mary Lincoln's connection to Eliza Browning faded away after she settled in Chicago in 1865. Building a new life with her two surviving sons took all the energy the grieving widow could muster.

When historian Theodore Calvin Pease edited Orville Hickman Browning's personal diaries for publication in 1927, he discussed the historical importance of Lincoln's friendship with Eliza Browning in the introduction. It was a rare acknowledgment of a woman's influence in Lincoln's life. However, he also wrote: "One may speculate on how far the country's history would have been different had the able, firm, temperate-minded Eliza Caldwell replaced the tempestuous Mary Todd as the wife of Lincoln."[16] In this outrageous speculation, Pease failed to understand that Lincoln never wished to wed the already-married Eliza Browning, and it missed the fact that Lincoln could want a woman for a friend and not for a wife. Pease's reasoning was also bizarre. He denigrated Mary Lincoln (and women) while at the same time giving Mary Lincoln credit for breaking American history and suggesting that Eliza Browning possessed the power to save our country.

Alleged almighty power to the contrary, Eliza Browning lived out her quiet life after the war in Quincy, a lady in a gracious house her husband built for her in the 1870s. She adopted several children, some with special needs. She and her husband lived a private, charitable life in Quincy, with occasional trips to Chicago, New York, and Colorado, the latter to benefit her frail health. Orville Browning died in August 1881, leaving his widow with debts. Eliza Browning died penniless on January 23, 1885, at the age of seventy-seven. Her obituary described her as "a woman of rare traits and great intelligence, and all her life given to charity." Eliza had contracted typhoid and died a week later from the resulting pneumonia. Memories in her final days were, no doubt, about her husband, children, and grandchildren. Memories may have also floated her mind back to the Civil War, back to the typhoid outbreak in Washington that claimed Willie Lincoln's life, and back to her old friend Abraham Lincoln.[17]

10. My Lincoln Friends

I hope you're having (or had) fun with Mary and Jen.
—@Mr_Lincoln to @StacyPhD,
Twitter, August 31, 2019

THEY WERE COMING FROM southern Ontario, northern Indiana, and Rockford, Illinois. I was driving from St. Louis to Springfield, Illinois, to meet these new friends, a blogger, podcasters, and Lincoln fans. I had arranged to introduce them to my old friends, a Lincoln curator, a history librarian, two Lincoln editors, and a Mary Lincoln presenter. It was a warm day in August 2019, and we convened in the beer garden at a microbrewery across Seventh Street from the Lincoln Home National Historic Site. Except for my friend Pam, dressed as Mary Lincoln for a living-history event in the Lincoln Home neighborhood, we looked like any group of friends sharing a pint, conversing, and laughing on a summer Saturday.

But we were not just friends.

We were Lincoln friends.

And Lincoln friends are a lucky, happy lot.

I first became acquainted with Mary, @Miss_Bellatrix, on Twitter through a mutual follow, @Mr_Lincoln, not long after I joined the platform as @StacyPhD in 2010. I had no understanding of Twitter and no clue about how hashtags worked, but I thought a wise, old historian like me could fill a void by offering the young folk smart daily tweets about Abraham Lincoln. I pulled together Lincoln documents and Lincoln on-this-day facts to post. I also prepared a list of what I call Lincoln Lunacies to share, like Lincoln dolls and out-of-time Lincoln images used in modern advertising. I was surprised to discover, however, a vibrant, brilliant history Twittersphere (#twitterstorians) and a crowded Lincoln-tweeting field. There was Geoff, aka @Mr_Lincoln, providing his nineteen thousand followers with excellent historical content. Despite his Lincolnesque modesty, Geoff is a history whiz. Mary, a blogger (aka Civil War Fangirl), has as much knowledge in her head about Civil War battles and generals as renowned Civil War historian James McPherson. And Mary is the most joyful Lincoln enthusiast I have ever known. Her tweets bridged the scholarly and the silly, delightful, springy expanse upon which I love to skip rope.

In April 2016, our virtual friendship became "real" (is that the word I'm looking for here? The modern world is so perplexing for a historian of the nineteenth century!). I had served as a panelist at a symposium on Mary Lincoln at the First Ladies National Historic Site in Canton, Ohio. The symposium had been an important engagement for me during a period of dark personal grief. It was also an opportunity to reconnect with a friend from my University of Illinois doctoral days. Geoff, who lives in northern Ohio, and Mary, a Canadian, had been real friends to each other for a good while already, and they planned to attend the symposium together in part to meet me. We convened at a picturesque winery for dinner the night before the symposium, and never before or since has conversation with new people been as effortless for me. It was a healing connection to meet face-to-face with good Lincoln people.

I have two marvelous co-editors in my current work on Jane Addams, and I have met fine scholars studying Addams and her Progressive Era contexts. But there is no such animal as a Jane Addams fan, and, sadly, many people I meet do not know who Jane Addams was. I do have a Jane Addams doll, but there is no great market for Addams kitsch, and I do not have Jane Addams friends in the way I have Lincoln friends. Lincoln is unique, and there is an unusual, wonderful kinship among people who study Abraham Lincoln for knowledge as well as for joy. We are Lincoln scholars *and* Lincoln fans, and the friendships meeting in the middle are special. Lincoln was right in saying: "If we have no friends, we have no pleasure."[1] And I am right in saying: "If we have Lincoln friends, we have a special kind of treasure."

The Springfield meeting with my new and old Lincoln friends brought Mary and me together in person once again, and another social media friend Jen from Indiana joined us. It was Mary's first trip to Springfield to see the Lincoln sites, and she spent the entire weekend on the verge of happy tears. I was emotional about meeting Jen, a brave woman beating cancer with grace who inspired me. Mary and her two podcast cohosts, Jeremy and Nick, two Rockford high school teachers, were in Springfield to record the one hundredth episode of their *Railsplitter* podcast. I had appeared on the podcast the year before and was excited to meet Jeremy and Nick in person, two more virtual friendships blooming into the real.[2] I rounded up my favorite Springfield Lincoln people—fellow Lincoln editors John and Marilyn, history librarian Kathryn, Lincoln curator James, Park Ranger Rose, and Pam. They all assembled to hang out with the out-of-towners, and I had never been more eager to make introductions. It was Lincoln magic with brilliant conversations passing across the picnic table and fast friendships forming before my eyes. Pam was there repping Mary Lincoln, and Kathryn thrilled everyone by talking about her work at the Lincoln Presidential Library and her portrayals of Harriet Tubman. James brought cool history books to show us, and Rose always has delightful stories to tell about visitors and their questions at the Lincoln Home. Mary, Jeremy, Nick, and Jen shared their own stories about how they came to admire Lincoln and how they shared their love for history. The beer garden lit up with Lincoln light.

I sat there and watched Lincoln scholars and avocational historians, museum professionals, and teachers, Lincoln enthusiasts all, bonding through a shared love for history and admiration for a man more than 150 years in the grave. Right there in Lincoln's adopted hometown, across the street from where he lived, we communed with one another and with Lincoln. It was a blast in the Midwestern summer sun. We were all engaged, learning about one another, our shared humanity across geography, discipline, and generation, ages running from thirty to sixty-five. As Mary later put it: "This community is incredibly accepting . . . we're all on equal footing. . . . We're all here, we're all laughing, we're drinking beers together, and we're celebrating this man who is the reason we've all been able to come together and do this . . . and that gets back to how much his spirit is here and still among us today."[3]

I already knew about Lincoln friend magic before the big Springfield Lincoln party, but James's presence sealed the deal. He is a serious Lincoln scholar, and while I had been friends with him for years, I had not counted him among my light-hearted Lincoln friends. I thought he was a Lincoln scholar who did not care to swing in the Lincoln playground. I invited him because I hoped to see him and catch up, and I knew my new Lincoln friends would be thrilled to meet James. I was not sure, however, that he would want to come out on a Saturday to hang out with a bunch of Lincoln Loonies. Not only did he join us, but the books he brought enthralled my new Lincoln friends, as did his knowledge and enthusiasm for history. My new Lincoln friends made a similar impression on him. He felt the Lincoln friendship magic, too.

There are old friends you grew up with. There are friends you meet along the way who come and go. There are friends who settle in forever. But if you are lucky, you also have friends who share your unique passion, the people who understand why you love what you love or do what you do. I am lucky, indeed, to have my Lincoln friends who understand my emotional connection to Abraham Lincoln. My Lincoln friends are a special and sparkling Lincoln treasure.

PART III

Mrs. Lincoln

11. *She Was Mary Lincoln*

> Do not come on the night train. It is too cold. Come in the morning.
>
> —Abraham Lincoln to Mary Lincoln, December 21, 1864

On November 11, 1842, one week after his wedding, Abraham Lincoln wrote a friend: "Nothing new here, except my marrying, which to me, is a matter of profound wonder."[1] Lincoln was not an effusive man, but there he was in awe, standing at the beginning of an unexpected, exciting, and perplexing new phase of his life. It is impossible to read anything into Lincoln's dramatic declaration other than delightful contemplation. He was no longer alone, his unsettled years in Springfield were behind him. There was innocence in his words and the wide-eyed hope of an adult who has made a big leap. He now had a partner, a lover, a friend, a woman who would make his house a home and give him children. And his new wife was a profound wonder all her own.

Like her husband, Mary Lincoln was beautiful and flawed and full of contradictions. She was whip-smart, curious, and social, but she was insecure, petty, and often reclusive. She loved with all her heart, and she hated with all her heart. She was a woman with a big personality when society expected women to sit quietly and be charming and pretty, but not too charming or too pretty. She was an intriguing woman who defined charming and pretty on her own terms and did not disguise her intelligence or wit. Mary Lincoln's sharp humor was, in fact, a trait she shared with her husband. The Lincolns teased each other and laughed together. In a letter to her sister in 1857, Mary Lincoln wrote: "I often laugh & tell Mr L. that I am determined my next husband *shall* be rich."[2]

Like all humans, Mary Lincoln was multiple people. She was President Abraham Lincoln's wife and a First Lady. She was a child, a daughter, a sister, a friend, a circuit-riding lawyer's wife, a churchgoer, a mother, a grieving mother, and a widow. She was a southern girl and a northern woman. She was an old-fashioned Victorian and also modern. She was a nineteenth-century woman doing the best she could. Sometimes her efforts exceeded even her own expectations, sometimes they were barely good enough, and sometimes they were devastatingly insufficient. Abraham Lincoln knew all these things about his wife. He accepted her complexities because he was not perfect and accepted his own messy contradictions. It is always within the gray space between our best and worst selves, in the middle of the dark and light sides of who we are, where our humanity resides. Mary Lincoln was a collection of experiences, actions, triumphs, and mistakes. As we all are, she was a sum far more worthy than her imperfect parts. Many Mary Lincoln stories are universal stories, and in myriad ways she is us. And to Abraham Lincoln, she was always his lovely, complicated, beguiling wife.[3]

SHE WAS MARY LINCOLN

Until her sister Ann was born, she was Mary Ann, and afterward she was plain Mary. When she arrived in Springfield, Illinois, in 1839, she was Mary Todd, Miss Todd, or Molly, her nickname. When she married Abraham Lincoln in 1842, she became Mary Lincoln, and afterward called herself Mary Lincoln, Mrs. Lincoln, or Mrs. Abraham Lincoln. She signed all her correspondence Mary Lincoln, Mrs. Lincoln, Mrs. Abraham Lincoln, or M. L. She was a typical nineteenth-century woman who took her husband's name and never used her family name again.

Do not call her Mary Todd Lincoln. She disowned her Confederate Todd family members, and the Todd name would offend her. Mary Lincoln was not a feminist who eschewed the patriarchy. She was opinionated and believed in her right to voice her opinions, but once she married, she never defined herself outside her marriage. Mary Lincoln always saw herself first as the wife, and later the widow, of Abraham Lincoln.

SHE WAS SMART

When people ask me about Mary Lincoln, I always start by describing her education, which for her era was extraordinary. In the nineteenth century's first three decades, few children, boys or girls, received a full, formal education. It was not until the 1830s that public education became widely accessible. Lexington, Kentucky, however, was an early educational center. All women in the Todd family were educated, but Robert Todd provided his third daughter with rare opportunities. Mary was a precocious child, and her father allowed her to study for an impressive ten years during a time when a lucky girl might hope to attend school for two or three. In two forward-thinking academies in Lexington, Mary Todd studied math, history, science, religion, and French. At Ward's Academy she participated in public recitations and in 1832 became a student of the avant-garde, French-born Charlotte Mentelle, whose school her father supported. Mary was the star actor at Mentelle's school, where she was encouraged to lose herself in reading, and her teacher's independence and eccentricities inspired Mary's own independence and eccentricities.[4]

Mary's elite education gave her a lifelong appetite for knowledge, a yearning to travel, and an open mind to try new and unusual things, like spiritualism and health spas. The public would often judge her interest in those unusual pursuits as indecent, but those interests were evidence of a forward-thinking mind and a searching spirit. Mary Lincoln found the common disappointing and sometimes inadequate, for example, spending her widowhood looking for remedies for her sorrow and health problems when mainstream medicine failed her.

Mary Lincoln was a voracious reader. She loved great literature, popular books, periodicals, and newspapers. The Civil War's partisan press criticized Mary Lincoln's lavish spending on the White House remodeling and on clothing, but they rarely mentioned the substantive items she purchased. Books she added to the White House library included Sir Walter Scott's series of Waverley novels, a history of birds, a volume of American Indian tales, and a book by American poet Lydia Sigourney. Mary Lincoln accounted for one $250 expenditure in a July 1862 letter to the Commissioner of Public Buildings: "I selected some books for the library—$75 worth were selected in W[ashington] and the remaining $150.00—in N.Y.—There is a very poor set of Waverley—also Shakespeare in the house library, so I replaced each with a fine new edition."[5]

SHE WAS A MAMA BEAR

In May 1860, Mark Delahay arrived in Springfield with a group of Republican men to convey to Abraham Lincoln their party's nomination for president. Delahay arrived at the Lincoln home with two campaign flags and promised one to a Lincoln boy, probably Tad. When Delahay left town, he inadvertently took both flags with him. On May 25, Mary Lincoln wrote to him: "One of my boys appears to claim prior possession of the smallest flag, is inconsolable for its absence. As I believe it is too small to do you any service, and as he is so urgent to have it again . . . I will ask you to send it to us, the first opportunity you may have, especially as he claims it, and I feel it is as necessary to keep one's word with a child, as with a grown person—Hoping you reached home safely, I remain yours respectfully Mary Lincoln."[6]

Mary Lincoln's boys hung her moon. She adored them as babies, indulged their joys as children, and worried herself sick over them, especially during the war. Although she would endure a long estrangement from Robert for his role in her incarceration in an asylum in 1875, in childhood Bobby, Eddie, Willie, and Tad were her darlings. Willie's death in 1862 damn near broke her, but Mary Lincoln continued breathing for her surviving sons. In a letter in December 1865, she wrote: "I must endeavour to make the best of life that is left for me, for the sake of my sons, who have had so much to try them."[7] That Mary Lincoln buried three children is the great tragedy of her life, and it has long been my contention that losing Tad was her hardest sorrow to endure. As she wrote David Davis in November 1871: "My beloved boy was the idol of my heart & had become my inseparable companion—My heart is entirely broken, for without his presence, the world is complete darkness."[8]

SHE WAS PASSIONATE

One of Mary Todd's closest friends in Springfield was Julia Jayne. Not long after Mary's wedding, Julia married Illinois secretary of state Lyman Trumbull. In the 1840s and early 1850s, Abraham Lincoln and Lyman Trumbull were legal colleagues, and the Lincoln and Trumbull families were friendly. In February 1855, political rivalry turned personal for Mary Lincoln when her husband was competing with Trumbull to fill a U.S. Senate seat. Mary Lincoln was in the gallery on the day the Illinois legislature voted (this was back before the popular election of U.S. senators). Mary was certain her husband would win the election, and he led on the first ballot. However, political wheeling and dealing favored Trumbull, and he was the victor. Mr. Lincoln was disappointed, but Mrs. Lincoln was furious. She was also embarrassed, because the party her sister Elizabeth Edwards was hosting to celebrate the new senator was now for Julia instead of for her. Mary Lincoln believed her husband was cheated, and she ended her friendship with Julia Trumbull. She was angry with Lyman Trumbull for his dirty politics, but she blamed Julia for failing to be a better influence on her husband. At that time, Trumbull was a Democrat, so Mary should have understood it was partisan politics that had bested her husband, not his rival's wife. Mary Lincoln was so fiercely loyal to her husband that she could not bear his political loss to an old friend. She could not see that most women of her era lacked her fierce passion for politics.[9]

Mary Lincoln interpreted her husband's political loss as a personal offense, and she never let it go. When she saw Julia Trumbull in 1859, she gossiped to a friend: "Mrs Trumbull made her first appearance last evening, looking as stately & *ungainly* as ever. Altho' she has been in the city 10 days, this has been about the first notice that has been taken of her. Tis unfortunate to be so unpopular."[10] Even after her husband's assassination, Mary Lincoln held her grudge against the Trumbulls, angry that "Mrs Trumbull has not yet honored me with a call, should she ever deign, she would not be received," and calling the senator a "sordid, selfish creature, without a *soul*."[11] Mary Lincoln's grudges were often childish, but this grudge was also evidence that she was Abraham Lincoln's most staunch supporter and no friend to anyone who stood between him and what he wanted.

Julia Trumbull's brother later remembered: "Mrs Lincoln was a woman of quick intellect & strong passions—decided in her friendships & intense in her dislikes."[12] Strong passions, indeed, which sometimes reflected poorly on her character but, in the end, only caused herself pain. In the Trumbull case, her strong passion cost her a dear friend. Yet passion is not always a negative trait. Mary Lincoln's support for her husband, his administration, and the U.S. Army's efforts to defeat the South's rebellion was also passionate. In 1861, she wrote: "In the hour of peace, the kind words of a friend are always acceptable, how much more so when a 'man's foes are those of their own household,' when treason and rebellion threaten our beloved land, our freedom & rights are invaded and every sacred right is trampled upon! Clouds and darkness surround us, yet Heaven is just, and the day of triumph will *surely* come, when justice & truth will be vindicated. Our wrongs will be made right, and we will once more taste the blessings of freedom, of which the degraded rebels would deprive us"[13]

SHE WAS A NORTHERN WOMAN

Mary Lincoln's support for her president and her country *never* wavered. She was pro-Union all the way, steadfast in her loyalty to the Lincoln administration, its policies, and the U.S. military effort to defeat the Southern rebellion. From the beginning of the war when she wrote: "In the battle for the Union, it would gratify me, to see the horses used, from my native state."[14] To after the war when she wrote to Charles Sumner, the day after passage of the Civil Rights Act of 1866, that the Emancipation Proclamation "is a rich & precious legacy, for my sons & one for which I am sure, and *believe* they will always bless God & their father."[15] Through to her widowhood in 1877 when she wrote her nephew about the "great mistake" President Rutherford B. Hayes made in placing a former Confederate in his cabinet when there were so many talented men "patriotic to the *true cause*."[16] Mary Lincoln was a Unionist. She was a patriotic American woman. She stood on the correct side of history.

There was no defined role for a First Lady and no modern press secretaries in Mary Lincoln's day, but reporters in Washington covered Mary Lincoln's activities during the Civil War. Therefore, we have abundant evidence about Mary Lincoln's visits with soldiers, perhaps the most important example of her support for the war effort. The *Evening Star* on August 29, 1862, for example, reported: "Among the many ladies who visit our sick soldiers with cheerful words and kind offices, none are more indefatigable than Mrs. Lincoln. She yesterday visited the Odd Fellows' Hall Hospital, Navy Yard, much to the gratification of the sufferers there, and kindly ministered their wants in various ways—bestowing gifts, kind words, &c. Among others Mrs. Lincoln visited the bedside of one soldier, over 60 years of age, who had expressed a desire to see her. After some conversation she bestowed upon the soldier a handsome donation. Her visit will long be remembered by the invalids."[17]

That particular visit took place six months after Willie Lincoln's death, and it seems clear that sitting with soldiers helped lighten Mary Lincoln's grief. With a maternal concern, she sat with sick and injured soldiers, wrote letters for them, brought them gifts and flowers, arranged holiday dinners, and joined her husband and others to review troops. On October 31, 1862, she accompanied General Winfield Scott to the Brooklyn naval yard, where she went aboard the *North Carolina* to meet the captain and crew. Soldiers who met her remembered her fondly. Although Mary Lincoln could be fearful and anxious, when she was with soldiers, witness to their dreadful, shocking injuries, she was calm and brave. Despite her personal sorrow, she fulfilled a duty as First Lady to be a symbolic mother to the country's soldiers.[18]

SHE WAS A SURVIVOR

While childhood privilege and education shaped Mary Lincoln's heart and mind, suffering etched its own defining marks upon her life. Physical pain and grief would be ever-present antagonists in her story. Mary Lincoln struggled with her emotions, anxiety, and debilitating headaches, both moods and migraines untreated at a time when medicine

Mary Lincoln, circa 1865. Photograph by Joseph Ward, Boston. Courtesy of Library of Congress, Prints and Photographs, https://www.loc.gov/pictures/item/2023630349/

was dominated by men and dismissive of feminine ailments. The difficult birth of her fourth son Tad, so nicknamed by his father because his head at birth was enormous like a tadpole's, left Mary Lincoln with an injury. That injury likely prevented her from having more children and caused her persistent gynecological problems. As she wrote to a friend in 1868: "I am *permitted* to sit up, whilst I write you a few lines, as for the past three weeks, I have been seriously sick. My disease is of a womanly nature, which you will understand has been greatly accelerated by the last three years of mental suffering. Since the birth of my youngest son . . . I have been more or less a sufferer. My physician, Dr Clarke . . . told me on yesterday, that he must prescribe an entire change of air, [and] scene, for me."[19]

Mary Lincoln understood the connection between mind and spirit, and empathy for her should be easy. Imagine suffering an injury during childbirth, endured without anesthesia, and that said injury still plagued you fifteen years after the child's birth; and then imagine having a male physician tell you what you need is a little fresh air. Imagine still that you are a woman who has buried two children when, at the end of a bloody Civil War, you are sitting next to your husband watching a comedic play when an assassin fatally shoots him in the head. Now imagine you are a widow of a martyred American president trying to get through a day without a negative story about you in the press, suffer the death of a third child, and have your last surviving child lock you up in a mental asylum.[20]

I am a mentally and physically healthy woman living with modern amenities and medications who has never witnessed a violent crime and who has buried only one child, but still there are days when my grief makes it hard to get out of bed. Today, anyone who suffered what Mary Lincoln suffered would have medicine and therapy and sympathy for living with PTSD. Mary Lincoln deserved empathy in her day, and she deserves empathy today. Mary Lincoln was not Andrew Jackson who killed Native Americans, Jefferson Davis who committed treason against his country, or John Wilkes Booth who assassinated an American president. Historians have considered all three of those flawed men with nuance, and Mary Lincoln deserves nuance, too. She was not a monster. She was a human woman who suffered physical and emotional trauma that would wipe out the best of us, and she got through it all under the critical eye of an unforgiving American public. Is it not well past time to let the woman rest in peace?

We cannot understand Abraham Lincoln's wife unless we acknowledge her suffering. Without empathy, there is no point studying Mary Lincoln, or Abraham Lincoln, or any figure in history at all. Mary's sorrows were part of her humanity, and how she moved forward was evidence of her resilience, a trait that is always illustrative of a person's spirit. After her son Eddie died in 1850, she was pregnant with Willie just a few weeks later. Two months after Willie died in 1862, she sent figs to her friend Emma Gurley along with a get-well message for her ailing daughter. Two months after her husband was murdered, she stared down powerful men who wanted to wrest from her a widow's right to determine the location of her husband's memorial. After fighting for her release from the asylum in Batavia, Illinois, where her son had her incarcerated, she fought for her legal independence, regained control over her finances, and moved to Europe for four years to curate a life of her own choosing.[21]

In 1953, Lincoln editor Roy P. Basler wrote: "It would be hard to find in all history a personality less equipped to bear the blows that fate dealt the pretty, gallant, spunky little woman who married Abraham Lincoln because she adored him. And yet she bore them and survived to reorient her spirit out of an insanity that nearly destroyed her."[22]

In 1865, Mary Lincoln wrote: "The world, without my beloved husband & our best friend, is a sad & lonely place."[23] She was forlorn, lost like a lone survivor of a shipwreck floating on a raft at sea. But she was alive, and she kept on living. In 1876 she was in Europe by herself, managing her finances, keeping up on political news in America, making new friends, and finding joy and a little much-deserved peace. In March 1878, she wrote home from Pau, France: "I leave here this afternoon, & will be in Naples in ten days time, where I join my lady friend."[24] Abraham Lincoln would have been so proud of his widow, out in the world, despite her sorrows, living in the gorgeous French Pyrenees, doing something that thrilled her, sightseeing throughout France and Italy.

Mary Lincoln was a challenging, difficult woman, but she was glorious, and she was brave. Love her or hate her, Mary Lincoln was a survivor.

12. Mrs. Lincoln's Household

> I consider myself fortunate, if at eleven o'clock, I once more find myself in my pleasant room & very especially if my tired & weary Husband is *there*, resting in the lounge to receive me—to chat over the occurrences of the day.
>
> —Mary Lincoln to Mercy Conkling, November 19, 1864

THE STORY OF MRS. Lincoln began in a small, humble room in a boardinghouse. As Mr. Lincoln wrote to a friend in the spring of 1843: "We are not keeping house; but boarding at the Globe tavern, which is very well kept now by a widow lady of the name of Beck. Our room . . . and boarding only costs four dollars a week. . . . Mary joins in sending love to your Fanny and you."[1]

A boardinghouse was a respectable, common first home for new couples in 1840s America, and this boardinghouse was perfect for the Lincolns. It was affordable and located on the Springfield town square. The yellow Sugar Creek limestone of the new Illinois State Capitol across the street was a gleaming symbol of the state's promise that matched the newlyweds' high hopes for themselves. A room lacking frills and privacy may have been an adjustment at first for Mary, who was used to servants and more gracious surroundings, but she seemed to relish the simplicity of her first home and the independence it offered. The living arrangement forestalled the heavy domestic responsibilities, and she was close to her sisters and the town's many amenities. The Globe was also convenient for Abraham Lincoln, close to his law office and the Sangamon County Courthouse. The Globe was a temporary love nest in which to begin life together, to become acquainted with each other, and to conceive a baby.[2]

A comfortable, domestic life was the best hope for most women of her era, but there is no evidence that Mary Lincoln was ever bitter about this truth. In contrast to contemporaries like Elizabeth Cady Stanton and Susan B. Anthony, who advocated for woman suffrage and legal rights for women, Mary Lincoln was never an advocate for women's equality. As an educated, middle-class woman, she had the luxury to feel entitled to hold and to express political opinions and to make decisions for herself and her family. She bristled a little against society's definition of appropriate and respectable because she believed (and her husband agreed with her) that she should be allowed to define appropriate and respectable for herself. However, she always defined her life and her purpose within the context of marriage and motherhood and her husband's professional success. In the little room in the Globe Tavern, as the first months of her marriage passed and her belly swelled with her first child, she dreamed of a long, happy domestic life. Her early married life would be typical of other women of her station, even as history awaited her.[3]

On August 1, 1843, nine months after her wedding, Mary gave birth to Robert, called "Bob" or "Bobby." The boy's arrival was both thrilling for his parents and terrifying, as it is for all first-time parents who have no clue what is coming. Abraham Lincoln, always teasing, declared to a friend: "I'm glad it is all over and that he is such a fine-looking little fellow. I was afraid he might have one of my long legs and one of Mary's short ones, and he'd have had a terrible time getting through the world."[4]

Whatever the length of his limbs, little Bobby's arrival pressed the Lincolns for space, so they rented a cottage with four rooms and a private yard where they spent the winter of 1843–44. Their improving family finances, based on Mr. Lincoln's thriving law practice, allowed the Lincolns to be on the move again in May 1844, when they purchased the first and only home they would ever own. It was a one-and-a-half-story cottage at the corner of Eighth and Jackson Streets, south of Springfield's town square.[5]

Constructed in 1839, it was a modest home, costing the Lincolns $1,500. Mary Lincoln was happy with the house, and her husband let her make it her own. Over the years she would make many improvements, including a dramatic addition increasing the house to a full two stories. Three Lincoln sons were born in the house. Edward, called "Eddie," arrived on March 10, 1846, and he died in the house on February 1, 1850. William, called "Willie," arrived on December 21, 1850, a pure joy to his parents who were still grieving four-year-old Eddie's death. Big brother Bob was seven years old when Willie was born, and Mary Lincoln was a busy mother. On April 4, 1853, when she had her fourth son Thomas, known as "Tad," she managed a big house and three boys under ten years old. Mary told her sister Emilie that she was a most content "staid matron, & moreover the mother of three noisy boys."[6]

Mary Lincoln did not receive a domestic education, raised as she was in an affluent household managed by enslaved women. But she and her husband were capable people, eager to learn. Mr. Lincoln taught himself the law, and Mrs. Lincoln taught herself how to keep a good house, learning the domestic arts from the era's literature for women, such as *The Mother's Book* by Lydia Marie Child.[7] Mary Lincoln did not just get by; she became famed among friends for her gracious hospitality and dinners at which she served Kentucky dishes that delighted her husband and their guests. Mary Lincoln managed her household in all the ordinary ways, cooking, cleaning, sewing, lighting and tending the fires, and minding her rambunctious boys.[8]

Over the years, she hired servants to help, but she mostly preferred to manage by herself. When Tad was born in the spring of 1853, Abraham Lincoln left just a week later for Bloomington to begin his legal work for the spring term of the Eighth Judicial Circuit. This trip would take him to Paris, Metamora, Pekin, Clinton, Danville, Urbana, and Decatur. With the exception of a possible quick trip home one weekend from Pekin, he would be gone for two months, while his wife was at home breastfeeding an infant, chasing a toddler, minding a young boy, and running a household. Lincoln's absences became the rhythm of Mary Lincoln's daily life, and the independence she developed was the melody of the Lincoln marriage.[9]

Mary Lincoln accepted her household arrangement and came to appreciate the autonomy it gave her, but she was sometimes lonely and fearful. For example, in the winter of 1857 when Tad was unwell, she wrote a friend about her husband's absence: "I am feeling troubled & it would be a comfort to have him *at home*."[10] Two years later, she lamented to another friend: "I am again at home and Mr L. is in Wisconsin."[11] Once during the Civil War she wrote her husband: "I have waited in vain to hear from you, yet as you are not *given* to letter writing, will be charitable enough to impute your silence to the right cause."[12] Although Mary saw her husband more regularly after they settled in the White House, the demands of his office increased his emotional distance from her. His health was a constant worry to her, and she worked hard to provide distractions for him. They attended plays and played with the boys, and she did her best to care for her overburdened husband. In 1864, she wrote: "The President is a little better today, was able to visit the 'blue room' tonight. I will try & persuade him to take some medicine & rest a little on the morrow."[13]

There is no evidence in the eight hundred or so of Mary Lincoln's surviving letters that she was disgruntled with the Lincoln family's household arrangement. In fact, her domestic contentment probably rested, at least in part, upon the independence the household arrangement provided her. When she wrote that letter to her husband about his silence, in fact, she was the one away from home. Mary Lincoln was independent when she arrived in Washington, and she continued to be independent during her time as First Lady. The Lincoln household was always Mary Lincoln's sphere, and Abraham Lincoln preferred it that way.

Mary Lincoln with sons Willie and Tad, December 1860. Frank Leslie's Illustrated Newspaper 11 (December 15, 1860): cover

If Mary Lincoln wanted to travel with Lincoln to Chicago, she did. If she did not want to go with him to visit their friends in Quincy or to a political debate, she stayed home. When she wanted to go to Congress in 1847, Lincoln took her and the boys with him. In Washington during the Civil War, she made her own decisions about traveling to New York or taking the family to their summer retreat at the Soldiers' Home. A statement Lincoln made during a whistle stop in Ashtabula, Ohio, on the inaugural train trip to Washington in February 1861 said everything anyone needs to know about Mary Lincoln. A newspaper reported that Mr. Lincoln told the Ashtabula crowd cheering for Mrs. Lincoln to make an appearance on the platform that she would not likely do so. The reporter paraphrased Lincoln that "he should hardly hope to induce her to appear, as he had always found it very difficult to make her do what she did not want to."[14]

Abraham Lincoln was joking, of course, but he was also dead serious.

Mary Lincoln was the queen of her domestic life, and Abraham Lincoln was content to let his wife handle management of family and household, which did not interest him much. Mary was sometimes hard to live with, but so was her husband. She was a feisty, opinionated, emotional woman who sometimes shopped to fill an emptiness inside her, but her husband's long absences from home put extra burdens upon her. When Lincoln was at home, he was often distant, melancholy, put his boots up on the divan, and answered the front door in his shirtsleeves. Abraham and Mary Lincoln were two flawed humans making a typical, imperfect life together. In their marriage, like every marriage, there were good days and bad days.

Abraham Lincoln once joked: "If you knew how little harm it does me and how much good it does her, you wouldn't wonder that I am meek."[15] Abraham Lincoln subscribed to the old Chinese proverb: happy wife, happy life. In Washington, when the burdens on Lincoln's shoulders were historically great, he let his wife take charge of things that were not important to him. Mrs. Lincoln wanted to buy pretty dresses, and Mr. Lincoln let her. When she wanted friends or family members to visit, even if one turned out to be an unrepentant Confederate, Abraham Lincoln let it happen. When she invited spiritualists to hold séances in the White House or Soldiers' Home, Lincoln did not interfere and, in fact, was present for at least one. Spiritualism was appealing to many people who were grieving during the Civil War; if it might soothe his wife's grief, Lincoln was willing to indulge her.[16]

He ran the country, and she ran the household. To Abraham Lincoln, Mary Lincoln was her own woman. She was his lover, his friend, the mother of his beloved boys, his political supporter, and the household manager. But she was also a human being with her own interests, her own delights, and her own life to live. Abraham Lincoln gave Mary Lincoln her autonomy, and he went along for the bumpy, beautiful ride.

13. Let's Hear It for the Boys

My Beloved Husband's great tenderness & gentleness of character is well established & in his great love for his children, it is well known.

—Mary Lincoln to Alexander Williamson, June 15, 1865

RAISING CHILDREN WAS the primary responsibility of women in the age of Lincoln. Regardless of social or economic status, women's lives were defined by childbearing, childrearing, and family life, and Mary Lincoln's life was spent tending her four spirited boys and making a home for them and their father. Mrs. Lincoln's greatest gifts to her husband were Bob, Eddie, Willie, and Tad, their nicknames illustrating their parents' adoration. Lincoln's "Dear rascals" deserved pet names.[1] The Lincoln boys paint a softer side of Abraham Lincoln, who was, in his bones, a family man. He and his wife were partners in child spoiling, crafting a childhood for their boys that looks a great deal like the modern, American, middle-class families we see today, childhood defined and coddled.

Together, Abraham and Mary Lincoln enjoyed their boys. Together, they grieved the death of two. The Lincoln sons were the strongest bond between them, and their indulgent parenting styles are another example of their companionable marriage. The Lincoln boys had pets and parties and permission to be children, to play and to romp through life, to be carefree and joyful. Abraham Lincoln had no heart to be stern; and Mary Lincoln was infrequently willing to be a disciplinarian. Lincoln's law partner William Herndon was horrified that the Lincolns spoiled those little boys a little rotten. In December 1859, for example, the Lincolns hosted an elaborate party for Willie's ninth birthday. Mary made invitations for the guests, and a noisy army of children attended the party, which featured cake, games, and chaos spilling onto the lawn and out to the street. Mary recalled the party to her friend Hannah Shearer:

Tad and Abraham Lincoln, February 5, 1865. Photograph by Alexander Gardner. Courtesy of Library of Congress, Prints and Photographs, https://www. https://www.loc.gov/pictures/item/2009630691/

"Willie's birthday came off on the 21st of Dec. and as I had long promised him a celebration, it duly came off. Some 50 or 60 boys & girls attended the gala . . . I wish your boy had been in their midst."[2]

It is not all good to spoil children rotten. The lack of discipline during the Civil War particularly, for example, resulted in Tad's educational delays. But the Lincolns adored their children, and so long as the boys kept out of their mother's parlor, they knew few boundaries. They wrestled in their father's Springfield law office and ran wild through the White

House, enjoying almost unfettered access to their father, the president of the United States, while he was working. They slept with their animals, chased cats through the White House, and rode ponies and played soldier on the White House lawns. They were allowed to skip their lessons, demand the attention of White House staff, and engage White House visitors no matter the political or military importance of their business with the president. When the boys required discipline, it was their mother who administered it and their father who, frequently, undid it. Once when she threatened to whip Tad for defacing his copper-toed shoes, which he had done as a gesture against Copperheads, his father said: "I guess I must exercise my executive clemency a little and pardon you, my patriotic boy. You shall not be whipped for this offense. Go and explain your case to your mother as it now stands."[3]

After Willie Lincoln's death in February 1862, his devastated parents clung tight to Tad, who was only nine years old when he lost his beloved brother. Robert Lincoln was a student at Harvard, so the Lincolns poured all their love and attention on Tad. Both parents spoiled him more, loved him harder, and drew solace from his joyful, mischievous spirit. Tad became his parents' hope for peace in the nation and for themselves. He offered a chance for them to heal their broken hearts, and they granted his every wish. "Capt. Dahlgren may let 'Tad' have a little gun that he cannot hurt himself with," Abraham Lincoln wrote. Tad thus received a miniature brass cannon. Lincoln made two requests on behalf of his son on April 10, 1865. One to Secretary of the Navy Gideon Welles: "Let Master Tad have a Navy sword." Another to Secretary of War Stanton: "Tad wants some flags. Can he be accommodated."[4]

Tad Lincoln is the Lincoln son who breaks my heart the hardest. He suffered his brother's death and his father's death, and he endured the sorrowful burden of being the most important solace to his grieving widowed mother. Photographs of Abraham Lincoln and Tad are a window into the relationship between them, which became a lovely muse for artists. Lincoln's love for Tad is inspiring to all of us who love Lincoln. His bond with the little boy is bittersweet and relatable; Tad's exploits and his father's joy of him give us a glimpse into Lincoln's soul. No story is more precious evidence of the love story of Abraham Lincoln and his children than the story of Tad and his goats. When Mary and Tad were away from Washington in the summer of 1863, Abraham Lincoln sent them troublesome news on August 8: "My dear Wife. All as well as

The author with statue of Abraham and Tad Lincoln, Rapid City, South Dakota, 2016. Sculptor James Michael Maher. Author's Photo

usual, and no particular trouble anyway. . . . Tell dear Tad, poor 'Nanny Goat' is lost. . . . The day you left Nanny was found resting herself, and chewing her little cud, on the middle of Tad's bed. But now she's gone! The gardener kept complaining that she destroyed the flowers, till it was concluded to bring her down to the White House. This was done, and the second day she had disappeared and has not been heard of since. This is the last we know of poor 'Nanny.'"[5]

Mrs. Lincoln sent a telegram to Mr. Lincoln on April 28 when she and Tad arrived in New York City: "We reached here in safety. Hope you are well. . . . Tad says are the goats well?" To which Mr. Lincoln replied by telegram on the same day: "Tell Tad the goats and father are very well—especially the goats."[6]

And then again in September, Lincoln sent more pet news for his son: "All well, including Tad's pony and the goats."[7]

14. *Love and Politics*

> My noble husband, who was my "light & life," and my highest ambition gratified . . . My husband became distinguished above all. And yet, owing to that fact, I firmly believe he lost his life & I am bowed to the earth with sorrow.
>
> —Mary Lincoln to Elizabeth Lee, December 11, 1865

When Abraham Lincoln won election to Congress, Mary Lincoln was determined to go with him to Washington. In 1847, it was uncommon for families to accompany congressmen, particularly those who were not wealthy and who lived a considerable distance from the U.S. capital. It would be complicated and expensive for the Lincolns to manage the temporary relocation with two little boys, but Lincoln agreed to take his family. His friend David Davis was aghast at the prospect, writing his wife: "Mrs. L., I am told, accompanies her husband to Washington city next winter. . . . She wishes to loom largely."[1]

Some of Abraham Lincoln's friends and political colleagues resented Mary Lincoln's influence on her husband. Their resentment, however, is all the evidence we need of Mary Lincoln's influence on her husband.[2]

In the fall of 1847, Abraham Lincoln rented the Springfield house, Mary Lincoln packed and prepared four-year-old Bob and nineteen-month-old Eddie, and the Lincoln family departed Springfield. Leaving on Monday, October 25, they headed first to Lexington for a visit with Mary's Kentucky family. She had not been home since before her marriage, and her husband and sons had not met all the Kentucky Todds. The family traveled overland, reaching St. Louis on Wednesday, and then took a boat south on the Mississippi River and then east on the Ohio River to Louisville, arriving in Lexington overland by Tuesday, November 3. I get exhausted just thinking about this journey, a nineteenth-century version of trains, planes, and automobiles with wiggling, impatient little boys in tow.

After a month-long stay in Lexington, the Lincoln family packed up again and headed to Washington on November 25, arriving on December 2. They checked in at Brown's Hotel until they found rooms in a boardinghouse. Mary Lincoln tended the children, she and her husband attended at least one musical event—the Ethiopian Serenaders at Carusi's Saloon in January 1848—and they took walks around the capitol grounds, which was opposite the boardinghouse. Mary Lincoln also enjoyed discussing politics with fellow boardinghouse guests who were members of Congress, even as it irritated some of them. The family lived together until sometime in the spring of 1848, when the situation became untenable with two active children.[3] The couple then decided Mrs. Lincoln would take the boys back to Lexington, but as soon as they were gone, Mr. Lincoln was lonely:

> Dear Mary:
> In this troublesome world, we are never quite satisfied. When you were here, I thought you hindered me some in attending to business; but now, having nothing but business—no variety—it has grown exceedingly tasteless to me. I hate to sit down and direct documents, and I hate to stay in this old room by myself. You know I told you in last Sunday's letter, I was going to make a little speech during the week; but the week has passed away without my getting a chance to do so; and now my interest in the subject has passed away too. Your second and third letters have been received since I wrote before. Dear Eddy thinks father is "*gone talipa*." [capital]. . . . I went yesterday to hunt the little plaid stockings, as you wished; but found that McKnight has quit business, and Allen had not a single pair of the description you give, and only one plaid pair of any sort that I thought would fit "Eddy's dear little feet." . . . And you are entirely free from headache? That is good—good—considering it is the first spring you have been free from it since we were acquainted. I am afraid you will get so well, and fat, and young, as to be wanting to marry again. . . . Get weighed, and write me how much you weigh. I did not get rid of the impression of that foolish dream about dear Bobby till I got your letter written the same day. What did he and Eddy think of the

little letters father sent them? Don't let the blessed fellows forget father. . . .

Most affectionately A. Lincoln.[4]

Mary Lincoln wrote from Lexington in May 1848:

My Dear Husband—
You will think indeed, that *old age* has set *its seal* upon my humble self, that in few or none of my letters, I can remember the day of the month, I must confess it as one of my peculiarities; I feel wearied & tried enough to know that this is *Saturday night*, our *babies* are asleep. . . . Our little Eddy has recovered from his little spell of sickness—Dear boy, I must tell you a little story about him—Bobby in his wanderings today, came across in a yard, a little kitten, *your hobby*, he says he asked a man for it, he brought it triumphantly to the house, so soon as Eddy spied it his *tenderness* broke forth, he made them bring it *water*, fed it with bread himself, with his *own dear hands*, he was a delighted little creature over it. . . . How much I wish instead of writing, *we* were together this evening, I feel very sad away from you. . . . Do not fear the children have forgotten you, I was only jesting. Even E's eyes brighten at the mention of your name. My love to all.

Truly yours M L.[5]

Mr. to Mrs. on June 12, 1848:

On my return from Philadelphia, yesterday, where, in my anxiety I had been led to attend the Whig convention I found your last letter. I was so tired and sleepy, having ridden all night, that I could not answer it till today; and now I have to do so in the H.R. The leading matter in your letter, is your wish to return to this side of the Mountains. Will you be a *good girl* in all things if I consent? Then come along, and that as *soon* as possible. Having got the idea in my head, I shall be impatient till I see you. . . . Come on just as soon as you can. I want to see you, and our dear—*dear* boys very much. . . .

Affectionately A. Lincoln.[6]

And husband again on July 2, 1848:

> My dear wife:
> Your letter of last Sunday came last night. On that day (Sunday) I wrote the principal part of a letter to you, but did not finish it, or send it till Tuesday, when I had provided a draft for $100 which I sent in it. . . . The music in the Capitol grounds on Saturdays, or, rather, the interest in it, is dwindling down to nothing. Yesterday evening the attendance was rather thin. Our two girls, whom you remember seeing first at Carusis, at the exhibition of the Ethiopian Serenaders, and whose peculiarities were the wearing of black fur bonnets, and never being seen in close company with other ladies, were at the music yesterday. One of them was attended by their brother, and the other had a member of Congress in tow. He went home with her; and if I were to guess, I would say, he went away a somewhat altered man—most likely in his pockets, and in some other particular. The fellow looked conscious of guilt, although I believe he was unconscious that everybody around knew who it was that had caught him. . . . Father expected to see you all sooner; but let it pass; stay as long as you please, and come when you please. Kiss and love the dear rascals.
>
> Affectionately A. Lincoln.[7]

These marvelous letters reveal a couple finding the way forward together. The Lincoln marriage was solid, companionable, and beneficial to both parties. Like all relationships, it was imperfect. Mary Lincoln was quick-tempered and sometimes selfish, and her emotional outbursts perplexed her calm, accommodating husband. Mr. Lincoln's melancholy, emotional detachment, and disdain for social graces frustrated his wife. Mary Lincoln once wrote about her husband that although he was a man of "deep feeling, he was not a demonstrative man, when he felt most deeply, he expressed the least." She also wrote that Mr. Lincoln was "Always—lover—husband—father & all all to me."[8]

Both Abraham and Mary Lincoln struggled throughout their lives to be mentally healthy. However, if scholars are correct to argue that depression was a challenge that fueled Lincoln's greatness, then perhaps we might consider that his wife's own struggle fueled her way forward as well. I suspect that since Abraham and Mary each experienced emotional pain, they understood the pain in the other. In the struggle, there was conflict of course, but there was also compassion. Abraham proved a tender, patient, beloved, and idolized husband, "the best man, that ever lived."[9] Mary was Abraham's dear wife, lover, and staunchest political ally, supporting him through political wins and losses. Theirs was a marriage of love and politics.

In the early morning on May 18, 1860, Mary Lincoln remained at home when her husband walked downtown to await the results from the Republican Convention in Chicago. Lincoln played handball in the lot next to the *Illinois State Journal* before going to his law office. When the telegram arrived announcing the Republican Party's nomination of Abraham Lincoln for president, the candidate enjoyed the moment with his assembled friends before telling them: "Well Gentleman there is a little woman at our house who is probably more interested in this dispatch than I am."[10]

Mary Lincoln's interest in politics was well known among her husband's friends; and Lincoln's desire to deliver the good news to his wife was widely reported in the newspapers in the following days. A family friend said the story spoke "eloquently of the affectionate relations" the Lincolns enjoyed.[11] When a supporter in New York read the story, he wrote to Lincoln:

> You will pardon me for saying, there was to me a touching tenderness & beauty, and a real wealth of affection in your remark upon the receipt of the telegraph announcing your nomination—"There's a little woman down at our house would like to hear this. I'll go down & tell her." To you, at that moment, the shouts of the great world had no music. Your heart in that moment of conscious pride was with the Mother of your boys—the chosen one of your affections; she was more than all the world beside. God bless her, & the boys; and I believe a kind Providence will take care of you. I hope to see that "little woman," The Lady President.[12]

Mary Lincoln and her husband certainly shared a laugh over the "Lady President" remark, but it would prove to be a little bit true.

Two weeks before the presidential election, Mary wrote to a friend: "I scarcely know how I would bear up under defeat. I trust we will not have the trial."[13] The Lincoln household was too hectic during the campaign for Mary to sit about fretting. She had guests to proudly greet in the elegant home she had made for the Lincoln family in Springfield. In the campaign, she was in her element, and her husband was in his element, and as a couple the Lincolns were on the cusp of political history. When the election results came across the wires in the night, Lincoln went home to wake up his wife: "Mary, Mary, *we* are elected!" Four years later, when he received the telegram confirming his reelection as president, he said to the clerk: "Send it right over to the Madam. She will be more interested than I am."[14]

Politics was an essential character of the Lincoln marriage. As a recent biographer notes: "Outwardly Mary honored the cult of domesticity. But she and Abe forged their own kind of marriage." John Todd Stuart, Lincoln's first law partner and Mary Lincoln's cousin, said: "His wife made him Presdt: She had the fire—will and ambition—Lincoln's talent & his wife's ambition did the deed."[15]

As First Lady, Mary Lincoln asserted her own political ideas, asked Lincoln's cabinet members for favors, and made her own promises to constituents. She kept the company of myriad politicians and political women. Elizabeth Blair Lee, the sister of Lincoln's postmaster general Montgomery Blair, became one of Mary's best female friends in Washington. Mary Lincoln's opinions and alleged interference annoyed some men. Lincoln's private secretaries clashed with her. They were jealous and did not wish to compete with her for the president's attention. Still there were many men who enjoyed her company and her intellect, like Illinois friend and U.S. senator Orville Hickman Browning and Commissioner of Public Buildings Benjamin French, the latter noting in his diary that Mary Lincoln was a woman of intelligence and independence. A Lincoln family bodyguard wrote in his memoir: "She was an interesting little woman, full of life and activities, and took great interest in her husband's welfare."[16]

Mary Lincoln endured "unprecedented mudslinging," which bruised her feelings but did not alter her personality or behavior. She was unflappable, although sometimes apologizing for her involvement in politics, which she had told her friend Mercy was an "unladylike profession." In a letter to David Davis arguing against an appointment of Norman Judd to Lincoln's cabinet, she said she was writing "for the good of the country, and Mr Lincoln's future reputation," and added: "If you consider me intrusive, please excuse me, our country, just now, is above all."[17]

When Lincoln's first secretary of war Simon Cameron apologized for complaining about her, Mary Lincoln wrote to him: "I understand that you forgive me for all past offences, yet I am not Christian enough to feel the same towards you as you pass me so 'lightly by' when you visit the White House." She went on to offer him more political advice. Lincoln's secretary of war Edwin Stanton, whose own wife kept to home and shadows, was even more perturbed than Cameron by what he defined as meddling. A woman stepping out of bounds was, to him, deviant. It drove Stanton crazy when Mary Lincoln sent him letters recommending people for posts, and he chastised her for interfering. Her response was to send him a bundle of negative newspaper articles about his War Department.[18]

When Mary Lincoln told her husband his secretary of state William Seward was a political enemy, Lincoln replied: "Mother, you are mistaken; your prejudices are so violent that you do not stop to reason. Seward is an able man, and the country, as well as myself, can trust him."[19]

Pillow talk in the Lincoln bedroom was often political. There is zero evidence Lincoln disliked his wife's interest in politics, although he did not always agree with her. On the contrary, he listened and debated the issues with her, validating her right to her opinions and a place in the discussion. All the men in the Lincoln administration had to deal with Mrs. Lincoln. Whether they liked her or not, they all understood her proclivity to involve herself and their boss's proclivity to let her. Some men objected to Mary Lincoln's voice, but most objected because it was a woman's voice.[20]

As an intelligent woman with a great knowledge and passion for politics, Mary Lincoln occupied an intriguing position in Washington. While she sometimes battled with cabinet members, she also entertained other politicians, like abolitionist senator Charles Sumner, who enjoyed her company. They discussed politics, and Mary Lincoln would relay details about those conversations to her husband. One Massachusetts newspaper reported that she was "ambitious of having a finger in every government pie; being much in conversation with cabinet members, and holding correspondence with them on political matters; making the political fortunes of men; suggesting to the president some of his ideas and projects."[21]

Surprisingly, however, Mary Lincoln's engagement with politics raised little public scrutiny. And, in fact, other women in Washington were also politically engaged and influential in the lives of their political relatives. The world was changing, and women in the war years were more public, more political, and more respected actors in public arenas. Many political, military, professional, and literary men were drawn to Mary Lincoln's Blue Room salons, some for the entertainment of her own company and others for the influence she had on President Lincoln. Abram Wakeman, a lawyer and Lincoln's New York City postmaster with higher ambitions, was one politician who spent time with her when she was in New York and used his friendship with her to curry favor. It is unclear how much influence Mary Lincoln had in Wakeman's appointment to the lucrative patronage position of surveyor of the Port of New York in 1864, but Mary Lincoln's fondness for him certainly did no harm.[22]

In early October 1861, George B. McClellan sent Mrs. Lincoln a box of grapes. It was common for people to send gifts to the White House, but given McClellan's contempt for the Lincoln administration, it was a curious gesture. I have always wondered if the Lady President's reputation had reached him all the way out in Cincinnati, from where he sent his goodwill grapes. If McClellan was trying to gain favor with the president by buttering up the First Lady, however, it did not work, although she enjoyed the delicious fruit. On November 2, she wrote to her husband from New York: "Your name is on every lip and many prayers and good wishes are hourly sent up for your welfare—and McClellan & his slowness are as vehemently discussed. . . . Many say they would almost worship you if you would put in a fighting General in the place of McClellan."[23]

Three days after his wife's letter, Abraham Lincoln relieved McClellan of his command. By juxtaposing these details, I am not suggesting Lincoln made such a monumental decision on his wife's advice. He had been for a long while perturbed by McClellan's hesitancy to engage the rebel army. Elizabeth Keckley remembered Mary Lincoln remarking that McClellan "talked so much and did so little" and Lincoln teasing his wife that perhaps he should give her charge of the army. I love every aspect of this story because it is indicative of the degree to which Mary Lincoln paid attention to politics and is evidence that the Lincolns talked to each other about politics, policy, and the war. Mary Lincoln once wrote that she had "a great terror of strong minded ladies."[24] She might not have been willing to admit that she was a strong-minded lady, but her husband knew it, and so did every man, woman, and child in the Civil War North.

Mary Lincoln's strong will, independence, and willingness to press people for favors and bargains became economically and politically problematic in one famous regard: the remodeling of the White House. To every administration since William Henry Harrison, Congress had appropriated $6,000 a year for Executive Mansion maintenance and repair. When Mary Lincoln arrived in Washington to find the building in a shabby condition, with tattered carpets and broken furniture, she determined to take full advantage of that appropriation. She saw her role to remodel the White House as an extension of her role as the head of her household in Springfield. And as First Lady, she believed it was her duty to create a gracious home becoming an American president and to present to the public the appearance of a functioning government despite war. In the first year, Mary Lincoln transformed the White House inside and out, from a rat-infested dusty old mess to comfortable elegance, remaking a home for her family and the nation. The problem was not that Mary Lincoln remodeled the White House. The problem was that Mary Lincoln likely exhausted the entire four-year budget in the first year, overspent by approximately $7,000, and played a little fast and loose with accounting.[25]

The opposition press went crazy over Mary Lincoln's lavish White House spending, which included extravagances such as $6,800 worth of French wallpaper. Abraham Lincoln was furious with his wife. He hated "flub dubs," considering chandeliers and fine China frivolous anytime, let alone during wartime. He was angry because it embarrassed his personal sense of frugality and stirred up political controversy. However, Mary Lincoln managed the extra spending by selling old White House furniture, negotiating prices, trimming White House staff, and, with the help of Building Commissioner Benjamin French, securing an extra congressional appropriation for $4,500 that easily passed.[26]

Mary Lincoln's lavish spending on clothes and jewelry would run up the real debts that would plague her later in her widowhood. The shopping sprees she enjoyed in New York during the war read like retail therapy in modern parlance, as spending and fashion-forward clothing became a balm to her. As she wrote a New York City milliner: "I am in need of a mourning bonnet—which must be exceedingly plain & genteel. . . . I want the crape to be the fast jet black . . . white & black face trimming."[27] Interestingly, Lincoln was far more tolerant of his wife's spending on clothing, enjoying for himself the results of her fine adornment. He delighted to watch her so lovely and charming at public receptions, one time commenting to a guest: "My wife is as handsome as when she was a girl and I, a poor nobody then, fell in love with her and what is more, I have never fallen out."[28]

On Good Friday, April 14, 1865, Mary Lincoln had lunch with her husband in the private dining parlor, after which he invited her for a long carriage ride in the afternoon. She asked if he wanted her to invite anyone to join them, and he replied: "No—I prefer to ride by ourselves today."[29] General Robert E. Lee had surrendered his rebel Army of Northern Virginia to General Ulysses S. Grant and the U.S. Army on April 9, Washington was ringing with jubilant celebration, and the Lincolns for the first time in four years were thinking about their future. About her husband's mood that day, Mary wrote:

> He was almost boyish in his mirth & reminded me of his original nature, what I had always remembered of him, in our own home—free from care, surrounded by those he loved so well & *by whom* he was so idolized. . . . I never saw him so supremely cheerful—his manner was even playful. . . . I said to him, laughingly, "Dear Husband, you almost startle me by your great cheerfulness." He replied, "and well I may feel so, Mary, I consider *this day*, the war, has come to a close"—and then he added, "between the war & the loss of our darling Willie—we have both been very miserable."[30]

The war had taken a horrific toll, but now, finally, blessedly, they could believe in happier days to come. That evening the Lincolns attended a performance of the comedy *Our American Cousin*. Although late arriving at Ford's Theatre, by 9 P.M. they were seated and laughing. Mary Lincoln cuddled close to her husband, his large hand enveloping her own. At approximately 10:13 P.M., while the audience erupted with laughter during act 3, scene 2, an assassin's bullet entered President Lincoln's brain. He slumped forward. Mary Lincoln screamed. Devastated, she had to be carried across the street to the boardinghouse, where her husband had been positioned in his death bed. She would spend the next nine dreadful hours kissing her husband's face, begging him to answer her, whispering endearments, her body, miserable with grief, sometimes draped across him. Throughout the night, she passed through waves of hysterics, pleading for her husband to take her with him, sobbing. Throughout the night, Robert Lincoln tried to soothe his mother, leading her from the room to wail in private, but Mary Lincoln was too distraught to notice his presence.

There was no relief in her agonizing vigil.

Until 7:22 and 10 seconds in the morning, April 15, when her husband stopped breathing.[31]

"Oh, My God," Mary Lincoln cried, "and have I given my husband to die."[32]

Politics made Mary Todd fall in love. Politics sustained Mary Lincoln's marriage. Politics made her husband president of the United States. And politics made her a widow.

PART IV

Women, the Law, and Lawyer Lincoln

15. Finding Forgotten Women

> This day came the complainant by her solicitor . . .
> —Court Decree, *Jane Dobbs v. Stephen Dobbs* (divorce),
> Abraham Lincoln for the Plaintiff, April 10, 1845

IT HAS BEEN YEARS since I have been in an Illinois courthouse looking for documents from Abraham Lincoln's law practice. I do not miss shivering in cold basements and sweating in attics. I hated the extreme temperatures as my asthmatic lungs struggled to breathe in grimy air. But I loved the thrill of the chase and the discovery. Legal documents brim with social history, community politics, crime, family drama, and women's stories worth mining. I lived for those moments when hours of frustration paid off and a new document emerged from the past. I was a historian, a detective, a hunter of lost treasure. I was a resurrector of the dead.

I can picture Lincoln, just a prairie lawyer at that time, years before he became president of the United States and left Mary Lincoln a widow. If I close my eyes and hold my breath, I can still smell the musky red rot on the massive, leather-bound court docket books, dusty with time and lost stories. The peculiar odor transports me to Lincoln's past and to my past, too. Vivid still in my memory is the image of the rusting towers of filing cabinets filled with tri-folded legal documents, stuffed into drawers precisely wide and tall enough to accommodate them standing upright. The memory of the courthouses where I first went looking for Lincoln treasures reminds me that it was in those unlikely spaces where I first began collecting my stories about Lincoln and women.

One courthouse was in Pekin, Illinois. A beaux-arts building constructed in 1914, it holds the records of the Tazewell County Circuit Court, which moved from Tremont after the county seat was relocated to Pekin in 1849. Lincoln represented clients in 266 cases in the Tazewell County Circuit Court. On the docket, circuit clerk John A. Jones entered case number 104. The book in which he recorded the case was new in the Spring Term 1845, the cover clean and the binding stitched up tight. In an elegant, swirling hand, which recommended him to his post, Jones wrote "Jane Dobbs vs. Stephen Dobbs, Libel for Divorce" in the middle of the left side of the two-page folio. In the column on the extreme left, the space reserved for the names of plaintiff attorneys, he wrote "Leonard & Lincoln."[1]

Who was Jane Dobbs? What was her story? What happened to this woman known to Abraham Lincoln but now lost to history? Because there she is, quiet in corroding, iron gall ink, waiting in a moldy old book for someone to tell her story. A woman's name in a docket book was always a first spark of joy for me. The fact-finding journey to uncover a story the second. Telling her story was a bright beam of sunlight from my heart, my happy purpose as a scholar. In studying Lincoln's law practice, I was compelled by the women I found in the records. To research Abraham Lincoln's life was my honor. To research the lives of the women in the docket books of Lincoln's cases became my calling.

Historians would define Jane Dobbs as an ordinary woman. Yet having collected the stories of hundreds of so-called ordinary women, I have come to see ordinary women as extraordinary. It is reasonable to define women of exceptional achievement, talent, wealth, fame, or historical importance as extraordinary. Yet I find women who made simple lives, worked hard, raised children, and built families and communities in humble circumstances more remarkable. While the experiences of Jane Dobbs were like the experiences of frontier Illinois women who shared her social, economic, and religious contexts, she was unique, and her life mattered to her, her family, and her community.

Jane Dobbs was born Jane Barker in 1797 in Kentucky (another Kentucky woman!) and grew up in Cave-in-Rock, Illinois, on the Ohio River. Her father served as a captain in the War of 1812 in a militia unit from Illinois Territory, and after Illinois statehood in 1818, he won election to represent Pope County as its first state senator. Jane was sixteen on November 7, 1813, when she married Isaac Perkins, with whom she had eight children. Her husband was successful, but her large family was financially insecure. Sometime in the 1820s, they settled in Sand Prairie Township in Tazewell County, where her husband served as the first recorder of deeds and purchased land in what would become Pekin, Illinois. In 1832, Isaac Perkins left his family to fight in the Black Hawk

War. On May 14, after a night of heavy drinking, his undisciplined unit fought in the Battle of Stillman's Run. A small group of Black Hawk's men attacked the sleeping Illinois Rangers in the early morning, killing twelve. Later that day, an Illinois militia company, led by a young captain named Abraham Lincoln, discovered the bodies of the fallen soldiers and buried them in makeshift graves. Isaac Perkins was among them.[2]

Jane Perkins was now a widow. Her husband left her land, so she was not destitute. However, she was a woman alone with small children to raise. Her best chance for security was to remarry, and on February 25, 1834, she wed Stephen Dobbs.[3] I know nothing of her life in the next eleven years, not until 1845 when Abraham Lincoln became her lawyer. Jane's second marriage was an unhappy one, and she had retained William Leonard to sue for divorce on the grounds of her husband's adultery. Leonard tapped Lincoln to join him in the case, and Jane Dobbs met Lincoln just before the start of the court term. The law was simpler then, but it was also more personal. When the cases involved intimate financial or personal details of a client's life, a good lawyer became a friend as well as an advocate.

I wonder if during their time getting acquainted Abraham Lincoln and Jane Dobbs made their connection to Stillman's Run. Probably not. Even so, there can be no diminishment of the power of coincidence. Our stories are always bound to the stories of others, making up one human narrative, whether we know it or not.

The clerk docketed Jane Dobbs's case on April 10, 1845. Along with the judge's docket book, there are two court record books with entries by the clerk providing general information about the Dobbs marriage and divorce. In box 76 in a rusty old drawer is a corresponding case file, containing forty-six documents, including Jane Dobbs's bill for injunction, signed with an "X" because she was illiterate. Among the case documents is the deposition of Margaret Hungerford, a woman who provided evidence of Stephen Dobbs's relationship with another woman with whom he had fathered a child. Hungerford testified that Mr. Dobbs was supporting the woman and child and had threatened to kill Jane Dobbs. When the trial began, Stephen Dobbs was not living in the state, and Jane Dobbs was in no immediate danger, but it would have been a terrifying threat for a woman alone with children. Twenty-three witnesses, including four women, testified in the two jury trials that ensued, but it was Hungerford's deposition in the second trial that was decisive. The jury granted Jane Dobbs a divorce and an injunction to keep her husband from interfering with rents from the land her first husband had left her. He might have married Jane Dobbs for her land, but Stephen Dobbs failed to take it from her.[4]

Jane Dobbs, with Lincoln's help, extricated herself from a disastrous marriage, retained her property, and, I hope, lived out her life in peace. She took back her first husband's surname and did not remarry, content to live on her own and capable of doing so. Her daughter Sibyl Perkins, who was two years old when her father died, married into the McKasson family, two members of which had testified on behalf of her mother in the divorce case. In 1860, Jane Perkins was living in Pekin with Sybil and Thomas McKasson and four of Jane's grandchildren. It was there she died in 1862, at the age of sixty-five.[5]

We can speculate about Jane Dobbs's daily life in her various roles as a pioneer woman, friend, neighbor, mother, wife, widow, divorced woman, and grandmother. Domestic duties, family connections, religious life, and the overlapping relationships with people in their communities defined women's lives in the first half of the nineteenth century. Jane Dobbs's life was so defined, but her agency to take advantage of Illinois law to end her unhappy marriage also shaped it. Because of those old courthouse documents, we know for certain that Jane Dobbs lived, loved, grieved, and divorced a rotten husband. Her peace was more important to her than the social stigma of divorce. In 1845, divorce was an available remedy in Illinois, more accessible than it was in most other states, but it required a brave woman to pursue it in an era when society frowned upon divorce.[6]

Abraham Lincoln helped Jane Dobbs navigate the legal system to make a better life for herself. Her individual impact on Abraham Lincoln's life was less dramatic than his impact upon hers. However, she paid him a fee, and her case furthered his knowledge of divorce law in Illinois. It also added another woman's story to the growing number of women's stories Abraham Lincoln collected on his way to the White House.

16. Polly Rogers and Her Husband's Lawyer

> The allegation of adultery against the said defendant was muted in the complainant's bill, for no other cause, than through tenderness to the said defendant's character.
>
> —Abraham Lincoln, affidavit for his divorce case client Samuel Rogers, October 20, 1838

On October 4, 1835, in Sangamon County, Illinois, Polly Offill married Samuel Rogers, a Petersburg farmer. She left him a week later. She must have had her reasons, because separation and divorce from husbands was not an easy path in antebellum America, even in Illinois where divorce law was progressive. While single women in America could own property and make contracts, a married woman's legal standing became one with her husband's. As well, women in antebellum America had limited economic opportunities outside the family home, and divorce was often met with harsh religious and social stigma. Legal and economic context and nineteenth-century expectations for women's obedience to their husbands be damned, Polly walked away from her new husband. Her desertion was, regardless of the circumstances, a brave assertation of independence.[1]

On November 7, 1835, Samuel Rogers published a public notice about his wife's desertion in the *Springfield Sangamo Journal*. The text, which was typical of such legal notices, revealed much about women's status in 1835: "My wife Polly, having left my bed and board, without any just cause or provocation, I hereby forewarn any person from harboring her on my account, as I am determined to pay no debts of her contracting after this date." In publishing the notice, Samuel Rogers was protecting himself from any debts his wife might incur in his name. For the next two years, the couple lived apart.[2]

In the summer of 1838, Samuel Rogers walked into Abraham Lincoln's second-story law office on Hoffman's Row, across from the Illinois State Capitol in Springfield. He explained to Lincoln that his wife had run off with another man and he wanted a divorce. Lincoln listened while Rogers shared all the details of his failed marriage, discussing his loneliness and her alleged adulterous relationship with a man named William Short. While Lincoln heard his client's tale of marital woe, he also envisioned the circumstances of the woman at the center of the tale. Even though she was not in the office telling her side of the story. Even as she might have been to blame for the breakup of the marriage. Even though Polly Rogers was not his client who would pay his fees.[3]

When Samuel Rogers finished explaining the details of his marriage to his lawyer, Lincoln explained that a divorce was possible on the grounds of his wife's desertion alone. Polly had been gone from his home for the two years Illinois law required for desertion as grounds for divorce. Lincoln urged his client to omit the adultery allegation. Lincoln would obtain the divorce so Samuel would be free to remarry, but there was no reason to drag his wife's reputation through public mud. Samuel Rogers trusted Lincoln's legal advice. Lincoln then drafted the one-page bill for divorce, which cited the grounds of desertion, and he filed the case in the Sangamon County Circuit Court.[4]

Polly Rogers defaulted in the case. Like Samuel Rogers, she wanted the divorce, and she saw no need to fight it. On October 20, 1838, the court granted the divorce based on desertion and ordered Samuel Rogers to pay his wife $1,000 in alimony. The award was a dear sum in 1838, and Samuel Rogers was shocked and annoyed with his lawyer. Abraham Lincoln, with help from his experienced law partner John Stuart, asked the court for leave to amend the bill for divorce. To reduce the alimony, he needed to introduce the adultery charge. In the affidavit Lincoln wrote and signed for himself, he admitted to the court he knew about the adultery charge but counseled his client against citing it. In the affidavit he prepared for Samuel Rogers to sign, Lincoln admitted he had muted the charge of adultery out of concern for the reputation of Polly Rogers. For no other cause than tenderness, Lincoln had made a legal blunder. His extraordinary admission of that blunder is striking.

With the adultery charge now in play, Polly Rogers hired an attorney, denied the accusation of adultery, and averred she left her husband to escape his abuse and adultery against her. The judge continued the case to the next court term. It was a he-said-she-said story, but two things were clear. First, the marriage was irreconcilable. Second, while Lincoln's advice to his client was a legal blunder, it is also a window into his character. It illustrates his concern for women, even a woman who was not his own client.[5]

On March 15, 1839, a jury heard the Rogers case. Female litigants, particularly those in divorce actions, were at the mercy of all-male juries to hear and to judge the most intimate details of their lives. These male jurors had the power to determine alimony and to make decisions about child custody. Polly Rogers had no children to worry about losing, and there is no indication she was in dire economic circumstances. The jury in her divorce case considered the evidence, which included a detailed accounting of Samuel Rogers's wealth and, typical of the era's trials, rendered a decision on the same day. The jury ruled that Polly Rogers had abandoned her husband but was innocent of adultery. The court ordered the marriage dissolution and Samuel Rogers to pay Polly Rogers an initial payment of $126 and subsequent $39 semiannual payments—a much more manageable settlement for Lincoln's client. Polly Rogers would remarry or move away before Samuel Rogers would have to pay her anywhere near $1,000. Both parties were now free to remarry, which Samuel Rogers did just three months later. The jury had muted the charge of adultery to spare Polly Rogers the stigma, but it had lowered the alimony because of it.[6]

Polly Rogers was one of 220 women who were litigants in divorce cases in Sangamon County from 1837 to 1860, during Lincoln's law career. While many lawyers of his era eschewed divorce cases, Lincoln handled 147 divorces during his twenty-five-year legal career. He was the attorney of record in 40 percent of all the divorce cases appearing on the docket in his home county. More than half of the divorce litigants Lincoln represented were women. The Rogers case was typical of divorce cases of the era, involving the most common ground of desertion. However, the rehearing on alimony and Lincoln's bad lawyer / good human mistake makes a messy, remarkable case out of a simple, good one.[7]

The rest of Polly Rogers's extraordinary story is lost to history, but one of the momentous events of her life tied her to Abraham Lincoln. I often wonder about the women who knew the lawyer Lincoln in quiet county seats in antebellum Illinois and what they thought about his rise to the presidency. I would have been telling all my friends and anyone who would listen: "Lincoln was my lawyer," or "He was my rotten ex-husband's divorce lawyer," or "I knew him before he was famous." Polly Rogers might have told her daughters, who told their daughters, who told their daughters, and the story is still alive in family memories somewhere out there in the world today. I hope so.

As for Abraham Lincoln, the Rogers case was instructive. Like any good novice learning on the job, Lincoln learned from his mistakes and moved on from them. The Rogers case was one of the first divorce cases he handled, not only acquainting him with Illinois divorce statute but also making clear to him the law could be a dangerous place for women. Lincoln would never repeat the blunder that jeopardized the legal outcome for his client Samuel Rogers, but I suspect, in his heart, he was not sorry he had first proceeded in tender consideration for his client's wife.

17. *Melissa Goings Goes Missing*

> She wanted to know where she could get a good drink of water, and I told her there was mighty good water in Tennessee.
>
> —Abraham Lincoln to Robert Cassell, October 10, 1857

MELISSA GOINGS WAS A sixty-nine-year-old farmer's wife living in western Illinois on the day she picked up a piece of kitchen firewood and whacked her husband Roswell Goings upside his head. The blow, which cracked his skull and injured his brain, was fatal. The husband died five days later, and the wife was indicted for his murder. All the mortal wound's gruesome details, the fight leading up to it, and the evidence in the case became part of the legal record in the Woodford County Circuit Court in Metamora. That Abraham Lincoln represented Melissa Goings is a historical fact. That Melissa Goings disappeared from the courthouse is also true. It is the extent to which her attorney participated in her unauthorized departure from the Woodford County Courthouse on October 8, 1857, that remains a historical mystery. It is Goings's flight from justice and her attorney's possible culpability that have made the story a legend, cast in bronze statues standing today outside the restored courthouse in Metamora.[1]

The facts in the Goings case are clear, her flight from justice less so. Most Lincoln biographies don't mention the murder case or the story. John Duff included two paragraphs on the Goings case in his important study of Lincoln's law practice in 1960, and he suggested the story could be true. A more recent author who examined the Goings case doubts that Lincoln suggested to his client that she flee the courthouse. I understand the scholarly hesitation, but to me the story rings true. Ringing true does not make a story true, but as an editor of Lincoln's legal papers who has read *all* the documents in Lincoln's nearly one thousand cases in which women were litigants, deponents, witnesses, and parties to legal actions and studied all the facets of Lincoln's legal career, I have been confident in my leaning toward true.[2]

Monica Melissa Lett was born in Frederick, Maryland, on January 19, 1788, to German immigrant parents. She married Roswell Goings in 1795 in Frederick, and she had seven children, all born before the family settled in Illinois sometime prior to 1839. The 1850 census taker reported the Goings family as residents of Worth Township in Woodford County, just west of Metamora and northeast of Peoria, where Roswell Goings was a farmer with real property worth a respectable $1,500. The Goingses' widowed daughter, Nancy Hibbs, and her eighteen-year-old son lived with the couple. Also in the household was Lucy Goings, a grandchild, and five people aged eighteen and younger with the surname of Flowers. The makeup of the family household in 1857 is unknown, but Josephus Goings, Melissa's son, lived nearby.[3]

On April 13, 1857, Melissa and Roswell Goings, who was in his late seventies, argued about the opening of a window. Roswell grabbed his wife's neck, but she escaped his hold and picked up a piece of firewood. Roswell told his wife to hush, and she dared him to make her. He came for her then, and she struck her blow. Melissa ran from the house to tell Josephus Goings what she had done. Josephus returned to the house to find his father on the floor, assisted him to his rocking chair, and washed off the blood. Roswell Goings was lucid for a time but soon exhibited diminished cognitive abilities. Josephus left the house to fetch a doctor. A physician and at least one other witness arrived to find the injured man in and out of consciousness, and during a moment of lucidity Roswell said: "I expect she has killed me."[4] He was correct. He died on April 18, 1857, and Josephus Goings arranged for his quick burial.

On April 20, the coroner Benjamin Kindig ordered Roswell Goings's body disinterred, and he conducted a coroner's inquest the following day at the gravesite. A doctor examined the body, and witnesses testified to the couple's quarrelsome relationship. Other evidence revealed that Roswell had grabbed Melissa by the throat, that she said she wanted to kill him, and that he had threatened to do her in if he recovered. The inquest found Roswell Goings "came to his death by violence" and "the following marks & wounds inflicted by Melissa Goings, the wife of the deceased; a bruise on the back, & a long, deep cut on the head & the skull much fractured, & the brains injured, to which the jury find did come the death of said person in five days from their infliction."[5]

On April 23, Melissa Goings appeared before Justice of the Peace Robert Cassell, who bound her over for trial in the next term of the Woodford County Circuit Court, setting bail at $1,000. Josephus Goings offered to pay him $10 to drop the charges, and the court charged him with bribery. Melissa Goings posted bond on the security of her son and Samuel Beck, a family friend. Authorities released Melissa on a recognizance bond, marked with her "X" because she was illiterate.[6] On October 8, a Woodford County grand jury indicted Melissa Goings for murder:

> Melissa Goings late of County of Woodford and State of Illinois not having the fear of God before her eyes but being moved and seduced by the instigation of the Devil on the fourteenth day of April . . . with force and arms . . . upon one Roswell Goings in the Place of the said People of the said State of Illinois then and there being unlawfully feloniously willfully and of her malice aforethought did make an assault and that the said Melissa Goings with a certain stick of wood . . . did strike and beat giving to the said Roswell Goings then and there with the stick of wood aforesaid in and upon the top of the head of him . . . one mortal wound of the breadth of two inch and the depth of one inch. . .[7]

Melissa Goings may have acted to save her life but protecting herself put her in serious legal trouble. Here entered Abraham Lincoln as attorney for the defendant.

On October 10, Goings appeared in court with Lincoln for arraignment and trial. Sometime after the court entered her not-guilty plea, the court took a recess. Lincoln might have requested a brief break for his client to collect herself before the trial commenced, but the clerk did not record an official adjournment that would have been customary. The next entry in *Common Law Record B* read: "And now afterwards on the same day this cause coming on further to be heard the defendant being called came not and also Armstrong Goings & Samuel W Beck the sureties being called came not to produce the body of Melissa Goings."[8]

Melissa Goings was gone.

The court ordered forfeiture of recognizance and issued an order for her return in the court's next term, but no one ever saw Melissa Goings in Woodford County again. In her absence, the court continued her case until the Spring Term of 1858 and then again to the Fall Term of 1858.

The penalty for murder in Illinois was death. No one seemed to have had the heart for Melissa Goings to die for killing a mean old man, as there was no sincere effort to find her. Court documents suggested there had been violence in the Goings marriage, enough evidence to suggest that Melissa Goings may have been an abused woman. If she was, everybody in town knew it. No sheriff pursued her, and the court also dispassionately pursued her sureties. On October 4, 1858, when Lincoln was in Metamora for a political speech, he had a private conversation with the States Attorney Hugh Fullerton about the Goings case. The following day, on Fullerton's motion, the Woodford County Circuit Court struck *People v. Goings* from the docket. Fullerton also told the clerk to enter into the record his unwillingness to further prosecute the sureties for failing to bring Melissa Goings to court.[9]

Robert Cassell later told this story, curiously preserved in a Woodford County chancery docket book: "Mrs. Goings was brought into court that Lincoln might talk to her. After a while I was told by the state's attorney to bring her up for her trial, but she could not be found. I asked Lincoln about her, and he said he did not know where she was. 'Oh, no, Bob,' replied Lincoln. 'I did not run her off. She wanted to know where she could get a good drink of water, and I told her there was mighty good water in Tennessee.'"[10]

Interestingly, or incidentally (or ironically?), John Hay, President Lincoln's personal secretary, recorded a version of this story years later. In his diary on July 18, 1863, he wrote: "[Lincoln] told one devilish good story about U. F. Linder, getting a fellow off who had stolen a hog, by advising him to go & get a drink & suggesting the water was better in Tennessee."[11]

The Melissa Goings case is a remarkable story of a woman, a lawyer, and justice beyond the fingers of the law. If Lincoln did, indeed, help a woman escape legal punishment for killing her husband, it is evidence that Lincoln was human, not always so honest, and willing to err on the side of one woman's life against a legal system that failed to protect abused women. As one Lincoln biographer has written: "Lincoln was well aware of injustice against women."[12] Abraham Lincoln had experience in hundreds of cases involving women by the time he took the murder case of Melissa Goings in 1859, and he may have acted through frustration with legal justice. Her case was evidence that the law in the Lincoln era did not always provide compassionate remedies for women's problems. When Abraham Lincoln was able, he was a great ameliorator of suffering; so perhaps he saw himself as mediating a kinder justice for Goings. As president of the United States, Lincoln also exhibited such compassion in the face of legal constraints. He would frequently overrule his secretary of war Edwin Stanton on matters of military pardons. Stanton would be legally correct in these cases, but Lincoln would make the more human decision to save young boys and men from the noose or a court martial. Lincoln arrived in Washington with a compassionate heart, which was informed in many ways by the legal cases he handled for women like Melissa Goings.[13]

Melissa Goings and Abraham Lincoln, Metamora, Illinois, 2021. Sculptor John McClarey. David Wiegers Photography

What we know for certain is that in 1860, Melissa Goings was living in Iowa with her son Benjamin Goings, whose home was next door to her daughter Nancy Hibbs. Melissa later moved with Benjamin to California, where she died in 1867. After her personal trauma, legal trouble, and escape from Woodford County, she lived her remaining years among her children and grandchildren. What we will never know is the true circumstances of her escape or Lincoln's belief in the good water in Tennessee. However, the fact that the story popped up in two such different contexts related to Lincoln—in the Melissa Goings legal documents and in John Hay's diary—makes the bell of truth ring even louder. I cannot help but wonder if in telling Hay the story, Lincoln was deflecting his own great (and very naughty) story onto another attorney from Illinois while also protecting his client, who was still alive.[14]

One thing I love about history is that it consists of stories we patch together from the facts we know and all the mysteries we cannot, even drawing meaning from the silences. Historical facts are often elusive, and evidence is open to interpretation. History is not science. It is storytelling with a narrator who is a million miles from omniscient. No historians are immune from their own biases, and published history always has an agenda. Besides, whatever I think, or you think, or anyone thinks, stories from the past often have a life of their own. Some history we can know, some we cannot. And some stories just ring true, revealing something eternally human we cannot always locate in the dusty records of history.

18. The Law and the New Salem Women

> Why, Hannah, I shan't charge you a cent, never. Anything I can do for you I will do for you willingly and freely without charges.
>
> —Abraham Lincoln, c. October 1857, as Hannah Armstrong remembered it to William Herndon in 1866

In November 1845, Nancy Green was a widow in possession of a one-hundred-dollar promissory note coming due. Mentor Graham, a New Salem neighbor, owed her money she had lent him the previous year at 12 percent interest. Her friend Abraham Lincoln was now practicing law in Springfield, and she decided to retain him to secure the debt for her. Since Lincoln had moved to Springfield in 1837, Green had stayed connected with him. In February 1842, he had honored her request to speak at her husband Bowling Green's graveside services after his death from a stroke. Lincoln's attendance at the funeral had been a comfort to Nancy Green. He had been happy to provide a kindness to an old friend, and his remarks at the service were in gratitude for the kindness Mr. and Mrs. Green had bestowed upon him when he was a poor, young man in New Salem.[1]

Although it was a busy fall court term for Lincoln, he took Green's debt-collection case, which the Menard County Circuit Court judge heard on Tuesday, November 4. Graham confessed judgment, and the court ordered him to pay the debt and interest, totaling $112.23 (worth approximately $4,200 in today's currency). Lincoln also asked the court to order Graham to cover court costs of $2.12. The legal case was important because it reinforced the debt Green was due. Graham was not trying to wheedle out of the debt, he was just poor and unable to pay it. In fact, he would not satisfy the debt until February 1855. Such was often the case in debt actions on the cash-poor Illinois prairie. Nancy Green was a little luckier than most, a creditor instead of a debtor, with the means to retain a lawyer. There is no record of the fee she paid Lincoln, but in such a case $2.50 was typical. Nancy Green might have also cooked Lincoln a meal or two during the four days he was in Petersburg for the court term. It is also possible Lincoln refused to charge her.[2]

Nancy Green was not the only friend who would turn to Abraham Lincoln for legal assistance. Neither is Nancy Green the most famous Lincoln friend who trusted him with legal problems. That distinction belongs to another New Salem friend, Hannah Armstrong. At a religious camp meeting on August 29, 1857, at Walker's Grove in rural western Illinois, Hannah's twenty-four-year-old son Duff Armstrong engaged in a drunken brawl leading to the death of James Metzker. On October 29, the grand jury in Mason County Circuit Court indicted Armstrong and James Norris for murder. Both men pleaded not guilty, and the judge moved Armstrong's case to neighboring Cass County on a motion for a change of venue. Hannah Armstrong was terrified that a jury would convict her son and sentence him to death, so she went to Springfield to see Abraham Lincoln. By this time, Lincoln was a prominent Illinois attorney commanding high fees, and he rarely practiced in Cass County. But because Hannah needed him, Lincoln agreed to provide his legal services pro bono, and the "Almanac Trial" became one of his most famous cases.[3]

Lincoln would not have defended Duff Armstrong, removed as the murder case was from his usual circuit in 1858 during a busy period in his life, if a cherished friend had not compelled him to do so. The case would not have taken its significant role in Lincoln biography if Duff Armstrong had not been the son of a New Salem friend. Lincoln's first biographer William Herndon focused his research and interpretative approach to Abraham Lincoln on what he defined as Lincoln's formative years in New Salem. All the folksy stories emanating from New Salem have endured, their romantic lure irresistible. In terms of illustrating Lincoln's skills as a litigator and his style of practicing law in front of juries, the Armstrong case is a good one. Lincoln's introduction of a *Farmer's Almanac* as evidence to counter testimony that the moon was bright enough on the night of the killing to see Armstrong strike the fatal blow is interesting, although it was not the only evidence, or the key factor, that led to an acquittal. For my money, however, at least a couple dozen other Lincoln cases are more illuminating and more important than *People v. Armstrong.* I do understand the legal interest in the murder trial and the romantic obsession with the case in Lincoln biography.

Too often the women in Lincoln's life are absent from the Lincoln narrative, ignored and undervalued, even when they were essential to Lincoln stories. *The Abraham Lincoln Encyclopedia*, for example, has an entry for Duff Armstrong, whom Lincoln barely knew, and not one for Hannah Armstrong, who was Lincoln's dear friend and for whom he took on Duff's case. In this 350-page encyclopedia, there are more profiles of male historians, male artists, and male manuscript collectors born after Lincoln's death than there are of the women Abraham Lincoln actually knew. Similarly, analysis of women's cases is often missing in the books about Lincoln's law practice, even though he represented hundreds of women over the years he practiced law in Illinois. Hannah Armstrong gets a little more credit than most, but when women's stories make it into Lincoln biographies, it is usually just to mention them in the sensational cases, not to consider them as a wider class of litigants.[4]

It is an unfortunate slight. Because thanks in good part to women, Lincoln built a law practice, earned a middle-class living, and learned about women's vulnerability before the law. From civil actions of debt, mortgage foreclosure, slander, and breaches of contract to criminal cases involving murder, theft, and destruction of property, and in all matters of estate settlement, Lincoln heard the stories of women's lives. He took great care with his female clients, and his representation of women made an imprint on his psyche and informed his concern for women pensioners during his term in Congress. As well, his legal practice provided the context for his understanding of and engagement with the individual troubles of women and families during the Civil War.[5]

We cannot understand Lincoln's legal career if we do not acknowledge women and the legal cases they brought to him, the law he learned while representing them, and the fees they paid him. One essential, straightforward way to understand women's importance in Abraham Lincoln's law practice is to see how Lincoln went above and beyond to use his legal expertise to aid women in his life who were dear to him. Women like Nancy Green and Hannah Armstrong. Women like Huldah Stout, a "near and favorite neighbor" in Springfield, who asked Lincoln to conduct legal research about family property in southern Illinois. Women like Maria Bullock, Mary Lincoln's beloved Kentucky aunt, who hired Lincoln to take on a foreclosure case on her behalf and to manage other legal matters for her. Women like Mary Welles, the wife of a close legal colleague who lost her husband and son to cholera in 1854 and needed Lincoln to assist her with several legal actions related to her husband's estate.[6]

In these cases, Lincoln often refused to accept fees. He added these additional responsibilities to his already busy legal practice without hesitation. He managed the cases with the same care and attention he managed all his cases, but there was an added weight of responsibility he was willing to assume. For these special women, Lincoln did his utmost. They trusted him, and he would have done anything to escape the sorrow of letting them down. In an interview in 1866, Hannah Armstrong remembered this special gift in her friend: "As to the trial—Lincoln said to me: 'Hannah your son will be cleared before sun down.' He and the other lawyers addressed the jury, and closed the case. I went down at Thompson's pasture. [Daniel] Staton came and told me soon that my son was cleared—and a free man—so did the court—so did Lincoln. We were all affected and tears streamed down Lincoln's eyes. He then remarked to me—'Hannah—What did I tell you.'"[7]

PART V

Women and President Lincoln

19. A Beardless Lincoln

> She advised me to let my whiskers grow, as it would improve my personal appearance; acting partly upon her suggestion, I have done so.
>
> —Abraham Lincoln, speaking about Grace Bedell in a speech at Westfield, New York, February 16, 1861

THE FIRST VERSION OF this book began in mid-November 2016, and the writing became a personal, life-saving effort. Two years after my daughter's death, I was struggling to breathe without her and failing to cope with the termination of my appointment to the Papers of Abraham Lincoln at the end of October. But a third grief had invaded my depleted body, filling me with despair. As a lifelong Democrat and feminist, I was distraught over Hillary Clinton's loss of the presidency despite winning three million more popular votes cast for her than for her unqualified and shockingly unpresidential opponent. I woke up the morning after the election nauseous and, like many people I later discovered, called in sick to work. After a full day sobbing, I realized I was not as upset over Clinton's loss as I was horrified by her opponent's win. There was a new wound in my broken heart. A dishonest, willfully ignorant, mean-spirited misogynist would occupy the same office as Abraham Lincoln.

A week or two after the election, with a mental clarity unfamiliar to me in those days of foggy grief, I decided an Abraham Lincoln project might be my salvation and my revenge. To focus my attention and energy on an honest, kind, compassionate American president who respected women and democracy and my country would be a healing balm. I began writing in a furious output of emotions, words and sentences banged out onto the pages of what became, six months later, an angry, crazed, 131-page manifesto I called *The Gentleman and the Ladies: Abraham Lincoln, Women, and the Power of Compassionate Politics.* It had been a therapeutic endeavor to write it, but it was not worthy of publication. The manuscript was a hot mess of rage. The focus and the tone were wrong in a million ways, and I struggled to maintain enthusiasm for serious revisions. The writing had gotten the anger off my chest, but that was the end of it. I simply could not bear the concentrated attention on the American presidency that finishing the book would require.

I set my mess of manuscript aside for three years. I concentrated my scholarly efforts on my new job and my new historical subject, Jane Addams. The fog of grief lifted, I began a daily practice of meditation and yoga, and my mind and my body were regaining health. I got divorced and moved back to Illinois to begin building a new life on my own terms. I did not think much at all about Abraham Lincoln during this busy and apprehensive time of recasting my personal and professional lives. And then one year into the COVID pandemic, I had a dream about Abraham Lincoln. In the dream he was clean shaven, and I was grinning. Upon waking from the dream, I had a certainty deep in my bones. I was ready to revisit my terrible Lincoln manuscript and to examine what being a Lincoln scholar had meant to me. I was ready to write a book about Lincoln reflecting my work and my historical passion, not a book to answer disappointment in the 2016 presidential election or to heal the wounds of my departure from Lincoln studies.

Whatever the project would become, it would not be a book about a great American leader. It would be a book about a good man who became a great leader. I was always more interested in the provincial lawyer than the president. I was a rare bird, a Lincoln scholar only mildly interested in the American Civil War. I preferred the bucolic Illinois context of Lincoln's family life and law practice to presidential politics and the turmoil of war. The bronze Lincoln bust sitting on my bookcase is not President Lincoln. It is a beardless, Illinois Lincoln. It was always the beardless Lincoln I loved.

Grace Bedell believed Abraham Lincoln would be more electable with a beard, and today it is the bearded Abraham Lincoln people recognize. Abraham Lincoln's beard is iconic, but to me it is one of those quiet milestones on a life journey. It documents a moment in a man's life when he sets his feet sturdy upon the ground, gathers all he has learned, loved, and lost, and commits the best parts of himself to a greater purpose. The Civil War did not make Abraham Lincoln. Abraham Lincoln took his fully formed, beautiful self to Washington. He continued to learn and to grow in the presidency, but this learning and his greatness were

The author with Abraham Lincoln figure, Second Illinois State Capitol, Vandalia, Illinois, 2017. Author's Photo

possible because his experiences and relationships of the fifty-two years he had already lived made him ready.

It is strange, I suppose, that a dream of a beardless Lincoln would set my own feet sturdy upon the ground, but it did. It is my milestone, my marker. My mission here does not balance on the historical scales of Lincoln's mission to save our country, but the lessons of living are no less important in a humble life than in a great one. If we are lucky, we all come to a point in our lives when we see that all we have experienced, loved, lost, and learned makes us ready to do a thing we could never have imagined.

In dreaming of a beardless Lincoln, I knew I was ready to let go of my fear of giving my voice to the full Lincoln narrative, to let go of my resistance to the Civil War Lincoln, and to believe that my perspective on women and President Lincoln would be as illuminating as my long study of his formative relationships with women before his historic presidency. I still love the beardless Lincoln finding his way in the world, but now I love the wise, old, bearded Lincoln, too. Because as you will see, the stories about President Lincoln and women are as inspiring as they are gorgeous and illuminating.

20. The Woman's President

> I have come to see you and allow you to see me and in this so far as regards the Ladies, I have the best of the bargain on my side.
>
> —Abraham Lincoln, Little Falls, New York, February 18, 1861

On August 23, 1862, Louise Paul, the thirty-year-old second wife of Gabriel René Paul, went to the White House to see President Lincoln. Her husband, a grandson of St. Louis founder Auguste Chouteau, was an 1836 graduate of the U.S. Military Academy and served with distinction in the Mexican War. Louise Paul was a determined, ambitious young wife who was, at the time, living in Washington, where her husband was inspector general for the defenses in the capital. Mr. Paul was an accomplished officer; however, it was Mrs. Paul who made an impression on the president. After she departed his office, Abraham Lincoln took out a piece of Executive Mansion stationery and, in his neat, steady hand, wrote: "Today, Mrs. Major Paul of the Regular Army calls and urges the appointment of her husband as a Brig. Genl. She is a saucy woman and I am afraid she will keep tormenting till I may have to do it."[1]

On September 5, Mrs. Major Paul became Mrs. Brigadier General Paul. Gabriel Paul had already risen to the rank of colonel in December 1861 and in April 1862 as lieutenant colonel, the rank at which he mustered out of the volunteer service at the end of May. After her husband's appointment as brigadier general in the regular army, Louise Paul became the beneficiary of his $315 monthly salary, twice as much as he was making as a major in April 1861. General Paul suffered a horrific injury at Gettysburg on July 1, 1863, but he survived the war. Louise Paul raised the couple's children while caring for her disabled husband until his death in 1886. Afterward, she drew her widow's pension of $50 and later $100 monthly until her death in 1898.[2]

Louise Paul's advocacy for her husband was important to her livelihood and the well-being of her family. She believed in her right to lobby the president of the United States, and Abraham Lincoln agreed with her.

The average woman who went to see President Lincoln was not saucy, although Louise Paul was not the only bold woman who asked him for a remedy or a favor or shared with Lincoln a strong opinion. On the spectrum, the women who met Lincoln in person or sent him letters or petitions fell somewhere in the middle of saucy and demure. They ranged from old Quaker ladies to young treasury girls, from generals' wives to poor widows, from journalists to the illiterate, from nurses to nursing mothers, from white women to Black women. There were women known to Lincoln, like Sarah Walworth, the widow of an Illinois friend, but most were not. None of these women could vote, but they viewed themselves as rightful members of Lincoln's constituency, and he viewed them as constituents, as well. Lincoln did not have to see these women or read their letters, but he saw them, and he read their letters. Despite the efforts of his personal secretaries to limit the public's access to an overburdened president, Lincoln obliged women with extraordinary access to his presidency. Secretary William O. Stoddard wrote that Lincoln in his "manner with the softer sex was kindly and courteous."[3]

Abraham Lincoln had enormous executive responsibilities, commanded a military of men, led a cabinet of men, negotiated with a Congress composed of men, and was, as a politician, beholden to voters who were all men. The burdens of prosecuting a civil war were heavy and endless, but Lincoln accepted the problems women faced as part of his responsibility as their president. As one woman who knew Lincoln well later described him: "President Lincoln had a genius for kindness and sympathy. He travelled out of his way to do good."[4]

Abraham Lincoln was available for women, even when their requests seemed trivial, like when he wrote Mary Motley, the daughter of his minister to Austria: "A friend of yours (a young gentlemen of course) tells me you do me the honor of requesting my autograph. I could scarcely refuse any young lady—certainly not the daughter of your distinguished father."[5]

Lincoln read the letters of women from across the country, answered them, endorsed them, and sent them on to governmental departments or military offices. He granted women interviews in the Executive Mansion, and he stood with the First Lady in receiving lines for hours at public receptions, shaking women's hands and listening to their stories. "All were greeted alike," wrote the *National Republican* in February 1864, "whether clad in homespun or flashing with jewels."[6]

Women in the nineteenth century could not vote, had limited economic opportunities outside the home, and had few legal rights, and married women assumed the legal identity of their husbands. Despite society's constriction of women, Lincoln believed in women's capabilities, and even once advocated their right to vote. These views reflected Lincoln's strong sense of fairness, a trait central to his political ethos. As the war progressed, Lincoln watched women demonstrate, over and over and over again, their service in the war effort and their importance in the life of the nation as well as in the lives of their families. Women mattered and, like men, could not escape history. As their president, he tried to be an advocate for women, to answer their worries, mitigate their difficulties, and ease their sorrows if he could.[7]

Women who appealed to Lincoln sought mercy for their soldier husbands and sons, wanted financial relief or government employment, asked for military passes or information, offered advice, or recommended individuals for appointments. Others sent gifts, good wishes, or blessings for the president's health and the well-being of his family, and, after Willie Lincoln's death, offered condolences. While there were prominent women among those who wrote to Lincoln or sought an audience with him, most were ordinary correspondents and visitors, facing the common problems war wrought upon families on the Northern home front. There were women Lincoln could help and others with problems beyond his control, but he always listened with sensitivity and compassion. The women who met Lincoln in Washington were impressed by his kindness and grateful for his time, sharing their stories of his magnanimity to friends, family, and newspaper reporters. That Lincoln took time with women is a testament to what he valued and to the breadth of his concern for all his constituents.[8]

Desperation often motivated women who sought an audience with President Lincoln. To tell their stories was their power and often their last chance for a remedy. Most women presented their cases with humility, apologizing for any appearance of unladylike pleading. Jessie Frémont, the spirited wife of General John C. Frémont, however, vexed Lincoln. She visited him to plead her husband's case after he overstepped his military authority in the border state of Missouri. She met Lincoln after a long journey from St. Louis, arriving at the White House unbathed, unrested, and rude. Lincoln apparently called her a "female politician." His wife was one of those, but Frémont took the term as a dismissal based on her gender and not on her argument. Their meeting was tense, but Lincoln was not dismissive because she was a woman. He disagreed with her on the merits of her case. General Frémont had overstepped his authority, but Lincoln heard his wife's plea anyway. Lincoln did not have to receive her, but he did; and meeting her validated her right to make her case, whatever the odds of its success. Lincoln always afforded women a hearing when it was possible, and "nothing showed his patience and kindliness more than his manner with the women who came to the Executive Office."[9]

Mary Buckley's story offers an interesting contrast to that of Jessie Frémont. Buckley was a widowed mother with three sons and three daughters who lived in Washington. In October 1861, she wrote to Lincoln: "I am poor and the mother of six children, the oldest of whom is not more than 12 years of age. I ask for employment for my brother Michael Donavan, who has been out of work for two months and who kindly helps to support me. He is well known as an industrious, honest man, who has been employed at the arsenal, and in various Departments of the Government." Mary Buckley was an Irish immigrant who previously operated a cake and butter store in Washington, but the war brought hard times for her and for women like her. Lincoln endorsed her letter: "Will Major Ramsey, or Capt Dahlgren, please find work for Michael Donovan?"[10]

Whether he pointed them out in an audience, shook hands with them in a receiving line at public receptions, or greeted them in his austere office on the second floor of the White House, President Lincoln saw the women. When he read their letters while seated at his mahogany desk with its stuffed pigeonholes at the top and cluttered with working models of weapons, he took in women's pleadings and tried to understand their problems. Along with far more men, there were women who tried Abraham Lincoln's patience, but for the most part he seemed to enjoy his interactions with female constituents. The access he provided women validated the idea that women, even those with ideas or determined opinions that caused him discomfort, had the right to make their cases. Even those who were hostile to Lincoln could not deny this truth. Jessie Frémont, who was so devoted to her husband's greatness that she failed to see the greatness of her president until years after his death, admitted it. In 1893, she wrote: "Mr. Lincoln's cruel death silenced

Abraham Lincoln's Last Reception, *1865. In the lithograph, by Anton Hohenstein, Abraham Lincoln greets a female guest as Mary Lincoln looks on.* Courtesy of Library of Congress, Prints and Photographs, https://www.loc.gov/pictures/item/93503162/

much truth, and since then he has been shaped and exalted into such 'a faultless monster as the world ne'er saw'—not content with his real greatness he has been made to appear incapable of error—and in short viewed in all ways from the altered conditions of a generation later."[11]

A saucy opinion, no doubt, but an admission of Lincoln's greatness and his humanity, nonetheless.

After conducting research for this section of the book, I came to the qualitative conclusion that President Lincoln engaged with his female constituency more than any president before him. I could not locate any substantive analyses about the first fifteen presidents and their relationships with women as constituents, there are no White House visitor logs for the nineteenth century, and rarely do the biographies of early presidents have the term "women" in their indices. Short of conducting a quantitative analysis from primary presidential sources, a task far beyond the scope of my humble book, I cannot know for certain, but there is a strong possibility that women's access to President Lincoln was unprecedented. The turmoil of the Civil War facilitated an increased urgency and compulsion for women, in the North and the South, to seek remedies from their political leaders. But as you have seen here, there is as much evidence to suggest that President Lincoln facilitated a stronger connection between his office and the women it served.

In its February 1918 issue, *The Ladies' Home Journal* published a color illustration of J. L. G. Ferris's 1912 painting, *Lincoln's Last Official Act*. The image depicts a compassionate Lincoln and a powerless, distraught woman, desperate to obtain the release of a Confederate prisoner of war. It is a romantic portrayal, published in a popular woman's magazine during a time of uncertainty, when women were emerging but still very much defined as the vulnerable sex in need of the protection of men. Ferris's painting depicts a human story, characterizing Lincoln as a man moved more by a woman's sorrow than by a rebel soldier's offense against his government and the nation. From the beginning to the end of his presidency, and depicted through the future definitions of his legacy, Abraham Lincoln was, indeed, the woman's president.[12]

Lincoln's Last Official Act *by Jean Leon Gerome Ferris, 1918. The Ladies' Home Journal* 35 (February 1918): 8

21. The Wants and Worries of Women

> I appeal to you as a Father who has lost a beloved son your "Willie;" that you may use your power in my behalf, the widowed mother of an only Son, that she may recover these beloved remains, to weep over the early grave, and lie beside it, after death . . .
>
> —Cornelia Liborius to Abraham Lincoln, August 13, 1864

CORNELIA LIBORIUS'S SON ERNEST was only nineteen years and three months old when he charged the rebel works at Petersburg on July 30, 1864, in the service of the Fifty-First Regiment of New York Volunteers in the U.S. Army. He died in that tragic Battle of the Crater, "shot through the Head, in that terrible Conflict," as his mother wrote to Abraham Lincoln in August 1864. The fifty-eight-year-old woman was bereft, and she appealed to her president's compassion as a fellow grieving parent. Searching for peace, she asked Lincoln to provide a pass for her nephew George Frost, a New York postal employee, to retrieve her son's body at Petersburg, where it was buried in a makeshift grave. Lincoln referred her request to Secretary of War Edwin Stanton, who provided the pass, and the body of Ernest Liborius was returned home to Brooklyn, New York, to his mother.[1]

Cornelia Liborius would suffer the death of another child, twelve-year-old Ann, two years later. Like so many women during the Civil War, she buried children, one she lost in battle and another to disease. Few women, in the North or the South, survived the war years untouched by death. When Liborius died in 1882, her final wish was granted when she was buried next to her children in Green-Wood Cemetery in Brooklyn. Abraham Lincoln could not save her from the grief she endured for eighteen years of her life, but he could and did answer one small prayer. This female constituent would be close to the spirit of her soldier son and rest with him in eternal peace.[2]

The Civil War years in America were years of immense suffering, and the wants and worries of women were many. Death transformed the nation into what historian Drew Gilpin Faust defined as a "republic of suffering." Women gave up their men and their boys, sacrificed their homes and their security, went to work to support their families, and contributed to the war effort in myriad ways. Women who had always worked worked harder in a world turned upside down; and women who would never have dreamed of employment outside of the household before the war went to work for the U.S. government. Women's wants and worries were unending, complicated, and constantly changing, and the wants and worries of Black women were made yet more poignant with the burning hope for freedom in their bodies. What women endured and what they did in the face of grief and terrifying instability was a marvel. Their stories, big and small and always brave, tiptoe through the documents of Lincoln's presidency, illustrating both women's experiences and the compassion of their president's heart.[3]

Abraham Lincoln recognized women's concerns, and their suffering weighed heavily upon his spirit. When he could offer to a woman a small kindness or grant her a significant request, he did so for his own sake as well as for hers. Mary Livermore, who was an associate member of the U.S. Sanitary Commission, wrote about witnessing Lincoln's joy when delivering news to a wife that he had stayed her husband's execution: "The expression of the President's face . . . will never leave my memory. His swarthy, rugged, homely face was glorified by the delight of his soul, which shone out on his features. He delighted in mercy. It gave him positive happiness to confer a favor."[4]

When the writer and editor Sarah Josepha Hale wrote to Lincoln on September 28, 1863, asking for a National Day of Prayer and Thanksgiving, she was communicating a national, emotional, and spiritual need to bind together a grieving nation through a shared holiday of gratitude. She was speaking on behalf of women across the North. When Lincoln issued his Proclamation of Thanksgiving on October 3, he acknowledged the suffering of that female constituency: "And I recommend to them that while offering up the ascriptions justly due to Him for such singular deliverances and blessings, they do also, with humble penitence for our national perverseness and disobedience, commend to His tender care all those who have become widows, orphans, mourners or sufferers in the lamentable civil strife in which we are unavoidably engaged."[5]

Anna Dickinson was another public American woman who spoke on behalf of a nation of women. An orator and women's rights advocate, she represented a generation of women abolitionists whose central worry was the enslavement of human beings. Abraham and Mary Lincoln attended her lecture in the U.S. House of Representatives on January 16, 1864, an event which raised $1,000 for the Freedman's Relief Association.[6] In her appeal to the audience, Dickinson was triumphant. As the *National Republican* reported:

> To have been invited by a committee of illustrious statesmen . . . to have been saluted by an unusually intelligent and fashionable audience . . . to have been presented by the one and supported by the other of the presiding officer of either House of Congress, with the President of the United States a charmed listener, were no common honors to accord to a mere girl, untitled and unknown; and it may be added that no such splendid tribute to feminine talent and patriotism would have been bestowed, or could have been hoped for, outside the limits of our own free and favored land.[7]

After the lecture, Lincoln met with Dickinson to congratulate her. He appreciated this woman who had taken on a cause bigger than herself, but it was not only the public women with grand missions to whom Lincoln responded. He had his country's survival upon his shoulders, but solving common problems of women helped him feel like he was doing something good and useful day to day. Some women Lincoln assisted needed work. Ann G. Sprigg, for example, whom Lincoln called a "most worthy and deserving lady," needed a job. Adèle Douglas, the widow of Lincoln's political rival Stephen Douglas, was worried about the confiscation of her children's property in the South.[8] Douglas's request was a delicate one about which Lincoln wrote:

> Yesterday Mrs. Douglas called, saying she is guardian of the minor children of her late husband; that she is being urged, against her inclination, to send them South, on the plea of avoiding the confiscation of their property there, and asking my counsel in the case. I expect the United States will overcome the attempt to confiscate property, because of loyalty to the government; but if not, I still do not expect the property of absent minor children will be confiscated. I therefore think Mrs. Douglas may safely act

> her pleasure in the premises. But it is especially dangerous for my name to be connected with the matter; for nothing would more certainly excite the secessionists to do the worst they can against the children.[9]

Sometimes the women seeking help were unknown to Lincoln, but the men they represented had known Lincoln in Illinois. After meeting with Lincoln if the fall of 1861, Mary S. Duncan wrote a follow-up letter: "When I called the other morning in view of a supposed vacancy of Inspector General, and in the hope you might give it to my husband, Major Thomas Duncan (3rd Cavalry), you were so considerate."[10]

Lincoln forwarded her request to the adjutant general on January 8, 1863, writing: "Major Thomas Duncan, now on duty on the border of Mexico, is an Illinoisian, and I had some acquaintance with him when he was young. His wife, whose father resides in this city, is now here, and tells me you know her husband. She is very anxious, as in duty bound, for him to be promoted, but especially for him to be assigned to duty here. Please write me what you know of him as an officer; and, if you can, tell me whether he can be brought here." Unfortunately for Mrs. Duncan, the U.S. Army needed her husband in New Mexico and would not reassign him to Washington, but Lincoln had done what he could for the time being. On April 25, 1863, Duncan became assistant provost marshal for Iowa, and his family reunited with him there.[11]

One interesting request came from a woman loyal to the North who was married to a man serving in the Confederate Army. Sallie Ward Hunt of New Orleans had left her husband, their political differences irreconcilable. She wrote to Mary Lincoln on March 31, 1864, asking for help obtaining personal items in New Orleans.[12] Mary Lincoln referred the letter to her husband, who endorsed it:

> I know nothing on the subject of the attached letter, except as therein stated. Neither do I personally know Mrs. Hunt. She has, however, from the beginning of the war, been constantly represented to me as an open, and somewhat influential friend of the Union. It has been said to me, (I know not whether truly) that her husband is in the rebel army, that she avows her purpose to not live with him again, and that she refused to see him when she had an opportunity during one of John Morgan's raids into Kentucky. I would not offer her, or any wife, a temptation to a permanent

> separation from her husband; but if she shall avow that her mind is already, independently and fully made up to such separation, I shall be glad for the property sought by her letter, to be delivered to her, upon her taking the oath of December 8, 1863.[13]

There goes Abraham Lincoln again giving a woman credit for knowing her own mind.

Some evidence indicates Lincoln sometimes was weary of desperate visitors, an understandable reaction of a human being under enormous pressure. Isolated examples show Lincoln becoming impatient with aggressive female petitioners, but there are far more examples of Lincoln becoming impatient with men, some much more difficult than Louise Paul. Salmon P. Chase and George McClellan immediately come to mind. There were hundreds upon hundreds of women with daunting wants and worries, but even as the war progressed, an overburdened, increasingly exhausted President Lincoln kept making time to see women and to read their letters. Women's access to Lincoln was policy.[14]

"Let this woman have her boy out of Old Capitol Prison," Lincoln wrote on January 3, 1863. When eighteen women died in an explosion at the Washington Arsenal, Lincoln attended the funeral on June 19, 1864. Lincoln pardoned sons and discharged ailing husbands because their wives and their mothers made their pleas. He talked to a governor's wife who wanted wounded soldiers moved away from the front. He listened to the suggestions of Dorothea Dix, the superintendent of women nurses in the U.S. Army. He issued passes to women. He gave permission to women to enter military camps so they could tend to the sick and wounded. He made appointments on the requests and upon the evidence of women, making this unusual note to himself in July 1861: "List of officers I wish to remember, when I make appointments from the officers of the regular Army . . . Lieut. Slemmer—His pretty wife says, a major, or first captain."[15]

Perhaps Abraham Lincoln's understanding of his responsibility for free Black and enslaved people is most illustrative of his compassion for women. He ended the use of slave labor in the White House, employing many free Black and formerly enslaved women, like the cook Mary Dines and Mary Lincoln's dressmaker Elizabeth Keckley. In contrast, there were at least twenty enslaved women and men in the Confederate White House in Richmond, Virginia, during the war, several of

Caroline Slemmer, 1861. Lithographer John L. Magee.
Courtesy of Library of Congress, Prints and Photographs, https://www.loc.gov/pictures/item/2003671577/

whom had to make their own way to freedom. There is much evidence of the dignity and respect with which Lincoln treated the women he employed. Keckley described Lincoln as kind and "generous by nature." Dines remembered fondly Lincoln's visits to the contraband camps, where he enjoyed conversations with the women there. Both Keckley and Dines kept fond memories of Lincoln. I wish there were Lincoln letters to confirm it, but I do not doubt Lincoln's affection for them. Previous American presidents did not give audiences to Black women, and confederate president Jefferson Davis certainly did not bear in mind their wants and their worries.[16]

Abraham Lincoln was more pragmatic than radical, the presidency constraining him. However, it could be said that simply by greeting Black people in the White House, by giving them access to the presidency, he was in radical territory. In receiving Sojourner Truth on October 29,

1864, for example, he acknowledged her worthiness and right to speak face-to-face with *her* president. Of her meeting with Lincoln, Truth said: "It was about 8 o'clock, A.M., when I called on the President. Upon entering his reception room we found about a dozen persons in waiting, among them two colored women. I had quite a pleasant time waiting until he was disengaged, and enjoyed his conversation with others; he showed as much kindness and consideration to the colored persons as to the whites—if there was any difference, more . . ."[17]

The Lincoln administration felt it had a duty not only to the brave men serving in the U.S. Colored Troops but also to the mothers, wives, sisters, and daughters of those soldiers. Lincoln viewed them all as his constituents. On January 1, 1863, Lincoln also made it an aim of his presidency to free four million enslaved people, half of whom were women. Sojourner Truth wanted to meet the man who had issued the Emancipation Proclamation, and Lincoln wanted to meet her, as he had wanted to meet Frederick Douglass. In a public statement, Truth said of her meeting: "I never was treated by any one with more kindness and cordiality than were shown to me by the great and good man, Abraham Lincoln."[18]

Truth's assessments of her meeting contrasts with that of Lucy Colman, the white woman who accompanied her to the White House. Remembering the visit years later, Colman claimed that Lincoln made them wait three hours while he talked with men and then talked down to them. She claimed Lincoln referred to Truth as "Aunty," a term that is hard from our modern view to see as anything other than condescending. Lincoln may have used the term, and he was probably busy with pressing military or political meetings that delayed his meeting with Truth. There were always too many people waiting to see the president, and Lincoln was notorious for spending too much time talking with people while others waited. Historian Nell Painter, Truth's best biographer, sides with Colman's account of the meeting, but a new study argues that Colman's version, written thirty years after the meeting, gets several facts wrong and should be carefully balanced with Truth's own public statements published in newspapers in 1864.[19]

We do know, however, that Lincoln received Sojourner Truth, shook her hand, met her eyes, and recognized her humanity. Abraham Lincoln was not perfect on race—far from it—but his compassion was not limited by race or by gender. It is hard for me to see his meeting with

Truth as anything other than historic. It is also more evidence of his willingness to make himself available to the women who had so much at stake in the war. Lincoln wanted to be answerable to them because he cared about them. He wanted to ease their burdens if it was at all in his power to do so. And in late October 1864, less than two weeks before an election he was uncertain he would win, no greater worry consumed Abraham Lincoln than the freedom of the human beings Sojourner Truth represented.

22. *Sanitary Fairs and the Ministrations of Angels*

> I have only to say that I accept this present of the ladies as an additional token of your confidence, but I do not need any further evidence of the loyalty and devotion of the women of America to the cause of the Union and the cause of Christian humility.
>
> —Abraham Lincoln to Ladies of the Sanitary Fair in Philadelphia, June 16, 1864

A CHEERING CROWD GREETED President Lincoln as he entered the packed grand hall of the U.S. Patent Office. He walked toward the speaker's platform, Mrs. Lincoln on his arm, as the Columbia Commandery of Knights Templars played "Hail to the Chief." People pressed forward to get closer to him. Young women squealed as they were squeezed in the crowd, and the cheers continued as Lincoln made his way to the stage. It was eight o'clock on Friday evening, March 18, 1864, the closing night of the "Ladies' National Fair." The Patent Office, an imposing Greek Revival building, just six blocks east of the White House, had played host to the month-long fair, entertaining 2,500 visitors each night. Women had planned and conducted the event to raise funds for the families of the city's soldiers, and it was an astounding $25,000 success. In the audience that evening for the fair's closing festivities were the women organizers, politicians, donors, private citizens, and soldiers. A series of speakers addressed the crowd, but it was the president the people wished to hear.[1] After loud calls, Lincoln stepped forward to enthusiastic applause:

> In this extraordinary war extraordinary developments have manifested themselves, such as have not been seen in former wars; and amongst these manifestations nothing has been more remarkable than these fairs for the relief of suffering soldiers and their families.

> And the chief agents in these fairs are the women of America. (Cheers.)
>
> I am not accustomed to the use of language of eulogy; I have never studied the art of paying compliments to women, but I must say that if all that has been said by orators and poets since the creation of the world in praise of woman were applied to the women of America, it would not do them justice for their conduct during this war. I will close by saying God bless the women of America! (Great applause).[2]

Abraham Lincoln's praise of the women at the close of this sanitary fair was more than public platitude. The work of women for the U.S. Sanitary Commission and the regional and national fairs that raised money to support soldiers and the U.S. war effort was evidence of women's political activity. Women were the heart and soul of the commission's work and its fundraising efforts, which centered on the fairs.[3] Lincoln also understood women's sacrifice as nurses, working for little or no pay. He appreciated their selfless dedication. It was clear to him that the U.S. military needed these women, that the United States of America needed women and would not win the war without them.[4]

Seal of the United States Sanitary Commission, 1861. Charles J. Stillé, *History of the United States Sanitary Commission*. Philadelphia: J. B. Lippincott, 1866, title page

Just four months before delivering these remarks at the national fair, Lincoln had traveled to Gettysburg, Pennsylvania, to dedicate a national cemetery. Before Lincoln delivered his now famous, two-minute address, the renowned orator Edward Everett spoke for two hours. When Lincoln wrote Everett the next day, he noted just two points from Everett's thirteen-thousand-word oration: "Of course I knew Mr. Everett would not fail; and yet, while the whole discourse was eminently satisfactory, and will be of great value, there were passages in it which transcended my expectation. The point made against the theory of the general government being only an agency, whose principals are the States, was new to me, and, as I think, is one of the best arguments for the national supremacy. The tribute to our noble women for their angel-ministering to the suffering soldiers, surpasses, in its way, as do the subjects of it, whatever has gone before."[5]

Lincoln was responding to a paragraph buried in the very middle of Everett's extravagant speech, delivered on that frigid winter day:

> Scarcely has the cannon ceased to roar, when the brethren and sisters of Christian benevolence, ministers of compassion, angels of pity, hasten to the field and the hospital, to moisten the parched tongue, to bind the ghastly wounds, to soothe the parting agonies alike of friend and foe, and to catch the last whispered messages of love from dying lips. . . . since this terrible war has been waged, the women of the loyal States, if never before, have entitled themselves to our highest admiration and gratitude,—alike those who at home, often with fingers unused to the toil, often bowed beneath their own domestic cares, have performed an amount of daily labor not exceeded by those who work for their daily bread, and those who, in the hospital and the tents of the Sanitary and Christian Commissions, have rendered services which millions could not buy.[6]

The compassionate president and commander in chief had seen women's work for himself. When he visited soldiers in military hospitals, he watched women tending to the sick and injured. He also had his own personal experience of such ministering angels. In February 1862, Willie and Tad Lincoln fell ill with typhoid fever, and Dorothea Dix offered the Lincoln family one of her nurses to tend to their critically ill boys. Lincoln replied: "The President's & Mrs L's thanks to Miss Dix for her kind inquiry by note of this morning. They do not, just now, need the nurse, but will preserve Miss Dix note, and call on her if occasion hereafter shall require."[7]

The following day, eleven-year-old Willie Lincoln died, and the White House went dark with grief. Mary Lincoln was inconsolable. Abraham Lincoln was devastated. Tad Lincoln was still ill. Two days later, Dix dispatched a nurse named Rebecca Pomeroy to the White House to care for Tad and the grieving Lincoln family. Pomeroy stayed with Tad, nursing him through his terrible illness until the end of February when he was out of mortal danger. Pomeroy stayed on at the White House, spending additional time with Tad but also with Mr. and Mrs. Lincoln. In May, when Mary Lincoln's sister Elizabeth Edwards was called home to Springfield to tend to a family illness there, Abraham Lincoln wrote to Dix, hoping Pomeroy could stay on for an additional two weeks. So helpful was Pomeroy that Mary Lincoln tried to keep her on indefinitely, but Pomeroy was keen to return to the soldiers for whom she had found a calling to attend. Not long after Pomeroy returned to her nursing post, Lincoln extended his gratitude by bestowing a favor to her sole surviving son.[8] Lincoln sent his personal request to Edwin Stanton:

> This young man—George K. Pomeroy—is the son of one of the best women I ever knew—a widow who has lost all her other children, and has cheerfully given this one to the war, and devotes herself exclusively to nursing our sick and wounded soldiers. I wish to do something for him, and, even, to strain a point for that object. I wish you would see him, and give him a second Lieutenancy in the regular Army, in the first vacancy not already promised. He has already served nearly a year in the volunteers. This shall be your voucher.[9]

Throughout the remainder of the war, Mary Lincoln brought presents to the soldiers in Pomeroy's ward at Columbian College Hospital where she was stationed. Mr. and Mrs. Lincoln would sometimes visit Pomeroy together and bring her flowers. After Mary Lincoln was injured in a carriage accident in July 1863, it was Pomeroy whom they called, and she spent three weeks nursing Mrs. Lincoln. Pomeroy returned to the First Lady's side in October 1864 when death threats against the president exacerbated her emotional anxiety. Rebecca Pomeroy felt a closeness to the Lincolns, and a sense of dread filled her heart at the close of the war. Just before the fall of Richmond on April 2, 1865, she wrote to a friend: "My soul is in the Lincoln family, and why I am distressed for them all God only knows. Sometimes I think God has put this heavy burden upon me for some wise purpose best known to himself. My heart cries out to God in behalf of Mrs. Lincoln and our dear, good President. I feel that I can pray for him hourly."[10]

Thirteen days later, her president was dead. On April 20, Pomeroy was discharged from her nursing duties. She had nursed over seven hundred patients and sat with eighty when they died. She had provided health care and emotional support to the Lincoln family and tended to the wounds Secretary of State William Seward and his son suffered in the assassination plot that killed Lincoln. She had done her duty to her country, and at war's end she returned home to Massachusetts. In 1872, she became the founding superintendent of a home for orphaned and destitute girls in Newton. Following her death in 1884, the home became known as the Rebecca Pomeroy Newton Home for Orphaned Girls.[11]

Pomeroy's good work throughout her life would not have surprised Abraham Lincoln. He knew a woman's worth. He appreciated such women as Pomeroy, like the nurse Abbie Beren from Troy, New York, whose personal worry compelled his request to Edwin Stanton: "This lady, Abigail C. [Beren], had a husband and three sons in the war, and has been a nurse herself, without pay, during nearly the whole war. Her husband was killed at Gettysburg, and one of her sons also has died in the service. One other son she is willing to leave in the service where he still is, but the youngest, James H. Benjamin, private in Co. K. 104 N.Y. vols. and who is in poor health, she asks to have discharged. Let it be done."[12]

Women like Annie Wittenmyer, Ella Hobart, and Emma Egbert knew something of Lincoln's capacity to see them, to help them if he could, and to appreciate their contributions. Wittenmyer was an Iowa woman who spent the war nursing soldiers. In 1864, she wanted a special pass, which Lincoln ordered: "Let this Lady have transportation to any of the Armies, and any privileges while there, not objected to by the commanders of the armies respectively." Hobart wanted an official appointment as chaplain of a Wisconsin regiment. She had recently been ordained, and the unit elected her to be their minister. Their colonel supported her, and when Lincoln heard her story, he agreed. He submitted her request to the secretary of war, writing: "This lady would be appointed Chaplain of the First Wisconsin Heavy Artillery, only that she is a woman.

The President has not legally anything to do with such a question, but has no objection to her appointment." When Egbert, the young wife of an oil magnate in Pennsylvania, made a staggering donation to fund a Christmas dinner for soldiers in military hospitals in 1864, her president sent her a note: "Col. Forney assures me that you will not be displeased if I tender, as I most heartily do, my sincere thanks for your munificent Christmas donation of five thousand dollars to the sick and wounded soldiers in the Philadelphia hospitals."[13]

Women across the north had knowledge of Lincoln's generous spirit. Mary Livermore and Jane Hoge, two Chicago women who organized the Northwest Sanitary Fair in 1863, made a special appeal to Lincoln on October 11 because of it:

> The patriotic women of the Northwestern States will hold a grand Fair in Chicago, on the last week of Oct., and the first of Nov., to raise funds for the Sanitary Commission of the Northwest, whose headquarters are in Chicago. This Commission labors especially for the sick and wounded soldiers of the South western States, of whose bravery, and persistent endurance, we are all justly proud. . . . [W]e confidently hope to realize from $25,000 to $50,000. . . . The Executive Committee have been urgently requested to solicit from Mrs. Lincoln and yourself some donation to this great Fair—not so much for the value of the gift, as for the éclat which this circumstance would give to the Fair. It has been suggested to us from various quarters that the most acceptable donation you could possibly make, would be the original manuscript of the Proclamation of emancipation . . . if it is at all consistent with what is proper, for you to donate it. There would be great competition among buyers to obtain possession of it, and to say nothing of the interest that would attach to such a gift, it would prove pecuniarily of great value. We should take pains to have such an arrangement made as would place the document permanently in either the State or the Chicago Historical Society.[14]

Lincoln answered the women on October 26 that he had "some desire to retain the paper; but if it shall contribute to the relief or comfort of the soldiers that will be better." The signed Emancipation Proclamation Lincoln sent to Chicago fetched $3,000 for the Northwest Sanitary Fair, which raised a total of $100,000. The document's buyer presented it to the Chicago Soldiers' Home to sell again to generate additional funds. The document was then reproduced in lithographs, thousands of which sold for $1 each. Between 1863 and 1865, women organized and managed more than two dozen sanitary fairs, raising more than $1 million.[15]

At the beginning of the Civil War, the U.S. military lacked basic infrastructure to collect wounded soldiers, transport them to hospitals, and care for them. When Lincoln established the U.S. Sanitary Commission in July 1861, he could not have known what women would contribute to creating a system of care and support to the U.S. military as nurses and cooks in military hospitals, as volunteers for organizations supporting the war effort, as donors and fundraisers, and as sanitary fair organizers. Women nursed soldiers, served them meals in military hospitals, collected blankets, made bandages, and donated and raised money. This work did not go unnoticed.[16]

When Abraham Lincoln had the opportunity, he was eager to express his gratitude, as he did in January 1864 when a wounded officer told him about Esther Stockton, an elderly widow in Pennsylvania to whom Lincoln wrote: "Learning that you who have passed the eighty-fourth year of life have given to the soldiers some three hundred pairs of stockings, knitted by yourself, I wish to offer you my thanks. Will you also convey my thanks to those young ladies who have done so much in feeding our soldiers while passing through your city? Yours truly, A. Lincoln."[17]

23. *A Lady Clerk and Abraham Lincoln*

> [I]t is certainly true in equity, that the laboring women in our employment should be paid at the least as much as they were at the beginning of the war.
>
> —Abraham Lincoln to Edwin Stanton, in response to the pleadings of twenty thousand working women of Philadelphia, July 27, 1864

WOMEN HAVE ALWAYS WORKED. Throughout history, they engaged in myriad labors both within their homes and outside of them. During the American Civil War, however, more American women left their homes for employment than ever before. The war brought horror and suffering, but it also offered opportunities for women as nurses, as laborers in a variety of skilled trades, and as government workers. In the absence of husbands and sons who were away at war, women went to work to support their families. Some filled vacated positions in business and industry in their communities to keep local economies going. Others sought work related to the army, military hospitals, or relief organizations. Thousands of unmarried women moved to Washington or other cities to take advantage of unprecedented prospects to enter the workforce, and hundreds found jobs in the U.S. government.[1]

Mary Anne Griffin was one. On her behalf, Abraham Lincoln wrote in September 1861: "I shall be very glad if any of the Heads of Departments, or Bureaus, can give this lady some suitable employment."[2]

Mary Ann Curry wrote Lincoln in March 1862: "Your humble servant kindly petitions your honor for some employment in any one of the Departments in any capacity where I should be competent . . . as it will enable me to aid my mother in supporting a large and fatherless family. Two of my brothers are with Gen. Burnside in North Carolina." Lincoln forwarded Curry's letter, which he endorsed twice, on April

14 and 26, 1862: "Sec. of Treasury please see Mrs. Curry, and give her employment if possible."[3]

President Lincoln supported, recommended, and nominated women for jobs in the federal government. In 1860, women worked as postmasters, but there were no women working in other departments of the

223.

Abraham Lincoln,

President of the United States of America,

TO ALL WHO SHALL SEE THESE PRESENTS, GREETING:

Know ye, That, reposing special trust and confidence in the Integrity, Ability, and Punctuality of Caroline F. Cowan, I have nominated, and by and with the advice and consent of the Senate, DO APPOINT Her Deputy Postmaster at Biddeford, in the State of Maine; and do authorize and empower ~~him~~ her to execute and fulfil the duties of that Office according to law: AND TO HAVE AND TO HOLD the said Office, with all the powers, privileges, and emoluments to the same of right appertaining, unto ~~him~~ her the said Caroline F. Cowan, for the term of four years, from the day of the date hereof, unless the PRESIDENT OF THE UNITED STATES, for the time being, should be pleased sooner to revoke and determine this COMMISSION.

In testimony whereof, I have caused these LETTERS to be made Patent, and the SEAL OF THE UNITED STATES to be hereunto affixed.

L. S.

Given under my hand, at the City of Washington, the Eleventh day of March, in the year of our Lord one thousand eight hundred and Sixty-three, and of the INDEPENDENCE OF THE UNITED STATES OF AMERICA the Eighty-seventh.

Abraham Lincoln

By the President:

William H. Seward, Secretary of State.

Caroline Cowan Appointment as Deputy Postmaster of Biddeford, Maine, March 11, 1863. National Archives and Records Administration, Washington federal government until Lincoln's appointment of Francis Spinner as the U.S. treasurer. The first to hire so-called "government girls," Spinner employed women as clerks, copyists, and currency counters. Lincoln endorsed the move to employ women with good pay. Salaries varied depending upon the job, but most women, working in the Treasury and Post Office Departments, earned $600 annually (about $22,000 today). Lincoln appointed more women as postmasters and deputy postmasters than any previous president, and he pressed hard for the appointment of widows.[4] In July 1863, he wrote his postmaster general:

> Yesterday little indorsements of mine went to you in two cases of Post-Masterships sought for widows whose husbands have fallen in the battles of this war. These cases occurring on the same day, brought me to reflect more attentively than I had before done, as to what is fairly due from us here, in the dispensing of patronage, towards the men who, by fighting our battles, bear the chief burthen of saving our country. My conclusion is that, other claims and qualifications being equal, they have the better right; and this is especially applicable to the disabled soldier, and the deceased soldier's family.[5]

Lady Clerks Leaving the Treasury Department at Washington, *by A. R. Ward, 1865. Harper's Weekly* 9 (February 18, 1865): 100

The mass employment of women during the Lincoln presidency was revolutionary, but it terrified many observers. One Illinois newspaper took aim at Spinner and his boss, Treasury secretary Salmon Chase: "There seems to be little doubt, from all the accounts, that the man placed there by Secretary Chase as superintendent of the note-printing turned his bureau into a brothel, appoint to place these women of loose morals." Even more sedate observers who understood the need for women workers fretted over the societal consequences of such a monumental shift in women's labor. As magazine editor Lydia Sayer Hasbrouck wrote in June 1861: "This war won't leave women where it found them, whatever may be said of men."[6]

No matter what anyone may have thought in 1861, including Abraham Lincoln, women's placement in government jobs and the appearance of them in the economic landscape became, by the end of the war, commonplace. In February 1865, the popular illustrated magazine *Harper's Weekly* published a scene of *Lady Clerks Leaving the Treasury Department at Washington*. The women depicted were respectable, not a prostitute among them. The few men in the lithograph are nonchalant as the rush of women in their wide skirts and bonnets crowd the street. It is a scene so comfortable, so normal, as to be unworthy of further comment. No detailed caption was necessary to describe the scene because it was just an ordinary day in America. Abraham Lincoln played a role in this revolutionary change.

There were 447 women employed as clerks and note cutters in the U.S. Treasury Department in February 1865, and one was Susan Dugger. She was a young woman whose journey from rural Illinois to the nation's capital was representative of women working for Lincoln's government. Susan Dugger was born on July 27, 1842, in Carlinville, Illinois. Her father died in 1847, her mother remarried, her sister died in 1856, and when the war came, her brother became a soldier. In 1864, Dugger left Carlinville and moved to Washington to find a job. On March 21, she and a Miss Beattie, also from Illinois, met President Abraham Lincoln in the White House, and Lincoln gave them an introduction to his postmaster general, Montgomery Blair: "These young ladies, Miss Dugger and Miss Beattie, are from Illinois, & want employment. They are loyal and worthy, and I shall be very glad indeed if places can be found for them."[7]

Dugger landed a job in the post office, but she soon transferred to the Treasury Department. The jobs of "treasury girls" ranged from menial work like cutting notes to clerkships for women with good penmanship, and Dugger quickly rose through the ranks. After the war, she stayed in Washington and lived her entire life as a government worker. In 1871, Dugger was earning nine hundred dollars a year as a clerk, supporting herself and residing in a boardinghouse with other treasury workers. She thrived in her professional life, choosing a lengthy career in the U.S. Treasury Department over marriage, becoming a foremost expert on counterfeit money, even testifying as an expert witness in a fraud trial in New Orleans in 1886.[8]

Susan Dugger rose to the level of a class-one clerk, handled billions of dollars, vacationed in the Blue Ridge Mountains, and lived among other working women in the District of Columbia. By 1897, she was earning $1,200 annually (about $44,000 today). She worked for the U.S. Treasury Department for forty-six years, serving under eleven presidents, from Abraham Lincoln to William Howard Taft. In mid-1910, she fell ill and could no longer work, age creeping into her bones. She was a lodger in the home of her friends Malvenia G. and Thomas Carmick, a married couple, the latter a clerk for the federal government. In April 1911, she went to see U.S. senator Shelby Cullom of Illinois, who had known Abraham Lincoln. They discussed the prospect of pensions for government clerks, and Dugger took with her a yellowed piece of paper, bearing the signature of Abraham Lincoln. It was the note Lincoln had written on her behalf in 1864, which she had kept as a treasure for five decades.[9]

Senator Cullom, who showed the letter to Secretary of the Treasury Franklin MacVeagh, said in an interview with a *Washington Post* reporter on April 5, 1911: "I am in favor of pensions for clerks who have grown old in the service of government. . . . Take, for example, the case of Miss Susan Dugger . . . who for 45 years she served the government faithfully, and today she is an invalid, chiefly on account of her old age. Clerks like that deserve a pension. This poor woman has no money, and if it were not for a friend who cares for her she would be without any of the necessities of life." Pensions were coming, partly because of Susan Dugger, although they would come too late for her. She died on December 28, 1911, of a cerebral effusion. She was sixty-nine-years old.[10]

As a young woman, Susan Dugger was brave. During the uncertain time of war, she traveled eight hundred miles to make a new start. She trusted enough in herself to leave her small hometown in Illinois to find a better life in the nation's capital. Abraham Lincoln had validated her courage and helped her find work. He believed in women's abilities and in their right to gainful employment. Susan Dugger lived up to Lincoln's faith in her and in women. For the rest of her fascinating, ordinary life, she never forgot the role Lincoln played in setting her upon a professional path created by the circumstances of war and the Lincoln administration's willingness to be as brave as the women they employed to keep the government running.

24. *Socks and Gratitude*

> Allow me to return my cordial thanks for your kindness in sending me a copy of your translation of the Comte de Gasparin's "America before Europe." I shall read it with pleasure and with gratitude.
> —Abraham Lincoln to Mary L. Booth, August 1, 1862

IN THE FALL OF 1861, Susannah Weathers, a widow, sat down by the fire in her home in Rossville, Indiana, to make a pair of socks for Abraham Lincoln. She was seventy-nine years old. Her husband had been dead since 1844. One of her children was also deceased, but she had two sons and a daughter and numerous grandchildren. I wonder what she was thinking as her old hands knitted those new socks. Perhaps it was her childhood in Kentucky that occupied her mind or raising her family in the infant state of Indiana or worrying about the future of her grandchildren and great-grandchildren and the country they would inherit. Perhaps her singular thought was of her president, bracing against the coming winter and facing the terrible arrival of a war.

After finishing the socks, Weathers penned a letter to Lincoln on November 26 and sent it along with her humble gift.[1] After receiving the letter and the socks, Abraham Lincoln wrote a thank-you note on December 4. On a busy day that included a tense meeting with a Canadian minister, a conference with senators from Iowa and Illinois about military appointments, attendance with Mrs. Lincoln at the presentation of colors to the Harris Light Cavalry near Arlington, Virginia, and an evening consultation with Assistant Secretary of the Navy Gustavus Fox,[2] Lincoln found time to write this thoughtful letter to an old woman:

> I take great pleasure in acknowledging the receipt of your letter of Nov. 26; and in thanking you for the present by which it was accompanied. A pair of socks so fine, and soft, and warm, could hardly have been manufactured in any other way than the old

> Kentucky fashion. Your letter informs me that your maiden name was Crume, and that you were raised in Washington county, Kentucky, by which I infer that an uncle of mine by marriage was a relative of yours. Nearly, or quite sixty years ago, Ralph Crume married Mary Lincoln, a sister of my father, in Washington county, Kentucky. Accept my thanks, and believe me Very truly Your friend A. Lincoln.[3]

The physical letter is as lovely as the sentiments conveyed within it. Written in his characteristic hand, every word deliberate, each line straight and tidy, no smudges of ink or unruly formation of letters, and no evidence of a hasty pen. Lincoln had the worry of a nation of 31.4 million people upon his mind, yet he sat at his desk and offered his heartfelt gratitude to a single female member of his constituency. The stationery on which Lincoln penned his gracious missive is yellowed with age, but the ink is still sharp, and the folds have been pressed flat to prevent deterioration of the ink that lies upon them. The letter is tucked up safe in an acid-free folder in pristine archival conditions in the Lilly Library at Indiana University in Bloomington. It was in the reading room of the Lilly Library in January 2006 that I held this treasure of the American president I study and a fellow Indiana woman.

In our digital age, historians rely more on scanned letters, diaries, newspapers, political and governmental documents, and other materials available online. As an editor who has spent a career in digital history, I celebrate the online accessibly of primary sources that enable scholars, educators, students, and history buffs to connect with collections in repositories they might never have the fortune to visit in person. However, there is magic in handling such a treasure as Lincoln's letter to Susannah Weathers. A digital image is an impoverished substitute, and no transcription of a document can do it justice. I knew about Lincoln's letter to Weathers before I conducted research at Indiana University because a transcription of it was included in the *Collected Works of Abraham Lincoln*. But holding the actual letter and seeing Lincoln's handwriting upon the page stirred my imagination in a way that printed text in a published book cannot do. A transcription of Lincoln's letter fails to convey the deliberation of his message as he put his pen to the paper on a busy day in the life of the president of the United States. A transcription fails to reveal the precious time he took to write the

Executive Mansion,

Washington, Dec. 4, 1861.

My dear Madam

I take great pleasure in acknowledging the receipt of your letter of Nov. 26; and in thanking you for the present by which it was accompanied— A pair of socks so fine, and soft, and warm, could hardly have been manufactured in any other way than the old Kentucky fashion. Your letter informs me that your maiden name was Crume, and that you were raised in Washington county, Kentucky, by which I infer that an uncle of mine by marriage was a relative of yours— Nearly, or quite sixty years ago, Ralph Crume married Mary Lincoln, a sister of my father, in Washington county, Kentucky—

Accept my thanks, and believe me very truly

Your friend

A. Lincoln.

Mrs Susannah Weathers
Rossville, Clinton Co, Ind.

Abraham Lincoln to Susannah Weathers, December 4, 1861.
Lilly Library, Indiana University, Bloomington

letter, his careful purpose to render in words his sincere gratitude and to create a beautiful keepsake for the recipient. The texture and depth of feeling of the document Susannah Weathers received in the post from President Lincoln was evidence of Lincoln's kind regard for a woman he had never met.

In the years since seeing the letter, which remains a personal favorite Lincoln document, I have thought a great deal about its meaning and importance. The socks Susannah Weathers made for her president were a humble gift, but they also represented her best self as a woman, as a nurturing human being, and as an American who appreciated Lincoln's responsibilities and worried about his poor, cold feet. Historians have mentioned the letter in passing as evidence of Lincoln's kindness and his beautiful way with words. Indeed, it is such evidence. However, it is also evidence of Lincoln's gratitude, his admiration for women, and his own sense of duty to his female constituents.

Susannah Weathers's gift was illustrative of a time when Americans felt an intimate connection to the president, when constituents often sent gifts and letters and hoped for or even expected letters in return. What might seem quaint to us today in our time of political disillusion was commonplace in the Lincoln era; and President Lincoln received hundreds of these letters. Women kept the good wishes, the gifts, and the gratitude coming throughout the Civil War. Eliza Hamilton wrote to make certain that Lincoln and his family members were enjoying good health. Mary Hancock Colyer sent Lincoln a letter signed by John Hancock, who was her uncle. To the latter Lincoln replied: "Permit me to express my cordial thanks for the interesting relic you were so kind as to send me, as well as for the flattering sentiment with which it was accompanied. I am with great respect Your Obdt Servt. A. Lincoln."[4]

Lincoln could have passed the Weathers letter on to a personal secretary, who would have dashed off a formulaic thank-you note. But he did not. And he did not dash off his own note, either. Lincoln's letter to Susannah Weathers is more than an example of Lincoln being a nice fellow whose mothers raised him up to be grateful and to express it. It is evidence of a deeper, abiding personal ethos. When President Lincoln replied to letters written by women, responsibility and respect compelled him. There was no vote or favor Lincoln was seeking when he penned these letters; and when he took the time to write them there were always a dozen other things of serious political, military, or personal import that he could have or should have been doing instead.

Lincoln did not respond to all his female correspondents. There were far too many. Lincoln's secretaries sorted through letters, responded themselves to some, and whittled down a stack before passing a few for Lincoln to answer. Sadly, Lincoln's secretaries were not always good judges of what letters would interest or amuse their boss. Before Lincoln's election in 1860, Libbie Bailey of New Jersey, for example, wrote to Lincoln to tell him that she had adopted him as a brother because of his antislavery convictions, signing her letter "Your Sister Libbie Lincoln." On the envelope a secretary wrote "needs no answer." Lincoln never saw Libbie's letter, and I am sorry for her and for all of us that he did not have a chance to respond.[5]

The letters Lincoln did write were gifts to the women who received them, an acknowledgment that they mattered. When the Quaker minister Eliza P. Gurney received Lincoln's letter about faith and a previous conversation they shared, she replied: "I like to address thee in thy own familiar way and tell thee how grateful to my feelings is thy valued and valuable letter, which I shall keep among my treasured things, and for which, allow me to return thee my sincere and grateful thanks."[6]

That Lincoln reached out to Gurney and responded to so many other women reflected his appreciation. The letters reveal his commitment to women. Offering a few personal words was his highest compliment. That Lincoln penned so many letters of gratitude in the middle of a terrible war is a testament to his character. Lincoln hated to shirk his responsibility to his female constituents, even as immense pressures crowded in on him. His letters were a gift to the women who received them, and they remain a gift to us all.[7]

PART VI

Women and Lincoln's Legacy

25. *The Widow and Oak Ridge Cemetery*

My determination is unalterable . . . that *the* Monument shall be placed over the remains of my Beloved Husband, in *Oak Ridge* Cemetery.
—Mary Lincoln to Richard J. Oglesby, June 10, 1865

In early June 1865, Mary Lincoln was grief-stricken and terrified. Having just left Washington on May 23, she faced the challenge of creating a new life for herself and her son Tad in Chicago. At forty-six, she was on her own for the first time in her life. Her husband and two sons were dead. Her country was torn apart. As a widow in nineteenth-century America, her future was precarious. And to trouble her further, a group of powerful Republican men in Illinois, without consulting her, were making plans to build a memorial for Abraham Lincoln on land of their choosing instead of at Oak Ridge, the pastoral cemetery she selected for her husband to be buried.[1]

Ten days after Abraham Lincoln's death, the Lincoln National Monument Association, consisting of old Lincoln family friends, organized to raise funds to erect a monument to the martyred president near the state capitol square in downtown Springfield. Mary Lincoln may have been a grief-stricken woman, but she was not stupid. She had read about the association's plans before she left Washington. She sent word that Abraham Lincoln's grave and monument would be in Oak Ridge Cemetery. She did not dictate monument design or object to the involvement of Lincoln's political friends. She simply wanted the remains and memorial to her husband to be in a quiet setting among trees where she would one day join him for their eternal rest together. The association ignored her.[2]

On June 5, 1865, one month after Abraham Lincoln's body was placed in a temporary vault at Oak Ridge Cemetery, Mary Lincoln wrote one of the most significant letters of her life. In that letter, she staked her claim, consequential for Abraham Lincoln's legacy and for me, 151 years later. Writing to sitting Illinois governor Richard Oglesby, leader of the association, she asserted her rights as Lincoln's widow and made clear her family's wishes. Throughout her life, Mary Lincoln spoke with candor, but this letter is a queen's example of a woman in possession of her own her mind at a time when people thought she had lost it to grief.

> I learn from the Newspapers & other sources that your association have it in contemplation to erect a Monument to my Husband's memory on the Mather Block in the City of Springfield, instead of over his remains, in Oak Ridge Cemetery. I feel that it is due to candor and fairness that I should notify your Monument association, that unless I receive within the next ten days, an Official assurance that the Monument will be erected over the Tomb in Oak Ridge Cemetery, in accordance with my oft expressed wishes, I shall yield my consent, to the request of the National Monument association in Washington & that of numerous other friends in the Eastern States & have the sacred remains deposited in the vault, prepared for Washington, under the Dome of the National Capitol, at as early a period as practicable. I remain, your deeply afflicted friend Mary Lincoln.[3]

Mary Lincoln did not play poker, but this letter was the poker face of a talented player—because Mary Lincoln was bluffing. On a walk through a peaceful, green cemetery in Virginia just days before his assassination, Mary's husband told her he wanted to be buried in such a peaceful place as that Virginia landscape. Although Mary Lincoln herself could not return to live in Springfield, where there were too many ghosts to haunt her, she chose Oak Ridge Cemetery to bury her husband, where he would be at peace among the trees in a spacious, quiet, green landscape. It was her express desire to respect her husband's wishes, her final gift to him. She also understood the political game well enough to know that those powerful Republican men would do anything to make certain that Lincoln's body remained in Springfield, that in perpetuity people would make pilgrimage to their state to pay respects to their martyred leader. Already Abraham Lincoln's meaning for the nation was clear. As an editorial in the *Illinois State Journal* put it: "His tomb will become a shrine at which Pilgrims will worship their God and send up prayers to Him for the preservation of our government and liberty."[4]

The Monument Association was too far forward in its mission to immediately submit to Mary Lincoln's demand, and so Oglesby and Ozias Hatch, a close Lincoln friend, made plans to see her in Chicago. They thought they could convince her, a little woman overcome with grief, that they knew best what should be done with her husband's memorial. Yet the fact that they made the effort to see her in Chicago at all revealed to Mary Lincoln and to anyone paying attention that as Lincoln's widow she held the stronger position. Mary Lincoln refused to see the delegation, and she reasserted her demands in a follow-up letter on June 10, renewing her threat to bury Lincoln in Washington. She gave them a June 15 deadline to produce, as she wrote, "formal & written agreement that *the* Monument shall be placed over the remains of my Beloved Husband, in *Oak Ridge* Cemetery, with the *written* promise that no other bodies, save the President, his Wife, his Sons & Son's families, shall ever be deposited within the enclosure."[5]

Mary Lincoln was dead serious. In a June 11 letter, she chastised the governor: "It is very painful to me to be treated in this manner by some of those I considered my friends, such conduct will not add very much to the honor of our state." Mary Lincoln knew the stakes. The association had acted so quickly after the president's death to ensure the honor of his memorial to Springfield. The association members underestimated her ability to advocate for herself and her dead husband, but they finally relented. On June 16, the *Chicago Tribune* reported that the association had adjusted its plans to Mrs. Lincoln's wishes.[6]

Mary Lincoln had been within her rights, but she was brave to stand up to powerful men. Because she was tenacious, the Lincoln Tomb is at Oak Ridge Cemetery. She and her husband rest in peace on a lovely hill with three sons (Robert is buried at Arlington National Cemetery). Oak Ridge Cemetery is still a green, serene landscape, and the monument erected to Lincoln over the bodies of the Lincoln family is a breathtaking and holy memorial among old oak trees. Mary's fight to honor Lincoln's wishes was important to her survival as a widow, and it was important to her memory of her husband. But it was also important to the collective, public memory of Abraham Lincoln.[7]

Had Lincoln been buried in Washington or downtown Springfield or anywhere else, he would have been there alone, more a god than a man; but at Oak Ridge he is buried among his many Springfield friends, more a man than a god. The erection of the monument over Lincoln's tomb also ensured the connection of Lincoln's body with a memorial structure dedicated to his memory, creating a space for visitors to commune with Lincoln's spirit and to contemplate his legacy. In taking up the fight to honor her husband's wishes, Mary Lincoln likely found the will she needed to survive her terrible, personal loss, but she also made the first and most human contribution to Abraham Lincoln's legacy.[8]

Today, we can go to the Lincoln Memorial in Washington, D.C., to feel Lincoln's power as an icon of American democracy. We can visit Lincoln's birthplace in Kentucky, his boyhood home in Indiana, and the reconstructed New Salem village to walk in the footsteps of his becoming. To immerse ourselves in the historical contexts of the Lincoln story, we can travel to Springfield to tour the only home he ever owned, his law office, and the Old State Capitol, where he delivered his House Divided Speech. We can see documents and artifacts and learn about his life at the Abraham Lincoln Presidential Library and Museum. But when we go to the Lincoln Tomb in Oak Ridge Cemetery, that is where Lincoln *is*. His human spirit whispers on every breeze under those mighty oaks, revealing history's power to connect us, across the ages, to our shared humanity.

I am not a religious person, but I have come to believe in the power of spirits to guide us and to humble us and to give us courage and hope. In my now thirty-year relationship with Abraham Lincoln, I can admit that my connection to this man I have studied for so long has been spiritual. In all my Lincoln work and travels I have seen the Lincoln magic. At conferences and Lincoln events and witnessing visitors breathing in that magic at historic sites, particularly in Springfield, I know that I am in good company in the belief that Abraham Lincoln is an inspirational life force.

I learned the truth of Lincoln's spirit in the peaceful sanctuary of Oak Ridge Cemetery when I buried my younger daughter Mackenzie there on a bitter cold and rainy day in January 2016. Her cremated remains had rested in a brass box in a closet for fifteen months, haunting her father and me, and making the decision to bury them at the bottom of a hill with a winter view of the Lincoln Tomb was the first step of my acceptance. On the day my darling girl was laid to rest in Oak Ridge Cemetery, with Mr. Lincoln, her spirit was released, and a feeling of solace held my heart. Peace. Inspiration. Magic. Whatever words I might employ to describe it, I know I owe this elixir to the legacy of Abraham Lincoln, and my gratitude for this soothing is for his wife.

Lincoln was right. We cannot escape history.[9] We cannot shield ourselves from tragedy. We cannot keep sorrow away from our hearts. We cannot choose the burdens that fall upon our shoulders. Not Abraham Lincoln. Not Mary Lincoln. Not me. Not you. Not my Mack. But there is comfort and perspective in our shared human mortality and in the hope we breathe while we walk upon this earth. Lincoln's most important legacy is situated in this knowing, and Oak Ridge Cemetery is a living

Gravesite of Mackenzie McDermott, with view of the Lincoln Tomb, Oak Ridge Cemetery, Springfield, Illinois, 2022. Author's Photo

monument to our honored dead and to the beauty of our potential in the terrifying face of our impermanence.

Mary Lincoln could not foresee what Oak Ridge Cemetery would become for pilgrims like me, more than three hundred thousand annually, seeking Lincoln's spirit. She wanted her husband to rest easy for his sake and for her sake, but in fighting for a serene landscape in which to place her husband's human remains she made possible a peaceful physical space for generations of us to feel Abraham Lincoln's spiritual legacy.

The chamber of the Lincoln tomb is silent. The air is cold, but it is not dank or unwelcome. It is a soothing blast upon my skin, hot from the Midwestern August sun. It is also a memory, a whisper, a message from the past. I step into the circular chamber, stroll past the bronze statues to the back of the tomb, above the Lincoln family's final resting place. I place my hand on the smooth marble wall next to Mary Lincoln's carved name. I close my eyes and take a slow, deep breath.

I open my eyes and turn my body to face the massive stone over the Lincoln crypt. I have stood here a hundred times, but this time feels different. It is different. I am different. Writing Lincoln from the perspective of women and allowing my own feelings for him to texture the writing has made him more real to me. It is strange to think I spent thirty years studying Abraham Lincoln and his family, living with the man through my historical work, and breathing inspiration in my life from his good spirit, yet it is only now I can say I know him. He was always, I suppose, high upon a pedestal to me, a myth and a legend, a bronze statue as far away as a distant planet. Now I know and appreciate his humanity. He was just a man, a good man, a man made better in good part by women.

Abraham Lincoln belongs to the ages.

And the angels.

He belongs to the women.

He belongs to my daughter and to me.

He belongs to all of us.

26. *Vinnie Ream's* Abraham Lincoln

> The success of the statue that I subsequently made
> was attributed to its trueness to the actual Lincoln.
>
> —Vinnie Ream, February 1913, as
> remembered by R. L. Hoxie

When Lavinia "Vinnie" Ream arrived in Washington with her family in 1861, she was already a dreamer, but she could never have envisioned the role she would play just ten years later shaping the public remembrance of President Abraham Lincoln. Educated at Christian College in Columbia, Missouri, she was fourteen years old when the Civil War broke out, the daughter in a family who was part of the great influx of military personnel and civilians who flocked to Washington. Her father Robert Ream was employed in the cartography unit in the War Department, and while his position was secure, his salary was insufficient to support a family in a city with an inflated war economy.[1]

To supplement the family's income, Robert Ream used his political connections to find work for his daughters. Vinnie landed a job in the post office with a six-hundred-dollar annual salary, one of hundreds of girls and young women who entered government employment during the Civil War. She was born with pluck but working in wartime Washington offered thrilling independence and broadened her mind and her ambitions.[2]

In 1863, while she was clerking part time for Missouri congressman James Rollins, Ream had a chance encounter that revealed her calling. She accompanied Rollins to the studio of the eminent sculptor Clark Mills, where the congressman was sitting for a bust. Mesmerized, she talked her way into a sculpting apprenticeship with Mills. She had talent and a voracious appetite to learn, and with hard work she quickly became a confident artist. Her political contacts opened doors, and she walked through them with youth's audacity and a fearless capacity to be a woman in a man's world.

Between December 1864 and April 1865, Ream visited the White House to study Abraham Lincoln for a bust, although the details of her visits are cloudy. Ream later said that Lincoln permitted her to sketch while he worked in his office. Some scholars have dismissed Ream's claims, but Ream's contemporary critics never questioned it, and the likeness she achieved in the bust she created suggests she saw Lincoln up close at least once. Ream believed Lincoln agreed to see her because she was "an ambitious girl, poor and obscure" and would have refused her had she been a famous male artist. As Ream's gender as an artist

Vinnie Ream with Bust of Abraham Lincoln, circa 1865–70.
Courtesy of Library of Congress, Prints and Photographs, https://www.loc.gov/pictures/item/2002712184/

made others curious, perhaps it made Lincoln curious, too. However, I suspect that Lincoln, who had always provided access to women in the White House, was happy to open his office door for Ream.[3]

In addition to her Lincoln bust, Ream completed commissions for busts and medallions of Ulysses S. Grant, Thaddeus Stevens, Horace Greeley, Richard Yates, and other political men in Washington. Congressman Rollins had taught her the art of lobbying, and her skill in landing commissions was becoming as brilliant as her skill with a chisel. The steady work honed her sculpting talents and helped her build a network of patrons. She endured criticism for daring to be a woman artist and withstood detractors who accused her of using her womanly wiles to win patrons. Yet Ream did not wilt from the scrutiny and may have even thrived on it. Whatever her approach, it worked, because she enjoyed more success than other talented female artists who struggled for public recognition. By the time Ream set her sights on a congressional commission to make a full-sized statue of President Lincoln for the U.S. Capitol Building, she had an impressive artist's portfolio to recommend her, and she had many political friends. And when Congress awarded her the $10,000 commission in 1866, Ream was the first woman so honored.[4]

Ream spent four years working on her Lincoln statue. She completed a clay model in her Washington studio and traveled to Europe to locate the perfect marble and casting. The public was impatient, and the criticism continued. Senator Charles Sumner questioned Ream's artistic competence. Others dismissed Ream because she was a woman. Eastern critics sneered because she was a Westerner. Publisher Jane Grey Swisshelm suggested that Ream seduced congressmen to win the job, others whined about her youth, and the papers all kept a close eye on Ream's progress and her critics.[5]

Finally on January 7, 1871, there was an official inspection of Ream's statue, and those in attendance praised the work and the artist. The formal unveiling took place on January 25. President Grant and a cadre of political and military men joined Vinnie Ream and her mother on the platform. The Marine Band performed, and the assembled crowd settled in for long-winded political speeches and the long-awaited unveiling. Seven sitting congressmen delivered remarks, discussing Abraham Lincoln, America, the statue, and the artist. James Brooks, a congressman from New York said: "But in the work here that we are unveiling, is the double memorial of not only a chief magistrate, in the prime of life, foully shot down, but the memorial of a woman's handiwork . . . here in this rotunda we now see the equal rights of woman are not at the ballot box, but in the pencil, the chisel, the artistic instruments, to perpetuate the human form divine."[6]

Brooks proclaimed the rightness of a woman's artistic contribution to public memorial, but he and all the other speakers underestimated the broader implications of Ream's achievement. The organizers had not even invited Vinnie Ream to speak, and at the end of the program, a man led her to the front of the platform, where she was posed like her statue.

Vinnie Ream was eighteen years old when Congress voted to grant her the monumental task of making a public sculpture of a martyred president. That she was so young is interesting, reflecting a rebirth and new hope for a grieving nation. That she was a woman was extraordinary. No one who supported Ream understood what a woman's statue of Lincoln in the great rotunda would portend. Neither did Ream fully comprehend that her statute represented Abraham Lincoln's promise of full citizenship and universal suffrage for women. Sculpture was a significant component of the crafting of historical memory after the Civil War. Few female artists were employed to create public art, but there was Vinnie Ream taking center stage, lending a woman's voice in the constructed meanings of the war.[7]

Vinnie Ream's *Abraham Lincoln*, cast in marble and red granite, was a triumph, a realist's interpretation of the human man who became a great leader. In his right hand, Lincoln holds the Emancipation Proclamation, and his left hand grasps the billowing folds of his coat, which hangs loosely from his right shoulder.[8]

"I think that history is particularly correct in writing Lincoln down as the man of sorrow," Ream later said. "The one great, lasting, all-dominating impression that I have always carried of Lincoln has been that of unfathomable sorrow, and it was this that I tried to put into my statue." In Ream's *Abraham Lincoln*, there is sadness as well as frailty, but there is also wisdom and hope. It is the combination of these four essential human qualities that makes Ream's *Lincoln* accessible, honest, and relatable. Ream's statue is not a god in a toga; it is human man in a crooked cravat, his down-turned glance and care-worn face reflecting the nation's grief. It is an image Abraham Lincoln would have recognized, and it casts an impression of "simplicity and naturalness," as one observer noted, making it feel like "the real Lincoln."[9]

Abraham Lincoln by Vinnie Ream, U.S. Capitol Rotunda, 1871. Architect of the Capitol, Washington

In its gleaming appearance, *Abraham Lincoln* is classical and staid, but with the movement of the coat and the toe of Lincoln's large right boot overstepping the pedestal, it faces the future, a point of change for women. For even the criticism of Ream's statue was situated in the moment of women's emergence into the public sphere. The very debate of it was evidence of their becoming. There were those who chafed at Ream's audacity while others embraced her and women's broader emergence, part of what one scholar calls the "changing conceptions of American nationhood and aesthetics."[10] These new conceptions opened toward the inclusion of women.

In a letter to her friend Charles Sumner, Mary Lincoln said she did not approve of Vinnie Ream's forwardness & unladylike persistence in lobbying for the commission. However, she later wrote: "This Miss Ream is an entire stranger to me and mine—and I expect very inexperienced in her work, but I trust very sincerely, she may succeed."[11] Even though Mary Lincoln was herself lobbying Congress for a widow's pension, she struggled to fully embrace a public life for women. Yet it also seems clear that Mary Lincoln, like so many women after the war, knew they were witnessing one of those rare moments in history when time stands still long enough to see the past sitting right next to the future. And a woman's statue of Abraham Lincoln in the U.S. Capitol was, and still is, a fitting marker to one such moment.

Today, *Abraham Lincoln* is appropriately flanked to the left by a statue depicting three icons of the woman's suffrage movement—Lucretia Mott, Elizabeth Cady Stanton, and Susan B. Anthony. Seen and appreciated by thousands of visitors every day, *Abraham Lincoln* still makes you feel like it is the real Lincoln you are meeting. It is the man we know. The human face and countenance Vinnie Ream captured 150 years ago still connects past to present. It tethers together the lives of the women who lost husbands and sons in the Civil War to the lives of suffrage pioneers and to every woman who has cast a ballot ever since.

None of these connections escaped Jane Addams, the social reformer and suffragist, when she delivered remarks at the dedication of the suffrage statue on February 15, 1921: "It is fitting that they should stand next to the great emancipator of another group, who has also long since transcended national boundaries."[12]

And all the better that the Lincoln standing there, looking on as Jane Addams spoke, was created by a woman.

27. Ida Tarbell's Lincoln

> It is Lincoln the man, as seen by his fellows and revealed by his own acts and words, that the author has tried to picture.
>
> —Ida M. Tarbell, preface, *Life of Lincoln*, 1900

IN 1894, THE JOURNALIST Ida M. Tarbell had a new assignment. Although she was still writing her serialized biography of Napoleon for *McClure's Magazine*, her publisher S. S. McClure wanted her to set her sights on Abraham Lincoln. She was not happy about the Lincoln assignment, but she liked her forty-dollar-a-week job at the magazine. In addition, McClure was determined. He believed that people could not get enough Lincoln, and he wanted Lincoln copy to sell his magazine. He charged Tarbell with digging up new material, but she was skeptical there was anything new to find. John Nicolay and John Hay, Lincoln's private secretaries, had published the definitive Lincoln biography with their ten-volume edition of *Abraham Lincoln: A History* in 1890. In addition, they had released the twelve-volume *Complete Works of Abraham Lincoln* in 1894.[1]

Tarbell was acquainted with John Nicolay and his daughter Helen, who were both members of the Washington Literary Society where she was a frequent guest. Sometime in mid- to late 1894, Tarbell went to see Nicolay. She wanted to ask for any unused letters, documents, or materials she could edit for *McClure's Magazine*. The interview was frosty. Nicolay was defensive. He told her that the collection of Lincoln letters and speeches was complete, that everything worthwhile was published in his volumes with Hay, that her task was hopeless, and that she was poaching on territory that belonged to the men who had lived the Civil War. "You are invading my field," he told her. "You write a popular Life of Lincoln and you do just so much to decrease the value of my property."[2]

Nicolay's terse response shocked Tarbell, but she was not discouraged. Nicolay's proprietary clinging to Lincoln only piqued her curiosity. His dismissal made her angry. The meeting compelled in Tarbell a desire to apply her skills as a reporter to find her own story about Abraham Lincoln. It sparked the journalist's passion she would later use to take on the Standard Oil Company. As one Tarbell biographer explained it, Nicolay's "rebuff had the effect all rebuffs had on Ida Tarbell—it inspired her to the exceptional."[3]

By February 1895, Ida Tarbell was already in Kentucky doing research for what would become a richly illustrated, serialized "Life of Abraham Lincoln." She had decided to start not with a great man in the White House but rather at the beginning, with a poor boy's birth and early childhood. She talked to people, collected photographs, found information in courthouses, and read newspapers and county histories. It was challenging work, and when she failed to find anything "smashing," Tarbell was frustrated. But then an acquaintance gave her an introduction to Robert Lincoln and set up a meeting for Tarbell in Chicago. The interview was warm. Lincoln was talkative and friendly. He did not rebuff her. Tarbell was delighted to be drinking tea with Abraham Lincoln's son.

At first Robert Lincoln said that Nicolay and Hay had used all the presidential papers available and William Herndon had used the earlier papers, but then he offered the smashing item: he had what he believed was the earliest image of his father, a daguerreotype that had never been published. He told Tarbell she could use it. She later remembered the thrill of it: "I held my breath . . . when the picture was finally in my hands for I realized that this was a Lincoln which shattered the widely accepted tradition of his early shabbiness, rudeness, ungainliness. It was another Lincoln, and one that took me by storm."[4]

The daguerreotype, which is the frontispiece of this book, was made around 1846. Tarbell described the man in the image as "remarkably handsome . . . the eyes deep and generous, the mouth sensitive, the whole expression something delicate, tender, pathetic, poetic."[5] Lincoln is, indeed, beguiling, clean-shaven and good-looking, the Lincoln I dream about. To Tarbell (and to me), it is no wonder Mary Lincoln cherished the image, keeping it to herself. Supplied by Abraham Lincoln's last surviving son, the daguerreotype was a generous gift to a woman Robert Lincoln barely knew. It was a gesture of respect for the project she had undertaken and a quiet endorsement of Tarbell herself. When it appeared in the October 1895 issue of *McClure's Magazine* in the advertisement for Tarbell's upcoming Lincoln series, which would begin the following month, it was a sensation. Readers responded to the image's suggestion that the frontier was not so rugged, not so lacking in refinement. It spoke to a new ideal of the western pioneer as the model American. The series also stirred readers to purchase the magazine, proved lucrative for *McClure's*, and made Tarbell a star.[6]

Ida Tarbell is best known to history as the hard-nosed muckraking journalist who exposed corporate greed and corruption in the age of the robber baron, but Lincoln studies claimed her first.

The photograph was not the only revelation in Tarbell's series on Abraham Lincoln. She uncovered dozens of new documents. Most refreshing was Tarbell's own perspective, which was readable and compelling. In a review of the first installment, the *Chicago Tribune* wrote: "The story is told very briefly in simple, easy style. . . . It is not only full of new things, but it is so distinct and clear in local color that an interest attaches to it which is not found in other biographies."[7]

Not only was Nicolay wrong that there was nothing new for Tarbell to report, but he was also wrong to assume that a new generation could not make its own claim to Abraham Lincoln and have its own way of telling his story. Tarbell's series reached thousands of readers, far more than previous bound biographies, multivolumed and expensive, had ever reached. The November 1895 issue of *McClure's* with the first installment

Ida M. Tarbell, c. 1905. Courtesy of Library of Congress, Prints and Photographs, https://www.loc.gov/pictures/item/2004670771/

sold 175,000 copies, and the December issue with the second installment sold 250,000. In contrast, Hay and Nicolay's ten-volume biography had sold just 7,000 copies.[8]

Tarbell's articles about Abraham Lincoln reached a vast audience and had a profound impact on readers and on the magazine. S. S. McClure wrote in his autobiography that Tarbell had saved *McClure's*: "A new sense of hope came to all of us," he said.[9] Based on the success of the series, Tarbell began publishing her articles in book form in 1896, and in 1900, she published a second, more expansive, two-volume set. Tarbell's *Life of Abraham Lincoln* also included a 196-page appendix of new documents, most of which did not appear in the *Complete Works of Abraham Lincoln*. One such document was a confidential letter Lincoln sent to John Stuart in March 1861 about the competitive appointment of a Springfield postmaster, which included his cousin-in-law Elizabeth Grimsley among the applicants. Tarbell obtained the letter from Stuart's grandson Stuart Brown, the son of Bettie Stuart Brown, the "tolerably nice fellow" Lincoln had known as a baby. The new material Tarbell included enhanced the value of her biography, which pleased readers, especially the most important reader, Robert Lincoln. Lincoln told his father-in-law he liked Ida Tarbell and recommended her biography, along with Nicolay and Hay, as the best works on his father.[10]

The *Chicago Tribune* wrote: "Miss Tarbell's work is probably the most complete and satisfactory life of Lincoln for the general reader. It does not aspire to the historical comprehensiveness of the work of Nicolay and Hay, but it is more entertaining." The *New York Times* called Tarbell's biography "new and striking." But not all reviews were positive. Biographer Henry Clay Whitney, who published his error-filled *Life on the Circuit with Lincoln* in 1892, was annoyed. He called Tarbell an "obscure Bohemian" and asked what right a woman had to have any opinion at all.[11]

"Poor Mr. Whitney," was Tarbell's response.[12]

Born in 1857 and coming of age in the 1870s, Ida Tarbell enjoyed the expansion of opportunities for women in the second half of the nineteenth century. After completing AB and MA degrees at Allegheny College in 1880 and 1883, Tarbell worked unhappily as a teacher before taking a job with *The Chautauquan*, where she wrote articles and performed editorial duties, work that revealed to her a calling for journalism. Just like me, Tarbell was journalist who became an accidental

Lincoln historian, resisting at first but then falling for Lincoln's charms. Tarbell's goal with her subject, which was always inspiration for my own, was "to bring out the real character of Mr. Lincoln, to give full attention to the picturesque and dramatic episodes of his life." She rejected the sensationalized stories sold by early biographers, like the illegitimacy of Nancy Hanks and the idea that Lincoln hated his wife. Tarbell, in fact, defended Lincoln's mother and his wife, offering family stories to depict the richness of his family life. She rejected the bleak narratives of Lincoln's boyhood poverty, instead celebrating Lincoln's brave pioneer origins and stressing his ordinary experiences. She painted a picture of a childhood that was common, buoyant, and adventurous.[13]

Tarbell's work on the life of Abraham Lincoln achieved a new objectivity unheard of in the Lincoln field to that time. That new perspective came not only from the passing of time and the contexts of a new generation but also from Tarbell's own talents as a researcher and the Progressive Era's emphasis on science, rationality, and realism. She was a popularizer of the Lincoln narrative. Her books on Lincoln were widely read until after the release in 1947 of the Lincoln Papers at the Library of Congress, when a new generation of biographers emerged. This wave of biographies based on the Lincoln Papers excited a new generation of readers, and Tarbell's work went out of fashion. Still, her human portrayal of Lincoln merged with her Progressive Era's articulation of Lincoln as an icon of American democracy to become part of the historical character of all the new biographies depicting Lincoln as a man as well as a hero. Ida Tarbell, a woman, had made her mark, the first conspicuous Lincoln biographer before Carl Sandburg.[14]

The great Lincoln scholar Benjamin Thomas wrote in 1947: "The biographers before Miss Tarbell were a stubborn lot, driven by their own opinions and agenda. Tarbell's biography of Lincoln was more nuanced, better contextualized, closer to modern historical practice." In 1952, Thomas again praised Tarbell, noting that her biography of Lincoln was "still worth reading because she understood Lincoln the man. While she liked to think the best of him, she had an open mind, a quality, singularly lacking in earlier biographers, that foretold and helped to make possible the work of modern writers."[15] In 2024, Tarbell's biography is still worth reading. It is accessible and engaging, and Tarbell's Lincoln is a man, not the myth, a quality lacking in too many recent works by modern writers.

As a Lincoln scholar, I have used Nicolay and Hay's Lincoln biography and their edited volumes of Lincoln's papers. Both have been surpassed, but as historiography goes, they still have worth. As a voracious reader who loves a good story, however, I have read Ida Tarbell's *Life of Abraham Lincoln* multiple times over the years. It never loses its vivid light, and, in fact, I enjoy it more every time I return to it. Tarbell brings Abraham Lincoln to life in a way few biographers have been able to do. Most modern Lincoln biographies do not quote Ida Tarbell, although I bet most writers of the best biographies have read Tarbell's work and are informed by it.

Bohemian women in all eras always have their male detractors. But Tarbell's Abraham Lincoln mattered and still matters, and her faith in herself to define Lincoln on her terms gives me faith to define Lincoln on my own. Ida M. Tarbell is my Lincoln storytelling superhero. She gives me courage to defend my right to tell Lincoln's story the way I want to tell his story, through the stories of women. Tarbell's work is my permission slip to sally forth in the face of rebuffing. Tarbell, for me, will always be the last Lincoln man standing.

28. Harriet Monroe and the Literature of Lincoln

But Illinois, even now, need not be ashamed of her art-history. She would not need to be ashamed of it if her list were limited to one name, that of Abraham Lincoln, the greatest literary artist the nation has produced, whose speeches are prose-poems of incomparable beauty.

—Harriet Monroe, *Poetry*, November 1918

Prairie child,
Brief as dew,
What winds of wonder
Nourished you?
Rolling plains
Of billowy green,
Far horizons,
Blue, serene;
Lofty skies
The slow clouds climb,
Where burning stars
Beat out the time:
These, the dreams
Of fathers bold,
Baffled longings,
Hopes untold,
Gave to you
A heart of fire,
Love like deep waters,
Brave desire.
Ah, when youth's rapture

Went out in pain,
And all seemed over,
Was all in vain?
O soul obscure,
Whose wings life bound,
And soft death folded
Under the ground;
Wilding lady,
Still and true,
Who gave us Lincoln
And never knew:
To you at last
Our praise, our tears,
Love and a song
Through the nation's years!
Mother of Lincoln,
Our tears, our praise;
A battle-flag
And the victor's bays![1]

For the centennial of Abraham Lincoln's birth in February 1909, this poem titled "Nancy Hanks" appeared in *The Century Magazine*, in a Lincoln commemorative issue. The poet was Harriet Monroe. She was a creative, visionary woman mostly lost to history now, but at the time she was a popularly published writer contributing a female voice to a special issue of the magazine to honor Lincoln. She was singing a song about a lost mother from an innocent past to the attention of a modern world celebrating Lincoln's life. For her, the connection of mother and son was the melody of Lincoln's story.[2]

The poem was widely read, reaching the magazine's more than ninety thousand readers as well as newspaper readers across the country whose papers reprinted the verse in full or in part. It is a haunting poem, as well as luminous. It is a woman's story, the beating heart of a mother who gives the world every life worthy of memorial. For Progressive Americans, Abraham Lincoln was an iconic figure of American democracy, but in Harriet Monroe's vision, he was also a son given to the world by a mother.[3]

I do not remember when or where I first encountered this poem that haunts me. Sometime shortly after I began my Abraham Lincoln studies, I suppose, long before I appreciated the author, or even considered the author, an oversight that also haunts me. Although moved by the poem upon that first, long-ago reading, I did not pause long to study its import as literature or as history. Yet it burrowed into my growing understanding of Lincoln and quietly nurtured the stories I collected about the women in his life. In recent months, I have read the poem aloud dozens of times, lingering on every word, line, and image. Now with a better understanding of the poet, I appreciate the depth of its meanings.

The poem haunts me as much today as it did upon my first reading, but now in the context of writing this book, it also stirs an abiding respect for the poet and a deep ache for history's mothers. Nancy Lincoln gave birth to a child whose inspiration to the world she would never know. I gave birth to a child whose spirit became my inspiration to survive in a world without her. It is in the wombs of mothers where humanity endures. It is in the hearts of mothers where history keeps time.

Harriet Monroe was born in 1860 in Chicago, and she grew up with the city as it stretched and groaned in beauty and in struggle, emerging together into modernity. It was in the context of the modern, industrial city, in progressive America, where Monroe penned her Nancy Lincoln poem. Monroe wrote in a world clinging to its historical heroes while at the same time shedding its traditional skin. She wrote as a woman raised up with a generation of women still limited in some ways by gendered boundaries and family claims but also reaching far beyond them. Monroe and her contemporaries were finding voice and purpose beyond motherhood and the home and stepping into public spaces in which to flourish as individuals. "Nancy Hanks" is a poem that sits at an important, historical intersection, looking back and looking forward, a rescue and a reimagining.

It was at my own intersection, immersed in the Progressive Era while putting Lincoln studies behind me, that I came to know Harriet Monroe. She lived for a time at the Hull-House social settlement in Chicago with Jane Addams, whose papers I now edit. Like so many inspirational paths of the Progressive Era's innovators, Monroe's path to the founding in 1912 of *Poetry: A Magazine of Verse* went through Hull-House. Harriet Monroe had limited success as a poet, but her gift to the world was inspired by the ethos of greater purpose that Jane Addams engendered. To launch a poetry magazine was bold and brave in 1912 in America, where the landscape for the form was somewhat barren. In the pages of *Poetry*,

Monroe promoted the work of young American writers and provided a forum for American poetry to flourish. She helped popularize the art form, but more importantly she validated American poetry and celebrated its unique voices and experiences.[4]

In getting to know Harriet Monroe, I could not stop thinking about her poem about Lincoln's mother; studying the poem, then, in the context of the Lincoln bicentennial celebrations for which Monroe wrote it inspired new meaning. Context is always the brightest color upon the historical canvas, especially when a new context, previously unseen, reshapes the portrait. Monroe's poem was as much a feminist protest of the political Chicago celebrations of the Lincoln bicentennial as it was a sweet memory of a mother. That Monroe focused her attention on Lincoln's mother when the entire country was looking directly at Abraham Lincoln elevated the poem from the spectral to the physical. The poem was not simply sweet and beautiful, it was also a feminist call for the centrality of women in every human story.[5]

To discover the poet who wrote a poem that had long inspired me was one thing, to discover that this same poet played a role in the rising careers of three prairie poets—Vachel Lindsay, Edgar Lee Masters, and Carl Sandburg—whose work I have loved, was a delicious revelation. Even gone from Lincoln studies, I was still collecting my stories about women and Abraham Lincoln. It is embarrassing to realize now that the poem's imagery of Nancy Hanks had been so poignant to me, but I had been so ignorant of the poet. Odder still that I would learn about Harriet Monroe while studying Jane Addams and not Abraham Lincoln.[6]

Harriet Monroe introduced a young poet from Springfield, Illinois, to her *Poetry* readers in June 1913: "And now, as the spring grows warm, comes from Lincoln's own country a poet of Lincoln's own breed, Nicholas Vachel Lindsay."[7] Monroe published and promoted Lindsay's work and had a direct role in his success. When Edgar Lee Masters began publishing in a St. Louis newspaper the epitaphs that would become *Spoon River Anthology*, Monroe made a failed effort to publish the collection herself. Yet so enamored with Masters's voice and certain of his promise, she praised the author and the book in *Poetry*, describing the Ann Rutledge epitaph as "a splendid burning candle-flame of beauty."[8]

Monroe also published two dozen poems by Carl Sandburg, and she reviewed his books in the magazine. Monroe was always particularly keen to support Sandburg's work on Abraham Lincoln. For her,

Sandburg, Lindsay, and Masters were perfect purveyors of the Lincoln story, a lifting of a Midwestern voice that was the thread between Lincoln and the present that could knit a strong fabric of American literature. As historian Mark Pohlad argues: "For Monroe, Lincoln's memory was changing how one was supposed to be an American poet, especially a midwestern poet. Accordingly, she came to regard each of the prairie poets as a unique reflection of Lincoln himself. Lindsay represented the young, love-lost, tragic Lincoln. Sandburg was the magnanimous, public Lincoln. . . . Masters embodied the side of Lincoln that was skeptical, pragmatic, and profoundly secular."[9]

As an editor and critic, Monroe used her platform at *Poetry* to shape the public perception of Abraham Lincoln as an approachable hero of American history and as a literary character. For her and the prairie poets, Abraham Lincoln belonged to the twentieth century as much as he had been a man of the nineteenth. Monroe believed that within Lincoln's humanity modern America could see herself. Monroe staked an additional claim through her literary criticism and her commentary on popular theater productions and art that sought to wrest Lincoln's image from truth. Of the play *Abraham Lincoln* by John Drinkwater, an Englishman, Monroe seethed: "Mr. Drinkwater picks [Lincoln] up out of his own place, and sets him down in a manufactured milieu, where people do not think his thoughts nor speak his tongue, and even the chairs don't look natural."[10]

Like her friend Ida Tarbell, Monroe adopted Lincoln's image for the new century. Toward an American progressive purpose, she aimed it. From a woman's perspective, she painted it. And in the pages of her magazine, she claimed Lincoln for poetry and prose and promoted him as a subject for great literature as well. She helped frame Lincoln's legacy for her generation, seeing him as a perfect historical inspiration for modern America, a figure to compel a more equal and more open society. She understood the power of language and the arts to tell stories that matter, endure, and reach vast audiences. As she did with her poem "Nancy Hanks," Harriet Monroe did with *Poetry* magazine and with the legacy of Abraham Lincoln. She cast her eyes in a different direction. She looked at poetry and Lincoln and the world a little sideways. And she gave us a new way to read Abraham Lincoln.[11]

29. *She Ruth*

> Throughout their married life there is an unbroken record of devotion between the Lincolns. He belongs to the nation, but they belonged to each other.
>
> —Ruth Painter Randall, *New York Times Magazine*, February 12, 1950

In 1934, in a paper delivered at a joint meeting of the American Historical and Mississippi Valley Historical Associations, historian James G. Randall asked the question: "Has the Lincoln Theme Been Exhausted?" He went on to argue that the answer was "no," because historically trained scholars had yet to take the Lincoln theme out of the hagiographic "hand of the amateur." He condemned "the collector, the manuscript dealer, the propagandist, the political enthusiast, the literary adventurer" who had dominated Lincoln studies to that point. He suggested avenues for historians to pursue, and he reaffirmed the answer to his question a decade later by publishing a four-volume history of Lincoln's presidency.[1]

Randall's call, as well as his mentorship of historians at my alma mater the University of Illinois, contributed to an excellent body of scholarship on Lincoln, but it did not discourage the voices outside of the academy.[2] Indeed, if the answer to Randall's question is revealed simply by the mind-boggling number of books about Lincoln published since he asked it, then the answer is a resounding "NO" from every possible direction and in every voice imaginable.

Randall's question has become something of an inside joke in Lincoln studies; and the academic-or-amateur test has not proven itself a worthy method of assembling a must-read Lincoln book list. I admit the sheer number of books by historians, politicians, writers, and random blokes every year is exhausting. Still, here I am writing my own book about Lincoln. But here's the deal: the endless stream of Lincoln publications, the good and the bad and the middling, says more about Lincoln than it does about the authors and the publishers who keep the books coming. The passion (or audacity) of the ever-going parade of Lincoln authors is magnificent because no other historical figure compels a writer to be so bold. Abraham Lincoln is not simply a historical figure who interests us; he is us.

For the four score and thousands of us, from every generation, who are compelled to read about him, write about him, and publish yet another and another and another book about him, Abraham Lincoln is in our bones. Every generation has produced and will continue to produce its own Lincoln folks who are compelled to write their own books about Lincoln, no matter the outrageous number of Lincoln books with which they will compete. The Lincoln theme will never be exhausted because Lincoln belongs to every generation. He belongs to *all* of us, woman, man, scholar, bloke. After years of pondering Randall's famous question, I have decided that the answer to the question will always be "NO!" and that Professor Randall himself provided the answer in the first paragraph of his 1934 paper: "Lincoln is everybody's subject."[3]

In 1934, Randall lamented that fact.

In 2024, I embrace it. It is on the evidence of Jim Randall's wife Ruth Painter Randall and the books she contributed to our understanding of Abraham Lincoln that I assert we should not only embrace it but celebrate it.

Ruth Painter was born on November 1, 1892, the youngest of six children, in Salem, Virginia. Her father was a professor of language and literature at Roanoke College, and her childhood was a privileged one. She graduated from Roanoke College in 1913 and went on to Indiana University, where she earned a master's degree in English in 1914. It was there, in Bloomington, where she met James Randall. The couple married in 1917, and in 1920 moved to Urbana, Illinois, where Jim Randall taught history at the University of Illinois for the next thirty years, and Ruth Randall was a dutiful, content faculty wife.[4]

With her graduate degree in English, Ruth Randall was from the beginning of her marriage an invaluable editorial assistant to her husband. She also conducted research and did writing for him. Jim Randall dedicated his first book to his wife and acknowledged her "valuable literary suggestions" in his second book, although he failed that time to mention her by name. In 1927, when he was writing an entry for the *Dictionary of American Biography* about Salmon P. Chase, Lincoln's secretary of the treasury who had been married three times and had six daughters, he asked Ruth Randall to handle "the problem of getting all those wives and children into one paragraph without confusion."[5] James Randall's final biography consisted of twenty-four paragraphs, some of them long and dull. The one paragraph on Chase's personal life, written by Ruth Randall, is tiny by comparison, too little space for love, grief, and family. However, Ruth Randall's paragraph is full of life. As she would later write in her memoir, she "loved writing about real people." She loved writing about life and the ordinary relationships that make people human and give them the ability to do great big historical things.

By assisting her husband over the years, Ruth Randall was "getting tremendously interested in Lincoln," falling in love with everyone's favorite historical subject. The Randalls had no children, and while they nurtured pets and Jim Randall's graduate students (among them the great Lincoln biographer David Donald), Abraham Lincoln became a central focus of their married life. Lincoln became a member of the Randall family. Her research resulted in some of the most humanizing sections in her husband's exhaustive study of the Lincoln presidency. The scenes of Lincoln's family life and of Mary Lincoln's activities in the White House illustrate Ruth's influence. In 1949, when Jim was at work on the third volume of *Lincoln the President*, Ruth admitted to herself that she "*had* to write a biography of Mrs. Lincoln. . . . By this time," she remembered, "Mary Lincoln had come alive to me, and I felt that I *must* go on with her story as a matter of historical justice."[6]

Ruth Randall was terrified, like I was once terrified, to weigh into Lincoln historiography. It seemed a daunting task, but she was compelled to be a voice for Mary Lincoln, in the same way I was compelled to be a voice for Mary Lincoln in my own work. Ruth Painter Randall published *Mary Lincoln: Biography of a Marriage* in 1953, and in the preface, she wrote: "Marriage involves two individuals and their relation to each other. It is impossible to understand a wife without knowledge of the husband. I have therefore planned the treatment as a double biography. It has been my purpose to present the personality and intimate life of Abraham Lincoln along with a full-length biography of his wife."[7]

Brilliant, Ruth. Thank you.

Randall's biography is a human portrait of an interesting woman with a unique education, a woman who had good qualities and flaws and who suffered physical and emotional pain deserving of empathy.

Randall's Mary Lincoln is the story of a woman Abraham Lincoln loved, and her Abraham Lincoln is a husband and a family man. The biography was well received by the public and scholars, and reviews of the book articulated the importance of Randall's nuanced interpretation. In his review, Lincoln editor Roy Basler argued that Randall's achievement was "not merely that she has brought to life in these pages Lincoln's warm, friendly, impetuous but insecure, erratic, and sharp tongued wife. She has also added a dimension to the portrait of Mary's husband. Despite their valiant efforts to limn Lincoln as a whole man, none of his [biographers] has done justice to him as a husband and father."[8]

Randall's biography predates the rise of women's studies and lacks the benefit of gender analysis that modern readers might expect, but it remains the most important biography of Mary Lincoln. It was grounded in impeccable research, offered a feminine perspective that was desperately needed at the time, altered prevailing views about Mary's character, and appealed to both scholarly and popular audiences. Most importantly, as Basler argued, it shed light on Abraham Lincoln. We cannot know Abraham Lincoln if we persist in villainizing the woman he married and shared a bed with for more than two decades. Mostly to the good, Jean Baker's 1987 biography of Mary Lincoln supplanted Randall's biography because of the former's rich context of women's history. Baker is the Mary Lincoln biographer that modern Lincoln biographers cite, if they cite any at all, yet in the ways that married people function as one unit—in love, in raising children, in the public persona they together define and inhabit—Randall's biography is more intimate and lusher with the sentiment that is sometimes lacking in feminist narratives.

After thirty years spent chafing against the hatred of Mary Lincoln in Lincoln studies and watching, dumbfounded, as new work on the most maligned First Lady failed to rescue her from the vitriol, I see a comfortable middle ground in Randall's rendering. Perhaps, it is time for a Ruth Painter Randall renaissance.

The first copies of *Mary Lincoln* arrived at the Randall home on January 12, 1953. In a Valentine's card to the new author on February 14, Jim Randall, who was gravely ill with leukemia, wrote: "To My Valentine, The lovely—and now most famous—Ruth Painter Randall." Carl Sandburg visited the couple on February 17, and Jim Randall collapsed the following day and was taken to the hospital by ambulance. He died three days later. Ruth was grief-stricken, but she had a financial future to secure. Her beloved history professor had not left her a wealthy widow, but he had given her something more precious: a purpose. He had encouraged her to write, and now she was a *New York Times* bestselling author, her publisher already talking about her next book. In the apartment she had shared with her husband in Urbana, Ruth Randall wrote nine more books, supporting herself as a historian until her death.[9]

Five of her books are directly related to Lincoln: *Lincoln's Sons* (1955), *The Courtship of Mr. Lincoln* (1957), *Lincoln's Animal Friends* (1958), *I Mary* (1959), and *Colonel Elmer Ellsworth: A Biography of Lincoln's Friend and First Hero of the Civil War* (1960). She also published biographies of Varina Davis, Jessie Benton Frémont, and Elizabeth Custer, putting three exclamation points on her argument that the wives of important historical men matter.[10]

In 1968, she published *I Ruth: Autobiography of a Marriage*, a loving portrait of her life with Jim Randall and a memoir about her own relationship with Lincoln studies. It is a modest story she tells, preferring to understand her work in the context of her life with her husband, who was the inspiration for her journey from faculty wife to prolific author and accomplished historian. The subtitle of the book almost makes me cry: *The Self-Told Story of the Woman Who Married the Great Lincoln Scholar, James G. Randall, and through Her Interest in His Work Became a Lincoln Author Herself.* In her mind, Jim Randall was great, and she was a wife. He was the Lincoln *scholar*, and she was just a Lincoln *author*, even though in her eighteen years as a widow, she published an impressive number of books and articles. Although she lacked a doctorate and had no status as a professor, she established herself as a historian. When she died in 1971, whoever wrote her brief obituary for the *Chicago Tribune* summed her up right, calling her a "noted writer and authority on Abraham Lincoln," best known for *Mary Lincoln: Biography of a Marriage*. Only in the last paragraph did the obituary identify her as the widow of James G. Randall.[11]

30. *Mary and Sally and Me*

> They were very, very bonded. Had there not been a Mary Todd, there would not have been an Abraham Lincoln. There were two sides of this coin that came together and were Abraham Lincoln.
>
> —Sally Field, *NPR Interview*, November 19, 2012

SALLY FIELD CAME TO St. Louis on September 21, 2018, to promote her memoir *In Pieces*. I am not a reader of celebrity memoirs, but the event was just up the street from my house and was part of a book festival hosted by Left Bank Books, my favorite independent bookstore. I enjoy book talks and had appreciated Field's portrayal of Mary Lincoln in Steven Spielberg's movie *Lincoln*, so I purchased a VIP ticket to attend a reception with Field following her appearance. Field's Mary Lincoln was a complex, human woman. She portrayed a woman I had come to know, and I wanted to ask Field how she had prepared for the role.[1]

A last-minute change in scheduling required Field to depart St. Louis earlier than planned, and my VIP ticket would offer only wine and petit fours. I was disappointed, but the organizers threw the VIP guests a consolation prize: the chance to submit questions for Field to answer from the stage. I prepared my question, hoping it would stand out in a sea of questions about Burt Reynolds and *The Flying Nun*, and I took my seat in the ballroom near the stage. Sally Field was adorable, a lovely, graceful seventy-two-year-old woman with no collagen-plumped lips or expressionless Botoxed face. She was smart and articulate, funny and genuine. I liked her. I *really* liked her. While Field discussed her life and her writing, I anticipated the Q&A, fingers crossed I would get my answer. After the interviewer sorted through the questions and asked one about *The Flying Nun* and another about Burt Reynolds, she asked my question.

Sally Field smiled and said something like "Oh goody," relieved, it seemed to me, to set Burt Reynolds well off to the side. I smiled and crossed my fingers and toes for a satisfactory answer. She nailed it: "Well, you know, there is a collection, a big book full of Mary Lincoln's letters. I read all of them!" She was animated through a lengthy explanation about how the letters helped her understand Mary Lincoln's sorrow and how Mary's words helped Field get to know a complicated, fascinating woman with flaws, especially when pressed to the breaking point by public scrutiny and grief.

Field talked about her feelings of responsibility to portray Mary Lincoln in such a way that it would shed light on Abraham Lincoln. She wanted to offer a sensitive performance that would show how Mr. and Mrs. Lincoln faced the Civil War, the incivility of politics and public life, and the death of a child on their own terms as a couple. It was lovely to learn that the movie's most poignant scenes were grounded in Sally Field's approach to her character, particularly the bedroom scene in which the Lincolns are arguing about Robert Lincoln's military service and the carriage-ride scene toward the end of the movie when Mary says: "All anyone will remember of me is I was crazy and ruined your happiness"; her husband responds: "Anyone who thinks that doesn't understand, Molly."

I have done no scholarly analysis of the opinions about Mary Lincoln that moviegoers possessed before and after seeing *Lincoln*. However, I have talked with dozens of people since the movie came out and most have said that Sally Field changed their minds about Lincoln's wife. They saw in Sally Field's Mary Lincoln a woman Abraham Lincoln loved. Movie magic, perhaps, but I will take it. Thank you, Sally Field, for reading Mary Lincoln's letters. Thank you for portraying Abraham Lincoln's wife as a complicated human being. Thank you for giving moviegoers the essence of the most important woman in Lincoln's life, a woman so many Lincoln biographers have failed to give their readers.

Dear Sally Field, I nominate you as a respectful keeper of Abraham Lincoln's legacy. You did your excellent work for love of your craft, not for history, but in thirty years of Lincoln scholarship, my favorite Lincoln folks have often hailed from outside of academia. I am happy to add a new one from the Academy of Motion Picture Arts and Sciences.

After Fields's Q&A that night, I sat back in my chair in that ballroom and beamed. There was a strange, warm feeling of validation tingling through my body. From an actress with no historical training, I felt the heady thrill of being seen. After years of seeking validation from Lincoln studies, I realized it was never about my relationship with Lincoln studies. It was about my relationship with Abraham Lincoln. I did not need Lincoln studies to validate my work. I did not need an actor to see me, either, even if the quiet feeling of connection with Sally Field that night opened me up to the idea of letting go.

Because it was time for me to let go, time to release the disappointment of failing to achieve what I thought I should have achieved in Lincoln studies. It was time to move on from the ridiculous expectations set by men who never saw and would never see Mary Lincoln's worth or my own as a Lincoln scholar. It was past time to trust my own abilities to tell stories of the past in my own way, with my love for Lincoln and all my emotions upon my sleeves.

When Abraham Lincoln died, Anna Lowell, a Boston woman, noted in her diary: "It seemed strange to love so much one whom we have never seen—but we did." As the historian Martha Hodes puts it: "President Lincoln had blurred the boundaries of leader and loved one, and at his death the categories blurred yet more."[2]

The boundaries and categories are blurry still, as is the space between the man and the legend. Yet there is historical truth and human beauty in that space. Abraham Lincoln is America's most enduring symbol of its greatness, its historic struggles, its beautiful complexities, its horrific contradictions, its boundless possibilities, and, most importantly, its humanity. In life, Abraham Lincoln was a good man, an honest lawyer, and a great political leader, but in death the man often gets lost in the crevices of legacy, etched in stone and printed on the pages of thousands of books (and a few movies), of which there are more than of any other figure in American history.

Lincoln is an icon. An ideal. An aspiration. But the best of Abraham Lincoln, his greatest legacy, is alive in the middle, breathing in that lovely, murky distance between man and legend. Women—a widow, an artist, three writers, an actress, and one humble historian—have delivered our beloved Abraham Lincoln down to the earth. It is the women in Lincoln's life who inspired me in my career in Lincoln studies to see Lincoln through my own feminine eyes. It is the women who have staked a claim to defining Lincoln's legacy who validate my personal relationship with Abraham Lincoln. Their stories soften the hard edges of the Lincoln myth, demand space for women's voices to come to life in the Lincoln story and refuse to betray the expansiveness of the human heart. Abraham Lincoln deserves this tender legacy, and he has it, thanks to the women.

Mary Lincoln.

Vinnie Ream, Ida Tarbell, Harriet Monroe, and Ruth Painter Randall.

Sally Field.

And me.

Epilogue

MARY LINCOLN IS NEXT to me at the front of the room, and behind me is her white, frosted, 196th birthday cake. People, mostly friendly-faced retirees, slowly file into the conference center of the Lincoln Home National Historic Site in Springfield, Illinois. Unwinding themselves from scarves, they greet one another and seat themselves in molded plastic chairs, lined up in careful rows. I breathe in the smell of the cold, which has wafted into the room upon their coats and gray hair, mingling with the smell of wool and coffee.

If the room is cold, its chill is lost on me. I am sweaty with nerves and menopause and grief. I long to grab a large, overfrosted corner of cake and escape this room. I want to run away from these bundled-up people who have assembled on a freezing-cold December evening to see me and to hear about my forthcoming biography of Mary Lincoln.

Mary Lincoln greets a friend, and the hooped skirts of both women rustle. The crinkling of fabric and the chatter of friendship snaps me out of my fixation on the temperature of the room. I am blasted awake from my daydream of eating a stolen piece of cake in my own home, alone in my bed. I am reminded of my unhappy presence here. Mrs. Lincoln, her friend, and all these people who showed up for a birthday party. But though there is such warm communion in this room, I am silent and still. I am apart from these people. I am not of this world. I am here for an obligation made before my life fell into ruin, and I am in no shape for celebration.

"What in the hell am I doing here?" I whisper to Kevin.

"You've done this a hundred times," he says. "You'll be great."

My husband always said this to me before a speech or presentation. The utterance so mindless and lithe on his tongue, there is no time for him to reconsider it. The muscle memory of it allows him no pause to remember that this time is different. I do not blame him for it, because I remember the meaning of the words when he used to say them, their power a balm to my public-speaking jitters. But this is not typical pre-lecture nerves. This is a grieving husk of my former self trying to do something I no longer have the mental and emotional capacity to do. This is one of those terrible, after-Mack firsts. I cannot even remember writing my Mary Lincoln biography, and now I am supposed to talk about it with an audience. Do they expect me to form words and to shape sentences when even my brain's capacity for reading novels has been given up to my grief?

I cannot do this.

I spy a lonely chair away from the traffic of the assembling people. I place my coat and bag upon the chair, and I turn to face the wall, pretending to consult my notes. Squeezing my eyes against the hot tears coming, I take a deep breath. I gather myself and my scripted, bony, uninspired lecture. I approach the lectern, leaning my bare, sweaty arm onto the coolness of the wood.

I cannot do this. Not yet. And, perhaps, never again.

A cool draft of air floats across my hot skin. I am cold. I am hot. I am ridiculous. These historical birthday guests are ridiculous. Mary Lincoln in her busy bonnet full of dried berries, now seated in a chair next to the lectern where I will soon be speaking, is ridiculous. The thought of me forming sentences is ridiculous.

Mrs. Lincoln has been dead since 1882. What matter now of her birthday and a cake? Mack has been gone just two months. What can I ever say that will matter to me, to these people, to anyone? It is 132 years too late for Mary Lincoln, and it is a million years too soon for me. I want Mary and all these ridiculous people waiting to hear me speak to go away, to go poof into the air, and to leave me be. I beg for transport from this room. Uber. Magic carpet. Whatever. I just need a vehicle big enough for me, my sorrows, and Mary's entire birthday cake.

Suddenly, at the back of the room, there is an excited murmur of voices. I look up and the necks of the birthday guests are all craning toward the door. A tall, lanky figure dressed in a black suit with a loosened, crooked tie enters. He doffs his stovepipe hat to the room.

"Well, of course, Mr. Lincoln is here," I say aloud.

How stupid I was for not noticing his previous absence. This is his wife's birthday, for crying out loud, and this is Springfield, where Lincoln never died. This is the town in which he walks the streets at midnight and shows up at history conferences. I release a short giggle. I roll my eyes. As the people settle back into their seats and Mr. Lincoln finds one, I laugh again. This time I let the laugh giggle through my muscles. I welcome the gentle relaxing of the tension in my jammed-up shoulders and my broken heart. Mr. Lincoln's arrival has calmed my nerves.

I am not laughing because it is ridiculous that Abraham and Mary Lincoln are here, and we all accept them as being here. I mean, yes, that is ridiculous, but it is also ridiculous because this time is the umpteenth time that I have delivered a lecture with Mr. Lincoln sitting in the audience. I laugh because this is what life for twenty years has been for me as a Lincoln scholar who lived on Lincoln Avenue in Lincoln's hometown, where the man's spirit is so much more than a ghost from the past.

It is all ridiculous, yes, but it is delightful and brilliant, and through the fog of my grief and across my worries over the capacity of my brain to be coherent, I see my daughter. Mack is present, right before my weary eyes. She is standing between me and Mrs. Lincoln, and she is laughing at the absurdity of my life as a Lincoln scholar. She is scoffing, a mischievous grin perched like an imp below her freckled nose. She then says to me what she has said to me a hundred times before: "Lincoln is dead, mom. You know that, right?"

"Not tonight he isn't," I say, "and not you either, my sweet girl. Mr. Lincoln is right over there, and you are here." I tap two fingers over my heart.

"I am here, too," I whisper, almost believing it.

This is me out in the world. At this moment, I am not hidden away in my darkened bedroom where my despair has no witness. I am alive. I am miserable, but I am breathing, and I am not alone. Mack is here. Mr. and Mrs. Lincoln are here. If I focus my eyes on the back of the room, where my husband and dearest friends in all the world have assembled to get me through this terrible first lecture after Mack, I might just get through this night. And when it's over, whatever happens, I'll reward myself with a giant piece of Mary's birthday cake.

I straighten my back and tell myself to draw power from Mr. Lincoln and all these Lincoln-loving people in the room. Anyway, there is absolutely nothing to get me out of it now because the host is introducing me. She is calling me to take the podium. People are clapping, waiting for me to take my place. I will do this for Mack. For cake. If not for me.

I step up to the lectern and face the room.

Four Abraham Lincolns in an audience in 2000 had given me courage when I stood on the unsteady legs of a young Lincoln scholar filled with doubt. Abraham Lincoln in an audience fourteen years later gave me courage once again, when I stood on the unsteady legs of a grieving mother. It would be the last time Abraham Lincoln would give me professional courage, and I would soon come to see those two physical and spiritual experiences as bookends of my professional relationship with Abraham Lincoln. I did not know it then, but my Lincoln party was almost over, and Mary Lincoln's almond cake would not be sweet enough to mask the bitter pills I would have to swallow in the coming months. Abraham Lincoln could not save me from the tsunami that was coming.

Nine months later, the foundation upon which the Papers of Abraham Lincoln had been situated for more than thirty years began to crumble. My position as assistant director and associate editor at the Papers was in jeopardy. All the desperate measures we would deploy and that would be deployed for our benefit would prove hopeless. A state budget crisis, bureaucratic dysfunction, and gross misunderstandings quickly became too much to withstand, soft-funded as our organization was and serving at the pleasure of a governor with no love for public institutions or cultural heritage. A terrible unraveling began in November 2015 with the first four staff layoffs. The Papers' director was suspended and later fired, my appointment to the Papers was terminated on October 31, 2016, and research operations at the National Archives were suspended in June 2017. Ten fine historians were out of work, the Papers of Abraham Lincoln decimated. National recognition, corporate sponsorship, and award-winning research and publications could not save us.

I was set adrift from work that for twenty years had been a privilege, and after my daughter's death in 2014, a lifeline. I had lost my daughter and my career. Lost to my grief, I clung to the details of the project's demise and my own expulsion from Lincoln studies for a long and bitter three years. Today, thankfully, the details no longer matter to me. There is not a thing anyone can do about it now. Life rarely unfolds the way we think it should or believe it might, and justice means nothing to the cosmos. When the world falls down around you, you can remain trapped inside the rubble, or you can stand up and move on.

In late December 2016, I landed a job as an assistant editor at the Jane Addams Papers Project. It was part-time and offered no benefits or permanent promise, but the position validated my belief in myself as a skilled historical editor. It was a first crucial step to regaining my professional confidence. It was the first brick I laid on a long path of letting go. I focused on Jane Addams and Progressive Era reform and tried not to think about the loss of my professional relationship with Abraham Lincoln. For the next four years, new and fulfilling research focused on the life of a brilliant and compassionate American woman, and a healthy work environment softened the chaos unfolding in my personal life. As I was learning to let go of Abraham Lincoln, I was also learning to let go of my thirty-two-year marriage, ending amicably but not without its gut-wrenching sense of loss and failure. Abraham Lincoln, Jane Addams, my old job, my new job, me, and my husband were all characters in a terrifying, horrible civil war raging inside of my body, a struggle threatening to kill me but that would eventually lead me to a peace I believed at the end of 2016 would never arrive.

Today, I am living alone with two dogs in a 1919 bungalow in a small college town, working as a full-time associate editor at the Jane Addams Papers. I earn a decent living, enjoy generous benefits, and work with two amazing women. We are a small, underfunded, and underappreciated project, but we are mighty and doing important work. I no longer pine for my old Lincoln days, and I am happy to keep to the twentieth and twentieth-first centuries. All the changes in my life, the leaving, the letting go, and the moving on have been an education I would never have chosen. But though I did not choose this path, I am on it now, walking at my own pace on steady legs.

Abraham Lincoln played a role in leading me here, to this place in my life where I am content. Although this odd little Lincoln biography is rooted in my professional work as a Lincoln scholar, writing it has been a personal journey. Now that I have had my peace, Abraham Lincoln can remain a joyful inspiration, divorced forever from disappointment and pain.

In the summer of 1894, when Chicago was reeling from violence sparked when federal troops arrived in the city to end the Pullman

The author with statues of the Lincoln family, Old State Capitol Plaza, Springfield, Illinois, 2018. Sculptor Larry Anderson. Author's Photo

Strike, Jane Addams, the leader of Hull-House, was weary. She needed inspiration and decided to make the 4.5-mile trek north, on foot, from her settlement house on South Halsted Street to Augustus Saint-Gaudens's statue of Abraham Lincoln in Lincoln Park. Recalling the experience in a 1906 article, she wrote:

> I walked the wearisome way from Hull-House to Lincoln Park—for no cars were running regularly at that moment of sympathetic strikes—in order to look at and gain "magnanimous counsel," if I might, from the marvelous St. Gaudens statue which had been but recently placed at the entrance of the park. Some of Lincoln's immortal words were cut into the stone at his feet, and never did a distracted town more sorely need the healing of "with charity

> for all" than did Chicago at that moment, and the tolerance of the man who had won charity for those on both sides of "an irrepressible conflict."[1]

Jane Addams drew inspiration from Abraham Lincoln like I draw inspiration from him. Addams and I have Lincoln in common. This Lincoln connection has made letting go of my professional connection to Lincoln a great deal easier. Lincoln's life inspired my professional work across three decades, and his human spirit will continue to be a personal solace to me. But it is time to take all my love and all my loss and write a new history. I am not leaving Mr. Lincoln. I am only completing my relationship with him and moving on. This book is not a bitter goodbye. It is the first step to a new beginning.

APPENDIX

LIST OF ABBREVIATIONS

NOTES

BIBLIOGRAPHY

INDEX

APPENDIX: THE WOMEN

ABRAHAM LINCOLN'S STEPSISTER BETSY HANKS died in 1864 and was buried in the Old City Cemetery in Charleston, Illinois. The small graveyard today is neglected, a lawn of ruins. The original stone marker has cracked and fallen; its etched words eroded away into silence. Standing upright next to it is a more recent marker, installed in the 1930s. It honors a "model pioneer woman who like her female peers made rude cabins warm homes." In the ground nearly one hundred years, its beauty is also diminishing, but it was and remains a beacon. In an era of scarcity and struggle, it was a message across the decades to women. We see you. We know your worth. Today in a lost place of ghosts, the marker is a special pleading. It is an urgent call from the 1930s to the present: never forget the women.

Elizabeth Abell (1807–69) was Lincoln's friend in New Salem. On January 22, 1861, Abell wrote President-elect Lincoln "to ask of you a favor, which if former friendships have deserved, I hope you will grant." She sought an appointment for her son Oliver Abell, and on April 1, 1861, Lincoln nominated him to a land office position, writing: "Mr. Abell is the child of very intimate friends of mine, and I would like, if possible, to oblige him." Oliver Abell became a messenger and later a clerk in the General Land Office in Washington. A footnote to the Lincoln appointment in *Collected Works of Abraham Lincoln* listed Bennett Abell as Lincoln's friend, failing to mention Elizabeth Abell and ignoring the fact that Lincoln wrote *friends*, plural, and it was a letter from Elizabeth, not Bennett, that appealed to Lincoln's friendship.[1]

Margaret Abell (Brundage) (1833–1912) was the daughter of Elizabeth Abell and knew Lincoln when she was a baby.[2]

Fanny J. Ames, a widow from Connecticut, asked President Lincoln to discharge her fifteen-year-old son from the U.S. Army. On July 6, 1864, Lincoln ordered: "Let this boy be discharged, on refunding any bounty."[3]

Hannah Armstrong (1811–90) was Lincoln's New Salem friend. In 1857, lawyer Lincoln successfully defended her son Duff in a now-famous murder trial.[4]

Libbie S. Bailey of Irvington, New Jersey, wrote to presidential candidate Lincoln in 1860 to show her support for his antislavery position.[5]

Grace Bedell (Billings) (1848–1936) was the young girl who wrote Lincoln in 1860 to encourage him to grow a beard.[6]

Abigail C. Beren (or Berea) (b. c. 1827) was a Civil War widow and nurse who appealed to President Lincoln to release her youngest son from the army. Beren's husband and another son died in military service, and thanks to Lincoln, her son James H. Benjamin was discharged. In June 1865 she was living with him in Troy, New York.[7]

Caroline E. Bibighaus (1818–1901), appointed by President Lincoln, was a postmaster in Lebanon, Pennsylvania.[8]

Pam Brown of Springfield, Illinois, portrays Mary Lincoln. A personal friend of the author, she has been presenting programs as Mrs. Lincoln since 2006. It is her calling to provide audiences with a nuanced portrait of Abraham Lincoln's wife.[9]

Eliza (Caldwell) Browning (1807–85) was a friend of Abraham and Mary Lincoln. In 1927 when her husband's diaries were published, the family requested entries critical of Mary Lincoln be redacted out of respect for an old friendship.[10]

Emma Browning (1848–1885) was the adopted daughter of Eliza Browning and spent time at the White House with the Lincoln family. She later married and gave her mother three grandchildren.[11]

Mary Buckley (b. c. 1828), who immigrated to the United States from Ireland sometime before 1851, was a widow with young children when she asked President Lincoln to find a job for her brother, on whose support she depended.[12]

Maria Bullock (1788–1861), of Kentucky, was Lincoln's aunt by marriage and his legal client.[13]

Emily J. C. Bushnell (1830–1913), appointed by President Lincoln, was a postmaster in Sterling, Illinois.[14]

Pamela K. Brown as Mary Lincoln, the author, and Fritz Klein as Abraham Lincoln, U.S. Grant National Historic Site, St. Louis, December 2017. Author's Photo, with permission of Pamela K. Brown and Fritz Klein

Harriet (Hanks) Chapman (1826–1915), Lincoln's niece, married Augustus Chapman in Coles County, Illinois, on September 8, 1847. Lincoln visited with her in 1861 before he left for Washington.[15]

Lucy Newhall Colman (1817–1906) was an abolitionist and women's rights activist who met President Lincoln in the White House in 1864.[16]

Mary (Hancock) Colyer (1816–72), a resident of New York City, corresponded with President Lincoln. She sent him a document signed by her famous uncle John Hancock.[17]

Caroline (Fenno) Cowan (c. 1814–93), appointed by President Lincoln, was a postmaster in Biddeford, Maine.[18]

Eliza Davis was a young niece of Lincoln's friend Joshua Speed. Lincoln met her on a visit to Kentucky in 1841.[19]

Anna Elizabeth Dickinson (1842–1932) became a public figure in 1856 when *The Liberator* published her letter in which she admonished the tarring and feathering of a Kentucky school teacher who had spoken out against slavery. She delivered her first public lecture, "The Rights and Wrongs of Women," in 1860, a sarcastic response to the idea that women were only good enough for homemaking. She became a popular orator of her day, and President Lincoln heard her speak in 1864.[20]

Mary Dines (b. c. 1801) was a formerly enslaved woman who worked for the Lincoln family during summers at Soldiers' Home. She was a cook, a nurse, and a gifted singer.[21]

Dorothea Lynde Dix (1802–87), who was an advocate for the mentally ill, became superintendent of U.S. Army nurses in 1861. During the Civil War, she advised President Lincoln and trained 180 army nurses who tended thousands of sick and wounded soldiers.[22]

Jane Dobbs (1797–1862) of Tazewell County, Illinois, was Lincoln's legal client. Lincoln helped her obtain a divorce from her husband in 1845.[23]

Nancy (Robinson) Dorman (b. c. 1820), Lincoln's legal client, was born in Gallatin County, Illinois. She inherited property from her father, which became embroiled in a lawsuit after her marriage to William Dorman on December 29, 1836. She was the mother of several children when Lincoln helped her retain her property in a case he argued before the Illinois Supreme Court.[24]

Susan Dugger (1842–1911) left Illinois for Washington in 1864, seeking employment in the federal government. After she met with President Lincoln, he helped her obtain a job in the U.S. Treasury Department, where she worked for forty-six years.[25]

Mary Shields (Wilson) Duncan (1830–1906), born in Washington, was the mother of two young children. She appealed to President Lincoln to station her army husband closer to home. After her husband's death in 1887, she lived the remainder of her life in Washington and is buried with her husband at Arlington National Cemetery.[26]

Adèle (Cutts) Douglas (Williams) (1835–1899), a Washington debutante, was the widow of Lincoln's political rival Senator Stephen A. Douglas. When she married Douglas in 1856, she became the stepmother of his two young sons; and she sought Lincoln's help regarding their property in the South. After the war, she married U.S. Army captain Robert Williams.[27]

Elizabeth Porter (Todd) Edwards (1813–88) was Lincoln's sister-in-law. She married Ninian Edwards in 1832 and had four children. President Lincoln appointed her husband commissary of subsistence in 1862. The eldest Todd sister, Elizabeth was a surrogate mother to Mary Lincoln, attended Lincoln's inauguration, consoled the Lincoln family after the death of Willie Lincoln, and took care of Mary Lincoln at the end of her life.[28]

Matilda Rachel Edwards (Strong) (1822–51) was a member of Lincoln's social circle in Springfield. Her father Cyrus Edwards was a political friend of Lincoln and a relative of his brother-in-law Ninian W. Edwards. Matilda married Newton Strong, a lawyer, in 1844.[29]

Emma Brower (Taft) Egbert (1846–1936), a wealthy woman from Pennsylvania, donated funds for the support of the U.S. military. President Lincoln acknowledged her generosity in a letter of gratitude.[30]

Sally Field, an Academy Award–winning actress, portrayed Mary Lincoln in the movie *Lincoln* in 2012. The role earned her a nomination for best supporting actress.[31]

Mary Fincher, a Lincoln enthusiast, is a blogger and podcaster with the blog *Civil War Fangirl* and the podcasts *The Railsplitter* and *Civil War Breakfast Club* to her credit.

Jessie (Benton) Frémont (1824–1902), the daughter of Missouri senator Thomas Hart Benton, was the wife of Civil War general John C. Frémont. "General Jessie" was an intelligent, ambitious woman with a head for politics. She was a trusted advisor to her husband, penning much of his correspondence, and she visited President Lincoln in the White House in 1861 on his behalf. Frémont published *The Story of the Guard: A Chronical of the War* in 1863 and became a prolific writer after the war. Lincoln biographer Ruth Painter Randall published a biography of Jessie Frémont in 1963.[32]

Mary Jane Frey (b. c. 1821), appointed by President Lincoln, was a postmaster in Columbia, Pennsylvania. In 1873, she was still postmaster there, earning $2,300 annually.[33]

Melissa (Lett) Goings (1788–1867), who raised seven children, lived in rural Woodford County, Illinois. In 1857, Lincoln became her lawyer when she faced a trial for murdering her abusive husband. Lincoln may have also helped her flee legal justice.[34]

Hannah Goode (b. c. 1796), a Lincoln legal client in a debt case, was born in Kentucky. When Lincoln was her lawyer in 1847, she was living in Christian County, Illinois, with her son, daughter-in-law, and four young grandchildren.[35]

Mrs. M. J. Green supported Lincoln's candidacy for president. On September 22, 1860, Lincoln wrote to thank her: "Your kind congratulatory letter, of August, was received in due course—and should have been answered sooner. The truth is I have never corresponded much with ladies; and hence I postpone writing letters to them, as a business which I do not understand. I can only say now I thank you for the good opinion you express of me, fearing, at the same time, I may not be able to maintain it through life."[36]

Nancy (Potter) Green (1793–1867) was Lincoln's friend in New Salem and his legal client.[37]

Sarah (Lincoln) Grigsby (1807–28) was Lincoln's sister. While a young wife in Indiana, she died from complications of childbirth.[38]

Elizabeth "Lizzie" (Todd) Grimsley (1825–95), Lincoln's cousin by marriage, grew up in Kentucky with Mary Todd and was a bridesmaid at her wedding. She married Harrison Grimsley, a Springfield merchant, in 1846, and in 1861 went to Washington to live with the Lincoln family for six months. Grimsley sought an appointment for the Springfield post office, but it was a competitive job and a delicate matter for Lincoln. As he wrote John Stuart about Grimsley in March 1861: "The question of giving her the Springfield Post-office troubles me. . . . Will it do for me to go on and justify the declaration that [Senator Lyman] Trumbull and I have divided out all the offices among our relatives?" Lincoln did not appoint Grimsley, but it is important to note that he considered Grimsley *his* family not just his wife's cousin.[39]

Eliza Paul (Kirkbride) Gurney (1801–81), a Quaker minister and poet, visited President Lincoln at the White House in October 1862. She found him in a fragile emotional state and soothed him with a gentle sermon.[40]

Sarah Josepha (Buell) Hale (1788–1879), the literary editor of the popular *Godey's Lady's Book*, inspired President Lincoln to proclaim a National Day of Thanksgiving.[41]

Eliza Ann (Wright) Hamilton (1833–1910) was the daughter of Lincoln's Springfield friend Erastus Wright. She was a minister's wife in

Keene, New Hampshire, when she sent good wishes to candidate Lincoln and his family in 1860.[42]

Elizabeth "Betsy" (Johnston) Hanks (1807–64), Lincoln's stepsister, married Lincoln's second cousin Dennis Hanks in 1821. She raised her family in Charleston, Illinois.[43]

Lucy (or Lucey) Hanks (Sparrow) (c. 1767–c. 1833), Lincoln's maternal grandmother, migrated to Kentucky with her young daughter Nancy in 1784. She married Henry Sparrow, a Revolutionary War veteran, in 1791.[44]

Sophia Hanks (1809–93), Lincoln's cousin, lived with the Lincoln family in Indiana.[45]

Rose Harmon was for many years a park ranger at the Lincoln Home National Historic Site in Springfield, Illinois. Tattooed up one of her arms is "A. Lincoln," a signature the author has authenticated.

Emilie Pariet (Todd) Helm (1836–1930) was Lincoln's sister-in-law. After her Confederate officer husband died at Chickamauga in 1863, she went to the White House. But when she refused to swear an oath of allegiance to the United States, President Lincoln sent her back home to Kentucky. In 1864, Helm presented a pass from Lincoln to prevent her arrest by authorities for the illegal transport of cotton, but Lincoln revoked her pass. To officers handling her case, he wrote: "Deal with her for her current conduct, just as you would with *any other*."[46]

Elvira "Ella" (Gibson) Hobart (1821–1901) became an ordained minister in 1864 and served as chaplain for a Wisconsin regiment. Secretary of War Edwin M. Stanton refused to recognize her, despite the support of President Lincoln and the soldiers to whom she ministered. She received no pay until 1876, when the government issued her a $1,201.56 check for service rendered to the First Wisconsin Heavy Artillery. In 2002, President George W. Bush posthumously appointed her to the grade of captain in the Chaplain Corp of the Army.[47]

Jane Currie (Blaikie) Hoge (1811–90) was an organizer for the U.S. Sanitary Commission during the Civil War. Educated at the Young Ladies' College in Philadelphia, she married Alexander Hoge, a merchant, in 1831. The couple settled in Chicago in 1848. Hoge nursed soldiers at Camp Douglas at the start of the war before teaming up with Mary Livermore to organize the Northwest Branch of the Sanitary Commission in Chicago.[48]

Matilda Ivers, a widowed resident of Washington, asked President Lincoln for a job in the treasury department.[49]

Louisa (Block) Jonas (1809–67), appointed by President Lincoln, was a postmaster in Quincy, Illinois. She was the wife of Lincoln's friend Abraham Jonas, who died in 1864.[50]

Elizabeth (Hobbs) Keckley (c. 1820–1907), a former enslaved woman, was Mary Lincoln's dressmaker and friend and had a close relationship with the entire Lincoln family.[51]

Juliette Augusta (Magill) Kinzie (1806–70), who corresponded with Lincoln, was a member of the fur-trading Kinzie family of Chicago. Her husband John Kinzie was a Lincoln supporter, and she was a historian and civic leader. In 1844 she published a history of the Battle of Fort Dearborn, and she was a founder of the Chicago Historical Society. One of her grandchildren living in Savannah, Georgia, during the Civil War, to whom Kinzie sent supplies with the help of President Lincoln, was Juliette Gordon (Low) (1860–1927), who founded the American Girl Scouts in 1915.[52]

Cornelia Margaret (Hitchcock) Liborius (1806–82), a grieving mother who corresponded with President Lincoln, was born in New York City. She married Charles Oswald Liborius in 1844. Her husband died (or left the family) sometime before 1850, and Cornelia raised her children alone in Brooklyn.[53]

Mary (Todd) Lincoln (1818–82) was arguably the first modern First Lady of the United States. She married Abraham Lincoln in November 1842 and had four sons. Much maligned in life and by Lincoln biographers, Mary Lincoln was a smart, interesting, complicated woman. As Abraham Lincoln's friend Isaac Arnold wrote: "Mrs. Lincoln has been treated harshly—nay, most cruelly abused and misrepresented by a portion of the press . . . there is nothing in American history so unmanly, so devoid of every chivalric impulse, as the treatment of this poor, broken-hearted woman, whose reason was shattered by the great tragedy of her life."[54]

Nancy (Hanks) Lincoln (1784–1818) was Lincoln's mother. An 1879 marker on her Indiana grave reads: "Nancy Hanks Lincoln, Mother of President Lincoln, died October 5, 1818. Aged thirty-five years. Erected by a friend of her martyred son."[55]

Sarah Bush (Johnston) Lincoln (1788–1869) married Lincoln's father in 1819. When Lincoln visited her in 1861, he promised to provide a stone marker for his father's grave. Mary Lincoln remembered his promise and sent money in a letter in 1867: "I cannot trust myself to write about, what so entirely fills my thoughts—my darling husband; knowing how well you loved him also, is a grateful satisfaction to me." Robert Lincoln erected a monument over the graves of Lincoln's parents in 1880.[56]

Mary Livermore (1820–1905) was an organizer for the U.S. Sanitary Commission during the Civil War. A journalist, abolitionist, and women's rights advocate, she graduated from a female seminary in Massachusetts in 1836 and in 1857 married Rev. David Livermore. The couple settled in Chicago. She supported Lincoln's campaign for the presidency and his administration throughout the war.[57]

Stacy Lynn (b. 1966), the historian formerly known as Stacy Pratt McDermott, edited Lincoln's papers for twenty years and published a biography of Mary Lincoln. Renowned Civil War historian James McPherson is her intellectual grandfather, having mentored her mentor Orville Vernon Burton, a Lincoln scholar and historian of the South. At her PhD graduation at the University of Illinois in December 2007, professors Burton and McPherson placed the doctoral hood over her head. For a Lincoln loony like her, this fact is cooler than the PhD itself.

Mackenzie "Mack" Kathleen McDermott (1994–2014), the author's daughter, is an inspiration for this book. She was born in Springfield, Illinois, and spent her entire childhood there in an antebellum house on Lincoln Avenue. In the spring of 2005, Mack played the role of Lincoln

Drawing of Abraham Lincoln, by Mackenzie McDermott, 2000. Author's Photo

in a performance of the Lincoln-Douglas debates for her fifth-grade living history program at the Lincoln Home. Lincoln was her subject in numerous school papers, including an essay she submitted to Truman State University, which arrived on the desk of an admissions counselor whose young son was named Lincoln for her favorite president. Mack liked to say that Abraham Lincoln got her into college. Mack, who studied creative writing and gender studies at Truman, died of complications from Addison's disease while studying abroad in Spain. Her spirit rests at Oak Ridge Cemetery, in the shadow of the Lincoln Tomb.

Harriet Monroe (1860–1936), a poet and founder of *Poetry* magazine, was a keeper of the Progressive Era legacy of Abraham Lincoln and promoted the "Prairie Poets" who made a literary tradition of the Lincoln story.[58]

Matilda (Johnston Hall) Moore (1811–78) was Lincoln's stepsister. She married Squire Hall in 1826 in Indiana, and after his death married Reuben Moore in Coles County, Illinois, in 1856. She once said: "My Mother, I think has given Abes character well."[59]

Mary Lothrop Motley (Sheridan) (1844–1918), born in Massachusetts, was the daughter of historian John Lothrop Motley, President Lincoln's minister to Austria. She asked for and received Lincoln's autograph in 1862. She married Algernon Sheridan in 1871 in England, where she lived until her death. Her fourth son William Frederic Sheridan died fighting in France during World War I.[60]

Mary Owens (Vineyard) (1808–77), whom Lincoln courted in 1836–37, married Jesse Vineyard in 1841. She settled in Missouri, where she raised four children. After Lincoln's death, she sent her Lincoln letters to Lincoln's biographer William Herndon. In one of her letters to Herndon, she wrote: "Really you catechize me in true lawyer style, but I feel that you will have the goodness to excuse me if I decline answering all your questions in detail, being well assured that few women would have ceded as much as I have, under the circumstances."[61]

Louise (Doxon Rodgers) Paul (1832–98), a native of Kentucky, was a widow with a young son when she married Major Gabriel Paul in April 1858. In 1862, she visited President Lincoln to press for a military promotion for her husband.[62]

Rebecca Rossignol (Holiday) Pomeroy (1817–84), born in Boston, was a U.S. Army nurse who also served as private nurse to the Lincoln family during the Civil War. Pomeroy had a difficult life. She lost her sea captain father in 1827 and was raised by her widowed mother, and her husband David Pomeroy had asthma and needed her constant care. She also buried her fifteen-year-old son William in 1856, her nine-year-old daughter Clara in 1857, and her forty-three-year-old husband in 1860. And then the Civil War threatened the life of her twenty-one-year-old son George, who enlisted in the U.S. Army. Lonely and lost, Pomeroy wrote to Dorothea Dix to render her services. Dix accepted her offer, and in the fall of 1860, Pomeroy reported to Georgetown Hospital to begin her long service as an army nurse.[63]

Marion Dolores (Bonsi) Pratt (1907–63) was an assistant editor of the first eight volumes and the index of the *Collected Works of Abraham Lincoln*. Born in Rockford, Illinois, she graduated from Rockford College in 1928 and earned a master's degree in history from the University of Illinois in 1929. She joined the *Collected Works* team in Springfield, Illinois, in 1945 before Roy Basler arrived as editor. She married Illinois state historian and Lincoln scholar Harry Pratt in 1950, and after his death in 1956 served as acting state historian. Since its publication in 1953, *everyone* who has written *anything* about Abraham Lincoln has consulted the *Collected Works*, and Pratt deserves as much credit as Basler for this important, enduring publication.[64]

Ruth Painter Randall (1892–1971), a historian and Lincoln scholar, published important books about Abraham and Mary Lincoln, the most influential of which was *Mary Lincoln: Biography of a Marriage* in 1953.[65]

Vinnie Ream (Hoxie) (1847–1914), the first woman to win a congressional commission, was a sculptor who created the Abraham Lincoln statue for the U.S. Capitol in 1871. *Abraham Lincoln* still resides in the Capitol Rotunda, greeting more than three million visitors annually.[66]

Polly Offill Rogers (b. c. 1803), the wife of Lincoln's client in a divorce case, married Samuel Rogers in 1835 and was divorced from him in 1839.[67]

Ann Rutledge (1813–35) was a young woman Lincoln knew (and maybe loved) in New Salem, Illinois. Of Rutledge, historian Benjamin Thomas wrote: "Ann Rutledge was a real girl, to be sure, and Lincoln probably sorrowed at her death, as any person with his keen sympathies would do, especially in a small community where people live together closely and knew one another well."[68]

Mary "Polly" Shelby (c. 1800–1879) was a mixed-race woman in Springfield, Illinois. Lincoln was her lawyer in two cases, in 1841 and

1858, indicating a long connection. In the early case, Shelby filed for divorce from her husband Mack, whom she had married in 1827, but the couple reconciled. After Mack's death in 1857, she hired Lincoln's law firm to settle her dower.[69]

Caroline "Carrie" Lane (Reynolds) Slemmer (Jebb) (1840–1930) was the young wife of Adam Slemmer, a U.S. Army officer who taught at the U.S. Military Academy before the Civil War. She asked President Lincoln to promote her husband, who then rose to the rank of major in May 1861. After her husband's death in 1868 of a heart attack while serving at Fort Laramie in Wyoming Territory, Carrie Slemmer went to England to visit family. In 1878, she married Richard Claverhouse Jebb, a British classical scholar. When her husband was knighted in 1900, she became Lady Jebb. Her husband died in 1905, and she returned to the United States during World War I.[70]

Ann Maria (Todd) Smith (1824–91) was Lincoln's sister-in-law. She married Clark Moulton Smith, a Springfield merchant, in 1846, and had six children. She named her eldest son Lincoln after her brother-in-law.[71]

Elizabeth "Betsy" (Hanks) Sparrow (1771–1818) was Lincoln's maternal great aunt who lived with the Lincoln family in Indiana. Along with Lincoln's mother, she died of milk sickness.[72]

Mary Speed (1802–84) was the half sister of Lincoln's close friend Joshua Speed. Lincoln met her in 1841 during his visit at Farmington, the Speed family plantation in Kentucky.[73]

Ann G. Sprigg (c. 1799–1870) was a native of Virginia who ran a boardinghouse in Washington where Lincoln once lived. When she appealed to President Lincoln for employment in 1864, he wrote his secretary of the Treasury: "The bearer of this is a most estimable widow lady, at whose house I boarded years ago when a member of Congress. She is now very needy; & any employment suitable to a lady could not be bestowed on a more worthy person." Sprigg gained an appointment as a clerk in the loan branch of the Treasury Department.[74]

Emma A. Stark, Lincoln's client in a divorce case, married Lafayette Stark in New York in November 1850. At the time she hired Lincoln, she was living in Atlanta, Illinois, seeking a divorce on the grounds of her husband's neglect and cruelty. On August 13, 1858, she wrote Lincoln: "I have concluded to address you, for the purpose of finding out what more it will be necessary for me to do if any-thing, in order that I may be successful—I fear this matter will seem rather unimportant to you (when compared with the subject that is principally occupying your attention at present) yet however much so, it may seem to you—to me, it is of the greatest importance that I should succeed, now that I have undertaken." Lincoln was preparing for his first senatorial debate with Stephen Douglas, scheduled for August 21. He helped Stark obtain a divorce and gain custody of her son.[75]

Esther (Clark) Stockton (1792–1868), the widow of the Rev. Joseph Stockton, lived in Allegheny City, Pennsylvania. She knitted stockings for soldiers during the Civil War, a task that President Lincoln graciously acknowledged.[76]

Bettie Jane Stuart (Brown) (1838–69) was the daughter of Lincoln's law partner John Stuart. She married Christopher C. Brown, a Springfield lawyer, in 1859. When Bettie died, Mary Lincoln wrote: "I am pained to hear of Bettie Stuart's death. She was a most amiable woman, and her father is a very dearly loved cousin—a most affectionate relative."[77]

Ida M. Tarbell (1857–1944), a journalist, was an early biographer of Abraham Lincoln. She published *The Life of Abraham Lincoln*, in 1900. If you read any Lincoln biography after reading this book, take a chance on Tarbell.[78]

Sojourner Truth (1797–1883) met President Lincoln in the White House in 1864. Born Isabella Baumfree, she was the daughter of enslaved parents. She gained her freedom in 1827, renamed herself Sojourner Truth in 1843, and dedicated her life to the cause of abolition and the civil rights of women.[79]

LuLu Waldron (1851–1929), the daughter of a judge in Dakota Territory, was a young constituent of President Lincoln when he wrote to her in April 1862: "My Dear Young Friend Allow me to express to you my very sincere thanks for your kindness in sending me those elegant studs of Pipestone."[80]

Frances Jane (Todd) Wallace (1815–99) was Lincoln's sister-in-law. She married William Smith Wallace, a Springfield physician, in 1839 and had six children. President Lincoln appointed William Wallace a paymaster in 1861.[81]

Mary J. Wallace (Baker) (1842–1911), Lincoln's niece, was the daughter of Frances Wallace, Lincoln's sister-in-law.[82]

Sarah Ellen (Hardin) Walworth (1811–74) was the widow of Lincoln's friend John Hardin, who died in the Mexican War. Sarah Hardin married Reuben H. Walworth, a congressman from New York, in 1851.

President Lincoln forwarded a recommendation from her to his secretary of state: "I know nothing of the gentleman recommend[ed] within; but the lady (Mrs. Walworth) in whose hands I find the paper is an old friend and acquaintance, and I would like for her to be obliged, in the way named, or some similar one." Sarah and John Hardin's daughter Ellen Hardin Walworth (1832–1915) became a well-known science writer, cofounded the Daughters of the American Revolution, and helped organize the women's exhibition at the 1893 World's Fair in Chicago.[83]

Sallie Ward (Lawrence, Hunt, Armstrong, Downs) (1827–96), a divorced Kentuckian living in New Orleans with her second husband, supported Abraham Lincoln in 1860. When her husband joined the Confederate cause, she left him and returned to Kentucky. She corresponded with Mary Lincoln, and President Lincoln wrote on her behalf about retrieving personal items from Louisiana. After the war, she earned a reputation for collecting wealthy husbands, which afforded her a luxurious lifestyle of parties and European travel.[84]

Susannah (Crume) Weathers (1782–1865), a widow from Indiana, knitted President Lincoln a pair of fine socks, and he thanked her in a letter she treasured until her death.[85]

Mary Louisa (Salter) Welles (1819–1900) was the widow of Lincoln's friend Charles Welles. She moved to Waverly, Illinois, in 1835 with her family, and in 1841 married attorney Charles Welles, with whom she had five children. She buried her first child in 1849; when cholera struck Springfield in 1854, her husband and infant son died, leaving her a widow with three young children, only one of whom reached adulthood. Lincoln was her lawyer in cases related to her husband's estate.[86]

Annie (Turner) Wittenmyer (1827–1900), born in Ohio and educated at a female seminary, settled in Iowa after her marriage. After her husband's death, she founded a free school for underprivileged children, and when the Civil War began, she collected supplies for Iowa's soldiers. Her relief efforts during the Civil War focused on food and nutrition, her special diet kitchen project drew national attention, and her relief work during the war earned the praise of President Lincoln.[87]

ABBREVIATIONS

In citing works in the notes and bibliography, works frequently cited have been identified by the following appreviations:

AL: Abraham Lincoln

ALPLM: Abraham Lincoln Presidential Library and Museum, Springfield, Illinois

ANB: *American National Biography*, New York: Oxford University Press, online https://www.anb.org/ (accessed Oct. 9, 2024)

CW: *Collected Works of Abraham Lincoln*, edited by Roy P. Basler, Marion Delores Pratt, and Lloyd A. Dunlap, 10 vols. (New Brunswick, NJ: Rutgers University Press, 1953, 1955, 1974, 1990)

DAB: *Dictionary of American Biography*, 1st ed., 20 vols. (New York: Scribner's, 1928 1936)

DLC: Library of Congress, Washington

HI: *Herndon's Informants: Letters, Interviews, and Statements about Abraham Lincoln*, edited by Douglas L. Wilson and Rodney O. Davis (Urbana: University of Illinois Press, 1998)

L&L: *Mary Todd Lincoln: Her Life and Letters*, edited by Justin Turner and Linda Levitt Turner (New York: Knopf, 1972)

LPAL: *The Law Practice of Abraham Lincoln* edited by Martha L. Benner and Cullom Davis (Urbana: University of Illinois Press, 2000, 2008), https://lawpracticeofabrahamlincoln.org/ (accessed Oct. 9, 2024)

ML: Mary Lincoln

NARA: National Archives and Records Administration

PAL: *Papers of Abraham Lincoln: Legal Documents and Cases*, edited by Daniel W. Stowell et al., 4 vols. (Charlottesville: University of Virginia Press, 2008)

NOTES

Preface

"Abraham Lincoln Walks at Midnight" was first published Oct. 18, 1914, in the *St. Louis Post-Dispatch*. It later appeared in Lindsay, *Collected Poems*, 53–54.

Introduction

1. AL to Jesse Fell, Dec. 20, 1859, *CW*, 3:511; Horrocks, *Lincoln's Campaign Biographies*, 70–71; *Speech of Henry Clay*, 18.
2. Books that have chipped away at the self-made myth include Angle, *Here I Have Lived*; Harris, *Lincoln's Rise to the Presidency*; Hofstadter, "Abraham Lincoln and the Self-Made Myth," 93–136; Reynolds, *Abe*; Winkle, *Young Eagle*; Wyllie, *Self-Made Man in America*.

   James K. Polk, Millard Fillmore, Franklin Pierce, and James Buchanan were all born in log cabins. *ANB*.
3. Eliza Browning to Ozias M. Hatch, May 23, 1860, box 1, Ozias M. Hatch Papers, ALPLM; Nelson, "Eliza Caldwell Browning," 37; Winkle, "Abraham Lincoln: Self-Made Man," 1–16.
4. AL, Farewell Address at Springfield, IL (A. Version), Feb. 11, 1861, *CW*, 4:190.
5. Baker, *Mary Todd Lincoln*, xi–xvii; McDermott, *Mary Lincoln*, 1–9; Thomas, *Abraham Lincoln*, 90–91.
6. Baker, "Biography as Social History," 204–5.
7. Banner, "Biography as History," 579–86; Tubbs, *Three Mothers*.
8. These titles particularly inspired my approach to this book: Nash, *Me-Search and Re-Search*; Nash, "Scholarly Personal Narrative," 39–52; Barnes, "History and Ordinary Womanhood," 98–108; Raymond, "I-Dropping and Androgyny," 478–83; Hunter, "Book Breaking and Book Mending"; Barnes, "History and Ordinary Womanhood," 98–108; Hodes, *My*

Hijacking; Lunden, *American Breakdown*; Saunders, *Lincoln in the Bardo*; Tarbell, *Life of Abraham Lincoln*; Gilder, *Lincoln the Leader*; Vidal, *Lincoln*; Borden, *A. Lincoln and Me*; Gates, *Colored People.*

1. Earthly and Angel Mothers

1. Family Record Written by Abraham Lincoln, c. 1851, *CW*, 2:94; Nancy Hanks-Thomas Lincoln Marriage Record, U.S. County Marriage Records, 1783–1965; Briggs, *Nancy Hanks Lincoln*, 18–21, 28, 35, 69–93; Donald, *Lincoln*, 17–21; Herndon, *Herndon's Lincoln*, 1:3–4; Neely, *Abraham Lincoln Encyclopedia*, 184, 188; Reynolds, *Abe*, 7–8, 36; Tarbell, *In the Footsteps of the Lincolns*, 22; Thomas, *Abraham Lincoln*, 6; Warren, *Lincoln's Parentage and Childhood*, 17–37; *DAB*, 11:242–43.
2. Family Record Written by AL, c. 1851, *CW*, 2:94; Autobiography Written for John L. Scripps, c. June 1860, *CW*, 4:61; Barton, *Women Lincoln Loved*, 41; Briggs, *Nancy Hanks Lincoln*, 64–88; Donald, *Lincoln*, 23; Neely, *Abraham Lincoln Encyclopedia*, 188; *DAB*, 11:243.
3. Autobiography Written for John L. Scripps, c. June 1860, *CW*, 4:61; Briggs, *Nancy Hanks Lincoln*, 81–82, 101; Dirck, *Lincoln in Indiana*, 8–10, 14–15, 29–33; Donald, *Lincoln*, 22–24; Haymond, *Illustrated History of the State of Indiana*, 181; Neely, *Abraham Lincoln Encyclopedia*, 187–88; Reynolds, *Abe*, 27–31; Thomas, *Abraham Lincoln*, 7–8.
4. Autobiography Written for John L. Scripps, c. June 1860, *CW*, 4:62; Dirck, *Lincoln in Indiana*, 12–13.
5. Dennis F. Hanks to William Henry Herndon, June 13, 1865, *HI*, 39; *HI*, 781; Dirck, *Lincoln in Indiana*, 6–7; Etchison, *Emerging Midwest*, 1–14; Hawes, *Family and Society*, 1–5, 37, 139; Meyer, *Making the Heartland Quilt*, 12–14; Neely, *Abraham Lincoln Encyclopedia*, 137, 188; Shenk, *Lincoln's Melancholy*, 15, 29, 37, 53.
6. James G. Randall, biography of AL, *DAB*, 11:243; Briggs, *Nancy Hanks Lincoln*, 115–16.
7. AL to Jesse W. Fell, Enclosing Autobiography, Dec. 20, 1859, *CW*, 3:511; Reynolds, *Abe*, 21–22.
8. Briggs, *Nancy Hanks Lincoln*, 9–12, 35; Dirck, *Lincoln in Indiana*, 18–21.
9. Swedlund, *Shadows in the Valley*, 2.
10. AL to Fanny McCullough, Dec. 23, 1862, *CW*, 6:16.
11. Dennis F. Hanks to William Henry Herndon, June 13, 1865, *HI*, 37, 40; Abner Y. Ellis (Statement), Jan. 23, 1866, *HI*, 173 (quote); Barton, *Women Lincoln Loved*, 67; Briggs, *Nancy Hanks Lincoln*, 30–38, 68, 116; Dirck, *Lincoln in Indiana*, 6–7; Neely, *Abraham Lincoln Encyclopedia*, 137, 184; *DAB*, 11:242.

12. Family Record Written by Abraham Lincoln, c. 1851, *CW*, 2:95; Coleman, *Abraham Lincoln and Coles County*, vii; Dirck, *Lincoln in Indiana*, 46–48.
13. Dirck, *Lincoln in Indiana*, 48–49.
14. Sarah Lincoln (Interview), Sept. 8, 1865, *HI*, 106–7 (quotes); A. H. Chapman (Statement), Sept. 8, 1865, *HI*, 99; John B. Helm to William Henry Herndon, Aug. 1, 1865, *HI*, 82; Barton, *Women Lincoln Loved*, 108; Neely, *Abraham Lincoln Encyclopedia*, 187.
15. Elizabeth Crawford (Interview) Sept. 16, 1865, *HI*, 126 (quote); AL to Thomas Lincoln and John D. Johnston, Dec. 24, 1848, *CW*, 2:15; AL to John D. Johnston, Jan. 12, 1851, *CW*, 2:96; Aug. 31, 1851, *CW*, 2:110; Autobiography Written for John L. Scripps, c. June 1860, *CW*, 4:62; Barton, *Women Lincoln Loved*, 108.
16. Barton, *Women Lincoln Loved*, 112–16; Donald, *Lincoln*, 19–37; Reynolds, *Abe*, 21–49; Thomas, *Abraham Lincoln*, 3–22.
17. AL to Martin S. Morris, Mar. 26, 1843, *CW*, 1:320 (quote); Autobiography Written for John L. Scripps, c. June 1860, *CW*, 4:63; Mar. 1, 1830, *Lincoln Log; McClure's Magazine* 5 (Nov. 1895): 502; *HI*, 780; Coleman, *Abraham Lincoln and Coles County*, 1; Dirck, *Lincoln in Indiana*, 87.
18. AL to John D. Johnston, Dec. 24, 1848, *CW*, 1:110; Jan. 12, 1851, *CW*, 2:96 (quote); Aug. 31, 1851, *CW*, 2:15; Nov. 4, 1851, *CW*, 2:110–11; Indenture of Thomas and Sarah Lincoln to Abraham Lincoln, Acknowledgement of Deed, and Bond, Oct. 25, 1841, *CW*, 1:262–63; ML to Sarah Lincoln, Dec. 19, 1867, *L&L*, 464–65; Sarah Bush Lincoln (Interview), Sept. 8, 1865, *HI*, 108; Matilda Johnston Moore (Interview), Sept. 8, 1865, *HI*, 109–10; Barton, *Women Lincoln Loved*, 107, 112–13; Coleman, *Abraham Lincoln and Coles County*, 31–32; Fraker, *Lincoln's Ladder*, xxiii, 8; *LPAL*.
19. AL Eulogy on Benjamin Ferguson, Feb. 8, 1842, *CW*, 1:268.
20. Family Record in the Abraham Lincoln Bible, Nov. 4, 1842–Apr. 4, 1853, *CW*, 1:304; Family Record Written by Abraham Lincoln and Memorandum of Births in the Hall Family, c. 1851, *CW*, 2:94–96; Resolutions Adopted by Springfield Clay Club on the Death of John Brodie, Aug. 7, 1844, *CW*, 1:341; AL to Joel A. Matteson, Jan. 10, 1853, *CW*, 2:187–88; Resolutions on the Death of Charles R. Welles, Nov. 29, 1854, *CW*, 2:289–90; AL to John McLean, Dec. 6, 1854, *CW*, 2:291; Endorsement: David Davis to John Wood Concerning Pardon of Thomas Patterson, Aug. 14, 1860, *CW*, 4:93–94; AL to Hiram Barney, Mar. 13, 1862, *CW*, 5:157; AL to Edwin Stanton, Nov. 22, 1863, *CW*, 7:28; Brooks, *Abraham Lincoln and the Downfall of American Slavery*, 21 (quote); Barton, *Women Lincoln Loved*, 114–16; Reynolds, *Abe*, 35–44.

2. Sisters and Girls

1. Family Record Written by Abraham Lincoln, c. 1851, *CW*, 2:94–95; AL to Samuel Haycraft, May 28, 1860, *CW*, 4:56–57; AL, Autobiography Written for John L. Scripps, c. June 1860, *CW*, 4:61; Dennis F. Hanks to William Henry Herndon, June 13, 1865, *HH*, 40–41; Elizabeth Crawford, Sept. 16, 1865, *HI*, 126; John Hanks (Interview), c. 1865–1866, *HI*, 456; Donald, *Lincoln*, 22–34; Reynolds, *Abe*, 25–31, 47; Thomas, *Abraham Lincoln*, 7–19.
2. Matilda Johnston Moore (Interview), Sept. 8, 1865, *HI*, 110 (quotes), 764; Family Record Written by Abraham Lincoln, c. 1851, *CW*, 2:94–95; Dennis Hanks to Abraham Lincoln, Apr. 5, 1864, AL Paper, DLC; Illinois Statewide Marriage Index, Illinois State Archives, Springfield; Elizabeth Hanks Gravestone, Old City Cemetery, Charleston, IL; Neely, *Abraham Lincoln Encyclopedia*, 165.
3. AL, "My Childhood Home I See Again," *CW*, 1:367–68.
4. Family Record Written by Abraham Lincoln, c. 1851, *CW*, 2:94–95; Sarah Lincoln Grigsby Gravestone, Pigeon Creek Baptist Church Cemetery, Dale, IN; Samuel E. Kercheval to Jesse W. Weik, Dec. 2, 1887, *HI*, 645; Donald, *Lincoln*, 22, 26; Louden, *Death in Childbirth*, 15–17, 49; Reynolds, *Abe*, 25, 29, 31, 47, 758.
5. Mar. 1, 1830, *Lincoln Log*; AL to John D. Johnston, Jan. 12, 1851, *CW*, 2:96; Matilda Johnston Moore (Interview), Sept. 8, 1865, *HI*, 110, 780; *McClure's Magazine* 5 (Nov. 1895): 502.
6. Frances Todd Wallace (Interview), c. 1865–1866, *HI*, 485; Berry, *House of Abraham*, vi–vii; Krause, 54–60, 78–80.
7. Elizabeth Todd Edwards (Interview), c. 1865–1866, *HI*, 445.
8. AL to John D. Johnston, Jan. 12, 1851, *CW*, 2:96–97; Family Record Written by AL, c. 1851, and Memorandum of Births in the Hall Family, c. 1851, *CW*, 2:94–95, 96; AL to John T. Stuart, Mar. 30, 1861, *CW*, 4:303; ML to Elizabeth Todd Grimsley, Sept. 29, 1861, *L&L*, 105; Berry, *House of Abraham*, vi.
9. AL to Grace Bedell, Oct. 19, 1860, *CW*, 4:129.
10. AL to John T. Stuart, Dec. 23, 1839, *CW*, 1:159.
11. Grace Bedell to AL, Oct. 15, 1860, *CW*, 4:130n1; AL to Grace Bedell, Oct. 19, 1860, *CW*, 4:129; AL Remarks at Westfield, NY, Feb. 16, 1861, *CW*, 4:219; Donald, *Lincoln*, 258–59, 274; Reynolds, *Abe*, 513; Thomas, *Abraham Lincoln*, 221.
12. Nov. 3, 1847, *Lincoln Log*; Randall, *Mary Lincoln*, 105 (quotes) 122, 162–64; Neely, *Abraham Lincoln Encyclopedia*, 142–43.

13. AL to Samuel Haycraft, June 4, 1860, *CW*, 4:69–70; AL to Simon Cameron, Apr. 16, 1861, *CW*, 4:335, 435n2; AL to ML, Sept. 24, 1863, *CW*, 6:478; AL to Lyman B. Todd, Oct. 15, 1863, *CW*, 6:517, 7:64n1; ML to Emilie Todd Helm, Nov. 23, 1856, *L&L*, 45–48; Sept. 20, 1857, *L&L*, 49–51, 155–56; Browning, *Diary*, 1:651; Baker, *Mary Todd Lincoln*, 223–26; Donald, *Lincoln*, 475; Helm, *Mary*, 219; McCurry, "Enemy Women and the Laws of War," 667–710; Randall, *Mary Lincoln*, 330–34 (quote); McDermott, *Mary Lincoln*, 110–11; Reynolds, *Abe*, 607–8.
14. Hay, *Inside Lincoln's White House*, 128.
15. Browning, *Diary*, 1:651; Donald, *Lincoln*, 475; Reynolds, *Abe*, 608.
16. AL to Whom It May Concern, Dec. 14, 1863, *CW*, 7:64; Emilie Todd to Abraham Lincoln, Dec. 20, 1863. AL Papers, DLC.
17. Emilie Helm to AL, Oct. 30, 1864, AL Papers, DLC.
18. Emilie Todd Helm to Jesse W. Weik, c. 1887, *HI*, 694.

3. A Mother's Fear

1. Augustus H. Chapman to AL, Jan. 3, 1861, AL Papers, DLC.
2. Jan. 30–Feb. 1, 1861, *Lincoln Log*; Donald, *Lincoln*, 271; Reynolds, *Abe*, 508; Thomas, *Abraham Lincoln*, 238.
3. *Illinois State Journal* (Springfield), Jan. 31, 1861; Feb. 2, 1861; *Chicago Tribune*, Nov. 14, 1873; Clayton, *Illinois Fact Book*, 107; Coleman, *Abraham Lincoln and Coles County*, 191.
4. *HI*, 743; Donald, *Lincoln*, 271.
5. Adams, *Illinois Place Names*, 312; Illinois State Historical Society, Moore House Historical Marker, on Lincoln Highway Road south of County Route 150N, near Lerna, IL.
6. Matilda Johnston Moore (Interview), Sept. 8, 1865, *HI*, 109 (quote); Coleman, *Abraham Lincoln and Coles County*, 209–10; "Mr. Lincoln Returns," *Illinois State Journal* (Springfield), Feb. 2, 1861; Augustus H. Chapman to William Henry Herndon, Oct. 8, 1865, *HI*, 135–36, 743.
7. Sarah Bush Lincoln (Interview), Sept. 8, 1865, *HI*, 106–7; Augustus H. Chapman to William Henry Herndon, Oct. 8, 1865, *HI*, 136–37; Augustus H. Chapman, (Interview), c. 1865, *HI*, 439.
8. Sarah Bush Lincoln (Interview), Sept. 8, 1865, *HI*, 108 (quote); Coleman, "Sarah Bush Lincoln," 26–27.
9. Coleman, "Sarah Bush Lincoln," 14 (quote); ML to Sarah Lincoln, Dec. 19, 1867, *L&L*, 465, 465n7. The obituary appeared in the *Charleston (IL.) Plaindealer* and was reprinted in the *Decatur Weekly (IL) Republican*, May 6, 1869, 4.
10. *McClure's Magazine* 5 (Nov. 1895): 511.

4. My Lincoln Family

1. Address Delivered at the Dedication of the Cemetery at Gettysburg, Nov. 19, 1863, Edward Everett Copy, *CW*, 7:21–22; *St. Louis Post-Dispatch*, Mar. 25, 1944; Boritt, *Gettysburg Gospel*, 1; White, *Eloquent*, 223–59.

5. A Good Man among Good Women

1. Donald, *Lincoln*, 40–60, 150–51; Reynolds, *Abe*, 121–23, 250–55; Thomas, *Abraham Lincoln*, 26–40, 159–60.
2. *HI*, 751; Thomas, *Lincoln's Old Friends*, 15–20, 39–41, 46, 103, 127.
3. July 1831, *Lincoln Log*; J. Rowan Herndon to William Henry Herndon, July 3, 1865, *HI*, 69–70, 775; Aug. 16, 1865, *HI*, 91; Donald, *Lincoln*, 32–33; Reynolds, *Abe*, 196–98; Thomas, *Lincoln's New Salem*, 80; Thomas, *Lincoln's Old Friends*, 116–23.
4. Sarah Bush Lincoln (Interview), Sept. 8, 1865, *HI*, 108; Ida Tarbell, "Abraham Lincoln," *McClure's Magazine* 6 (Jan. 1896): 118; Thomas, *Lincoln's Old Friends*, 39; Winkle, *Young Eagle*, 22–131.
5. AL to Eliza Browning, Apr. 1, 1838, *CW*, 1:117; Elizabeth Abell to Abraham Lincoln, Jan. 22, 1861, RG 107, NARA; Abner Y. Ellis (Statement), Jan. 23, 1866, *HI*, 171.
6. Abner Y. Ellis (Statement), Jan. 23, 1866, *HI*, 171; Etcheson, *Emerging Midwest*, 1–14; Meyer, *Making the Heartland Quilt*, 25–32; Thomas, *Lincoln's New Salem*, 3–38; Winkle, *Young Eagle*, 61–66.
7. Elizabeth Abell to AL, Jan. 22, 1861, RG 107, NARA; Oliver Abell to Abraham Lincoln, Apr. 1861, with AL Endorsement, DLC; Memorandum: Appointment of Oliver G. Abell, c. Apr. 1, 1861, *CW*, 4:310; J. Rowan Herndon to William Henry Herndon, July 3, 1865, *HI*, 69; Hannah Armstrong (Interview), c. 1866, *HI*, 526 (quote); Elizabeth Abell to William Henry Herndon, Jan. 13, 1867, *HI*, 544 (quote); *People v. Armstrong*, May 1858, Cass County (IL) Circuit Court; *Green v. Graham*, Nov. 1844, Menard County (IL) Circuit Court, both in *LPAL*; *People v. Armstrong*, in *PAL*, 4:1–48; Schnell, "Two Lincolns," 4; Thomas, *Lincoln's New Salem*, 44–46, 80; Thomas, *Lincoln's Old Friends*, 127.
8. *HI*, 738; Thomas, *Lincoln's Old Friends*, 40; Winkle, *Young Eagle*, 56–68.
9. J. Rowan Herndon to William Henry Herndon, July 3, 1865, *HI*, 69; Aug. 16, 1865, *HI*, 92, 755; Hannah Armstrong (Interview), c. 1866, *HI*, 526; Jason Duncan to William Henry Herndon, c. late 1866–early 1867, *HI*, 541 (quote), 746; Elizabeth Abell to William Henry Herndon, Feb. 15, 1867, *HI*, 557 (quote); Wilson, *Honor's Voice*, 111–12; Thomas, *Lincoln's Old Friends*, 16, 40, 46.

10. *HI*, 738; Burlingame, *Oral History of Abraham Lincoln*, 19; Thomas, *Lincoln's Old Friends*, 39 (quote).
11. Mentor Graham to William Henry Herndon, May 29, 1865, *HI*, 8–11, 750; Duncan, *Mentor*, 39, 46, 129–34; Herndon, *Herndon's Lincoln*, 1:143; Neely, *Abraham Lincoln Encyclopedia*, 126, 230.
12. Family Record Written by Abraham Lincoln, c. 1851, *CW*, 2:94–95; Autobiography Written for John L. Scripps, c. June 1860, *CW*, 4:61; Elizabeth Abell to William Henry Herndon, Feb. 15, 1867, *HI*, 556; Thomas, *Lincoln's Old Friends*, 20, 23, 39–41.
13. AL to Joshua F. Speed, Feb. 25, 1842, *CW*, 1:281.
14. Communication to the People of Sangamon County, Mar. 9, 1832, *CW*, 1:5–9; Muster Roll of AL's Company, May 27, 1832, *CW*, 1:10–11; AL to the Editor of the *Sangamo Journal*, June 13, 1836, *CW*, 1:48 (quote); Baker, "Biography as Social History," 209; Etcheson, *Emerging Midwest*, 27–32; Etcheson, "Manliness and the Political Culture of the Old Northwest, 59–77; Guelzo, "'Public Sentiment Is Everything,'" 78–79; Smith, "Abraham Lincoln, Manhood, and Nineteenth-Century American Political Culture," 29–41.

6. Much Ado (or What to Do) about Ann Rutledge?

1. Donald, *Lincoln*, 55–57; Emerson, *Giant in the Shadows*, 142–46; Gannett, "The Ann Rutledge Story," 21–60; *HI*, 374; Randall, *Mary Lincoln*, 36–40; Randall, *Lincoln the President*, 2:321–36; Reynolds, *Abe*, 150–59; Schwartz, "Ann Rutledge in American Memory," 1–27; Simon, "Abraham Lincoln and Ann Rutledge," 13–33; Thomas, *Lincoln's New Salem*, 121–24; Wilson, "William H. Herndon and Mary Todd Lincoln," 1–26.
2. Elizabeth Abell to William Henry Herndon, Feb. 15, 1867, *HI*, 557.
3. AL to John McNamar, Dec. 24, 1836, *CW*, 1:60; Nov. 9, 1843, *CW*, 1:330.
4. Abner Y. Ellis (Statement), 23 January 1866, *HI*, 171; David Davis (Interview), Sept. 20, 1866, *HI*, 350; Wilson, *Honor's Voice*, 127.
5. Ann Rutledge Gravestone, Old Concord Cemetery, Petersburg, IL; Hardin Bale to William Henry Herndon, May 29, 1865, *HI*, 13; William G. Greene to William Henry Herndon, May 30, 1865, *HI*, 17–21; Lynn McNulty to William Henry Herndon, July 30, 1865, *HI*, 80; Henry McHenry to William Henry Herndon, Jan. 8, 1866, *HI*, 155–56; William G. Greene to William Henry Herndon, Jan. 23, 1866, *HI*, 175; Mary Owens Vineyard to William Henry Herndon, May 1, 1866, *HI*, 248; Benjamin F. Irwin to William Henry Herndon, Aug. 27, 1866, *HI*, 325; Robert B. Rutledge (Ann Rutledge's brother) to William Henry Herndon, Nov. 1, 1866, *HI*,

382–83; Isaac Cogdal (Interview), c. 1865–1866, *HI*, 440; Neely, *Abraham Lincoln Encyclopedia*, 265; Thomas, *Lincoln's New Salem*, 121–24.
6. ML to David Davis, Mar. 4, 1867, *L&L*, 415.

7. Courting Mary Owens

1. ML to Josiah G. Holland, Dec. 4, 1865, *L&L*, 293; ML to Sally Orne, Dec. 12, 1869, *L&L*, 533–34.
2. AL to Eliza Browning, Apr. 1, 1838, *CW*, 1:117–18; Elizabeth Abell to William Henry Herndon, Feb. 15, 1867, *HI*, 556; Donald, *Lincoln*, 67–69, 87; Lystra, *Searching the Heart*, 28–55, 1158–64, 166; Reynolds, *Abe*, 150–63; Thomas, *Abraham Lincoln*, 56–58, 69–71; Thomas, *Lincoln's New Salem*, 126–28; Winkle, *Young Eagle*, 149–55.
3. AL to Eliza Browning, Apr. 1, 1838, *CW*, 1:117–19; Mary Owens Vineyard to William Henry Herndon: May 1, 1866, *HI*, 248; May 23, 1866, *HI*, 255–56; July 22, 1866, *HI*, 262–63; Aug. 6, 1866, *HI*, 265; Oct. 29, 1866, *HI*, 380; Caleb Carman (Interview), Oct. 12, 1866, *HI*, 374 (quote); Donald, *Lincoln*, 68; Thomas, *Lincoln's Old Friends*, 55–66.
4. AL to Eliza Browning, Apr. 1, 1838, *CW*, 1:117–18; Mary Owens Vineyard to William Henry Herndon: July 22, 1866, *HI*, 263 (quote); Dec. 5, 1839, *Lincoln Log*; Donald, *Lincoln*, 67; Neely, *Abraham Lincoln Encyclopedia*; Ida Tarbell, "Abraham Lincoln," *McClure's Magazine* 6 (Mar. 1896): 317, 323–25; Thomas, *Abraham Lincoln*, 56.
5. AL to Mary Owens, Dec. 13, 1836, *CW*, 1:54–55.
6. Mary Owens Vineyard to William Henry Herndon, July 22, 1866, *HI*, 262.
7. Lincoln earned his license to practice law on Sept. 9, 1836. *Lincoln Log*.
8. Mary Owens Vineyard to William Henry Herndon, July 22, 1866, *HI*, 262; Jan. 1–5, 1837; March 7–12, 1837, *Lincoln Log*; Thomas, *Lincoln's Old Friends*, 87–88.
9. John T. Stuart (Interview), late June 1865, *HI*, 63; Apr. 15, 1837, *Lincoln Log*; Duff, *A. Lincoln*, 21–50; Krause, "Abraham Lincoln and Joshua Speed," 35–37; Reynolds, *Abe*, 138–40; Thomas, *Abraham Lincoln*, 67.
10. AL to Mary Owens, May 7, 1837, *CW*, 1:78–79; Elizabeth Abell to William Henry Herndon, Jan. 13, 1867, *HI*, 544.
11. AL to Mary Owens, Aug. 16, 1837, *CW*, 1:94–95.
12. Mary Owens Vineyard to William Henry Herndon, May 23, 1866, *HI*, 256.
13. AL to Eliza Browning, Apr. 1, 1838, *CW*, 1:119; Mary Owens Vineyard to William Henry Herndon, July 22, 1866, *HI*, 263 (quote); Nov. 16, 1866, *HI*, 399; Thomas, *Lincoln's Old Friends*, 88–97.

14. Mary Owens Vineyard to William Henry Herndon, July 22, 1866, *HI*, 263.
15. Mary Owens Vineyard Gravestone, Pleasant Ridge Cemetery, Weston, MO.
16. AL to Eliza Browning, Apr. 1, 1838, *CW*, 1:119.
17. Winkle, *Young Eagle*, 155.

8. Mary, Molly, Lover, Wife

1. Baker, *Mary Todd Lincoln*, 74–75; Berry, *House of Abraham*, 24–30; *HI*, 747, 775; Neely, *Abraham Lincoln Encyclopedia*, 95; Randall, *Mary Lincoln*, 28–35; *L&L*, 9–10.
2. Elizabeth Edwards (Interview), c. 1865–1866, *HI*, 443.
3. William Jayne to William Henry Herndon, Aug. 17, 1887, *HI*, 624 (quote); Mary Todd to Mercy Ann Levering, July 23, 1840, *L&L*, 14–19; *L&L*, 9–14; Baker, *Mary Todd Lincoln*, 77–81.
4. Mary Todd to Mercy Ann Levering, Dec. 15, 1840, *L&L*, 21–22.
5. Mary Todd to Mercy Ann Levering, Dec. 15, 1840, *L&L*, 20–21; Neely, *Abraham Lincoln Encyclopedia*, 68.
6. Elizabeth Todd Edwards (Interview), c. 1865–1866, *HI*, 443 (quote); ML to Mercy Conkling, Nov. 19, 1864, *L&L*, 187; ML to Abram Wakeman, Sept. 23, 1864, *L&L*, 180; Arnold, *Life of Abraham Lincoln*, 72; Baker, *Mary Todd Lincoln*, 94–95; Fehrenbacher, *Recollected Words*, li; Randall, *Mary Lincoln*, 47–49.
7. Anderegg, *Lincoln and Shakespeare*, 18, 33; Winkle, *Abraham and Mary Lincoln*, 28–38.
8. AL to Joshua F. Speed, June 19, 1841, *CW*, 1:258; "Riding on a Dray" was written by Dr. E. H. Merriman. Alice Conkling (Mercy Levering Conkling's daughter), "A Story of the Early Days in Springfield, and a Poem," 144–46; Baker, *Mary Todd Lincoln*, 81–82; McDermott, *Mary Lincoln*, 41–42.
9. Elizabeth Edwards (Interview), c. 1865–1866, *HI*, 444.
10. AL Communication to the People, Mar. 9, 1832, *CW*, 1:8; *HI*, 760; Ida Tarbell, "Lincoln's Engagement to Miss Todd," *McClure's Magazine* 6 (Mar. 1896): 435–48; Temple, *Abraham Lincoln*, 127–28.
11. ML to Alexander Williamson, June 15, 1865, *HL*, 251 (quote); ML to Ozias M. Hatch, Feb. 28, 1859, *L&L*, 53; ML to Adeline Judd, June 13, 1860, *L&L*, 64–65; ML to James Gordon Bennett, Oct. 25, 1861, *L&L*, 110–11; ML to Josiah G. Holland, Dec. 4, 1865, *L&L*, 292–94; AL to ML, April 16, 1846, *CW*, 1:465–66; June 12, 1848, *CW*, 1:477; June 16, 1863, *CW*, 6:283; Aug. 8, 1863, *CW*, 6:371–72; Thomas, *Abraham Lincoln*, 303; Winkle, *Young Eagle*, 205–12.

12. ML to Mercy Ann Levering, June 1841, *L&L*, 27.
13. AL to Joshua F. Speed, Mar. 27, 1842, *CW*, 1:282–83.
14. Jan. 13–18, 1841, *Lincoln Log*; AL to John T. Stuart, Jan. 20, 1841, *CW*, 228; Jan. 23, 1841, *CW*, 229.
15. AL to Joshua F. Speed, Feb. 3, 1842, *CW*, 1:267–68; Randall, *Mary Lincoln*, 36–51, 58 (quote).
16. AL to Mary Owens, May 7, 1837, *CW*, 1:78; Randall, *Mary Lincoln*, 47–51.
17. AL to Joshua F. Speed, July 4, 1842, *CW*, 1:288–90; Oct. 5, 1842, *CW*, 302–3; Donald, *Lincoln*, 85–93; Randall, *Mary Lincoln*, 52–74; Reynolds, *Abe*, 169–70; Thomas, *Abraham Lincoln*, 81–91.
18. AL to Jesse W. Fell, Enclosing Autobiography, *CW*, 512; AL to Joshua F. Speed, July 26, 1843, *CW*, 1:328; Baker, "Managing Home," 9–10; Baker, *Mary Todd Lincoln*, 85–98; Martin H. Quitt, "New Year's Day 1841: A Puzzling Triptych," *Journal of the Abraham Lincoln Association* 39 (Winter 2018): 1–25; Randall, *Mary Lincoln*, 36–51.
19. Mary Todd to Mercy Ann Levering, Dec. 15, 1840, *L&L*, 22.
20. Mary Todd to Mercy Ann Levering, Dec. 15, 1840, *L&L*, 19; *L&L*, 16n, 52, 186; Elizabeth Todd Edwards (Interview), c. 1865–1866, *HI*, 443; Arnold, *Life of Abraham Lincoln*, 70; Baker, *Mary Todd Lincoln*, 97–98; Berry, *House of Abraham*, vi; McDermott, *Mary Lincoln*, 50–56; Reynolds, *Abe*, 196–204; Thomas, *Abraham Lincoln*, 89–91.

9. Our Friend Mrs. Browning

1. Browning, *Diary*, 1:530; Pease, "Special Introduction," Browning, *Diary*, 1:xix–xx; Nelson, "Eliza Caldwell Browning," 28, 38–40; Reynolds, *Abe*, 628; Thomas, *Abraham Lincoln*, 303.
2. Dec. 5, 1838, *Lincoln Log*; Clayton, *Illinois Fact Book*, 204–5; Nelson, "Eliza Caldwell Browning," 23–29; Pease, "Special Introduction," in Browning, *Diary*, 1:xiii; Barton, *Women Lincoln Loved*, 197.
3. Nelson, "Eliza Caldwell Browning," 23–33; Wilson, *Honor's Voice*, 131.
4. AL to Eliza Browning, Apr. 1, 1838, *CW*, 1:117–19.
5. AL to Eliza Browning, Apr. 1, 1838, *CW*, 1:119.
6. Barker, *Abraham Lincoln and Mary Owen*, 16; John George Nicolay, "The Springfield Interviews," in Burlingame, *An Oral History of Abraham Lincoln*, 4; Zall, *Lincoln on Lincoln*, 43.
7. AL to Eliza Browning, Dec. 11, 1839, *CW*, 1:156 (quote); Petition of AL and others to Eliza Browning, Dec. 11, 1839, *CW*, 1:156–57; Nelson, *Eliza Caldwell Browning*, 25, 31.
8. Pease, "Special Introduction," in Browning, *Diary*, 1:xiii.
9. AL to Orville Hickman Browning, June 24, 1847, *CW*, 1:395.

10. AL and ML to Orville Hickman Browning, Invitation, Feb. 5, 1857, *CW*, 2:388; Browning, *Diary*, 1:59, 370; Pease, "Special Introduction," in Browning, *Diary*, 1:422.
11. Eliza Browning to Ozias M. Hatch, 23 May 1860, box 1, Ozias M. Hatch Papers, ALPLM; Nelson, "Eliza Caldwell Browning," 37; Pease, "Introduction," in Browning, *Diary*, 1:xiv, xix.
12. Eliza Browning to AL, June 8, 1861, AL Papers, DLC.
13. Browning, Diary, 1:532–33, 546, 608; *L&L*, 134; Nelson, "Eliza Caldwell Browning," 28, 38–40.
14. Eliza Browning to Catharine Hickman Prewitt, Mar. 1862, Eliza Browning File, Historical Society of Quincy and Adams County, Quincy, IL.
15. ML to Orville Hickman Browning, Sept. 24, 1866, *L&L*, 391; Dec. 3, 1866, *L&L*, 397; AL to Orville Hickman Browning, Sept. 22, 1861, *CW*, 4:531–33; Apr. 18, 1861; Apr. 22, 1861; Apr. 30, 1861; Sept. 24, 1861; Nov. 8, 1861; Aug. 25, 1862; Sept. 25, 1863, all in AL Papers, DLC; *L&L*, 613; Browning, *Diary*, 1:595–96; Barton, *Women Lincoln Loved*, 197; Neely, *Abraham Lincoln Encyclopedia*, 38–39; Nelson, "Eliza Caldwell Browning," 38–41; Pease, "Special Introduction," in Browning, *Diary*, 1:xvii–xviii.
16. Pease, "Special Introduction," in Browning, *Diary*, 1:xiii.
17. *St. Louis (MO) Globe-Democrat*, Jan. 24, 1885, 7 (obituary); Browning Gravestones, Woodland Cemetery, Quincy, IL; Nelson, "Eliza Caldwell Browning," 42; Pease, "Special Introduction," in Browning, *Diary*, 1:xxx–xxxii.

10. My Lincoln Friends

1. AL to Joshua F. Speed, Feb. 25, 1842, *CW*, 1:281.
2. Episode #35 on Mary Lincoln, *The Railsplitter* (podcast) on Feb. 1, 2018, https://www.podbean.com/media/share/pb-64mci-86354a (accessed Apr. 28, 2024).
3. *The Railsplitter* (podcast), Sept. 6, 2019, https://therailsplitter.podbean.com/e/100-episode-the-hundredth/ (accessed Oct. 13, 2024).

11. She Was Mary Lincoln

1. AL to Samuel D. Marshall, Nov. 11, 1842, *CW*, 1:305.
2. ML to Emilie Todd Helm, Sept. 20, 1857, *L&L*, 50.
3. Clinton, "Wife Versus Widow," 1–19; Schroeter, "Julia Butler Newberry and Mary Todd Lincoln," 264–74.
4. Emile Todd Helm to Jessie W. Weik, c. 1887, *HI*, 694; Baker, *Mary Todd Lincoln*, 37–45; Myron Marty, "Schooling in Lincoln's America and Lincoln's Extraordinary Self-Schooling," in Fornieri, *Lincoln's America*, 56–61; McDermott, *Mary Lincoln*, 23–29; Neem, *Democracy's Schools*, 62–64, 177.

5. ML to Benjamin Brown French, July 26, 1862, *L&L*, 129–30 (quote); Emile Todd Helm to Jessie W. Weik, c. 1887, *HI*, 694; Arnold, *Life of Abraham Lincoln*, 439; Baker, "Biography as Social History," 204–7; Baker, *Mary Todd Lincoln*, 43–45; Berry, *House of Abraham*, vi–vii; Brownstein, *Lincoln's Other White House*, 79; McDermott, *Mary Lincoln*, 23–24; Reynolds, *Abe*, 749–50; Pratt, *Personal Finances*, 180–81; Runyon, *The Mentelles*, 95, 182–85.
6. ML to Mark Delahay, May 25, 1860, *L&L*, 63–64.
7. ML to Francis Bicknell Carpenter, *L&L*, 298.
8. ML to David Davis, Nov. 9, 1871, *L&L*, 597–98; Randall, *Mary Lincoln*, 423–35.
9. Baker, *Mary Todd Lincoln*, 78, 95–96, 149–50; *L&L*, 29–30, 43–44; Thomas, *Abraham Lincoln*, 152–55.
10. ML to Hannah Shearer, June 26, 1859, *L&L*, 56–57.
11. ML to Anson G. Henry, July 26, 1865, *L&L*, 264 (first quote); ML to David Davis, Sept. 12, 1865, *L&L*, 274 (second quote).
12. William Jayne to William Henry Herndon, Aug. 17, 1887, *HI*, 625.
13. ML to James Gordon Bennett, Oct. 25, 1861, *L&L*, 110–11.
14. ML to Thomas A. Scott, Oct. 3, 1861; ML to Montgomery Meigs, Oct. 4, 1861, both in *L&L*, 107.
15. ML to Charles Sumner, Apr. 10, 1866, *L&L*, 356.
16. ML to Edward Lewis Baker Jr., Apr. 11, 1877, *L&L*, 633.
17. ML to AL, Nov. 2, 1862, *L&L*, 139–40; *Evening Star* (Washington), Aug. 29, 1862 (quote); Dec. 26, 1862; *National Republican* (Washington), Aug. 27, 1862; Oct. 31, 1862; Dec. 25, 1862; Baker, 185–87; *L&L*, 145; Laura Mammina, "Southern Woman, Republican Partisan: Mary Lincoln's Wartime Identity," in Sibley, *Southern First Ladies*, 133–49; Randall, *Mary Lincoln*, 231–32, 297–98, 322–23, Winkle, *Abraham and Mary Lincoln*, 77–114.
18. Arnold, *Life of Abraham Lincoln*, 439–40; Bach, "Acts of Remembrance," 37–38; Randall, *Mary Lincoln*, 230–32; 388–89; Reynolds, *Abe*, 611–20.
19. ML to Rhoda White, May 2, 1868, *L&L*, 475–76 (quote); *L&L*, 41; AL to ML, Apr. 16, 1846, *CW*, 1:465–66; Baker, *Mary Todd Lincoln*, 129, 142; Dye, "Mother Love and Infant Death," 329–53; McGregor, *From Midwives to Medicine*, 3–7; Randall, *Mary Lincoln*, 147–49; Reynolds, *Abe*, 395.
20. Emerson, *Giant in the Shadows*, 155–68; Randall, *Mary Lincoln*, 429–35; Ross, "Mary Todd Lincoln," 5–34; Swedlund, *Shadows in the Valley*, 5–6.
21. ML to Emma Gurley, May 16, 1862, *L&L*, 126; ML to Rhoda White, May 2, 1868, *L&L*, 475; Baker, *Mary Todd Lincoln*, 129; Clinton, *Mrs. Lincoln*, 88–89, 197; McDermott, *Mary Lincoln*, 121–51; L&L, 618–20; Randall, *Mary Lincoln*, 97–101.

22. Roy P. Basler, "Paradoxical, 'Hellcatical' Mary Lincoln; Kinder Light on Much Maligned Woman," *Chicago Tribune*, Feb. 8, 1953.
23. ML to Eliza Henry, Aug. 31, 1865, *L&L*, 272.
24. ML to Jacob Bunn, March 22, 1878, *L&L*, 665; 685–86; Baker, *Mary Todd Lincoln*, 281–303; Irvine, "Mary Lincoln and Her Visit to Wisconsin's Wild Region," 2–11; Krueger, "Mary Todd Lincoln Summers in Wisconsin," 249–53; McDermott, *Mary Lincoln*, 123–51; Wayne C. Temple, "'I Am So Fond of Sightseeing': Mary Lincoln's Travels Up to 1865," in Williams, *Mary Lincoln Enigma*, 140–81.

12. Mrs. Lincoln's Household

1. AL to Joshua F. Speed, May 18, 1843, *CW*, 1:325.
2. AL to Joshua F. Speed, Jan. 18, 1843, *CW*, 1:306; May 18, 1843, *CW*, 1:325; *L&L*, 30–31; McDermott, *Mary Lincoln*, 57.
3. Baker, *Mary Todd Lincoln*, 130–36; Reynolds, *Abe*, 196–206.
4. Fehrenbacher, *Recollected Words*, 164 (quote); *L&L*, 32.
5. Family Record in AL's Bible, *CW*, 1:304; *L&L*, 31.
6. ML to Emilie Helm, Nov. 23, 1856, *L&L*, 46; Family Record in Abraham Lincoln's Bible, *CW*, 1:304; Baker, *Mary Todd Lincoln*, 116–17, 125–27; Donald, *Lincoln*, 197–98; Fleischner, *Mrs. Lincoln and Mrs. Keckley*, 149–58; *L&L*, 10; McDermott, *Mary Lincoln*, 60–62.
7. Baker, *Mary Todd Lincoln*, 110–13; Green, *Light of the Hearth*, 59.
8. Theodore Dwight, *The Father's Book* (1834); John Abbott, *The Mother at Home* (1833); Lydia Maria Child, *The Mother's Book* (1844); Catherine Beecher, *A Treatise on Domestic Economy* (1848); Arnold, *Life of Abraham Lincoln*, 82–83; Baker, "Managing Home," 1–12; Winkle, *Abraham and Mary Lincoln*, 39–76; Kenneth J. Winkle, "The Middle-Class Marriage of Abraham and Mary Lincoln," in Fornieri, *Lincoln's America*, 94–114.
9. Apr. 4–June 6, 1853, *Lincoln Log*.
10. ML to Ozias M. Hatch, Feb. 28, 1859, *L&L*, 53.
11. ML to Hannah Shearer, Oct. 2, 1859, *L&L*, 59.
12. ML to AL, Nov. 2, 1862, *L&L*, 139.
13. ML to Daniel E. Sickles, Feb. 20, 1864, *L&L*, 169.
14. AL Remarks at Ashtabula, Ohio, Feb. 16, 1861, *CW*, 4:218; AL to Joshua F. Speed, Nov. 19, 1860, *CW*, 4:141; ML to Hannah Shearer, Jan. 1, 1860, *L&L*, 61.
15. Fehrenbacher, *Recollected Words*, 124; Thomas, *Abraham Lincoln*, 90–91.
16. Brooks, *Lincoln Observed*, 83; Epstein, *Lincoln's Men*, 76; Mast, "Mary Lincoln's Séance at Soldiers' Home"; Randall, *Mary Lincoln*, 293–94; Winkle, *Abraham and Mary Lincoln*, 77–114; Winkle, *Lincoln's Citadel*, 206.

13. Let's Hear It for the Boys

1. AL to ML, July 2, 1848, *CW*, 1:496.
2. ML to Emilie Helm, Sept. 20, 1857, *L&L*, 49; ML to Hannah Shearer, Jan. 1, 1860, *L&L*, 61–62; ML to Robert Todd Lincoln, June 19, 1876, *L&L*, 616; ML to William A. Newell, Dec. 16, 1862, *L&L*, 143; Party Invitation, ML to "Little Isaac Diller" (son of a Springfield pharmacist), ALPLM; Keckley, *Behind the Scenes*, 181; Brownstein, *Lincoln's Other White House*, 75; McDermott, *Mary Lincoln*, 77–78; Wilson, *Honor's Voice*, 244.
3. AL to Joshua F. Speed, Oct. 22, 1846, *CW*, 1:391; ML to AL, May 1848, *L&L*, 36–38; ML to Emilie Helm, Sept. 20, 1857, *L&L*, 49–51; ML to Ozias M. Hatch, Feb. 28, 1859, *L&L*, 53; ML to Eliza Stuart Steel, 23 May 1871, *L&L*, 588–89; ML to David Davis, Nov. 9, 1871, *L&L*, 597–98; ML to Edward Lewis Baker Jr., June 22, 1879, *L&L*, 682; *Sangamo Journal* (Springfield, IL), May 17, 1858; Oct. 18, 1854; Interview, *Washington Chronicle*, June 18, 1865; Keckley, *Behind the Scenes*, 181; Fehrenbacher, *Recollected Words*, 415 (quote); Baker, "Managing Home," 7; Brownstein, *Lincoln's Other White House*, 75; Humphrey, "Springfield of the Lincolns," 37; Pratt, *Personal Finances*, 145, 147; Reynolds, *Abe*, 201–3, 289, 295–96, 620–29.
4. AL to John A. Dahlgren, Oct. 14, 1862, *CW*, 5:463; AL to Gideon Welles, Apr. 10, 1865, *CW*, 8:395; AL to Edwin M. Stanton, Apr. 10, 1865, *CW*, 8:395; Randall, *Lincoln's Sons*, 118–31.
5. AL to ML, Aug. 8, 1863, *CW*, 6:371–72 (quote), *CW*, 5:492n1; Randall, *Lincoln's Sons*, 125–26.
6. ML to AL, Apr. 28, 1864, *L&L*, 175; AL to ML, Apr. 28, 1864, *CW*, 7:320.
7. AL to ML, Sept. 8, 1864, *CW*, 7:544.

14. Love and Politics

1. David Davis to Sarah Davis, Aug. 15, 1847, David Davis Papers, ALPLM; Winkle, *Lincoln's Citadel*, 4–5.
2. Rosa, "Abraham Lincoln and Women," 113–18.
3. 1847–1848, *Lincoln Log*; Randall, *Mary Lincoln*, 106–9.
4. AL to ML, Apr. 16, 1846, *CW*, 1:465–66.
5. ML to AL, May 1848, *L&L*, 36–38.
6. AL to ML, June 12, 1848, *CW*, 1:477–78.
7. By April 1848, Mary and the boys were back with her family in Lexington, where they remained until their reunion in Washington in July 1848. AL to ML, July 2, 1848, *CW*, 1:495–96; July 23, 1848, *Lincoln Log*.

8. ML to Josiah G. Holland, Dec. 4, 1865, *L&L*, 293 (first quote); ML to Sally Orne, Dec. 12, 1869, *L&L*, 534 (second quote).
9. ML to William Henry Herndon, Aug. 28, 1866, *L&L*, 384 (quote); ML Todd to Mercy Levering, July 23, 1840, *L&L*, 18; AL to Samuel D. Marshall, Nov. 11, 1842, *CW*, 1:304–5; AL to ML, Apr. 16, 1848, *CW*, 1:45–66; June 12, 1848, *CW*, 1:477–78; July 2, 1848, *CW*, 1:495–96; Winkle, *Abraham and Mary Lincoln*; Shenk, *Lincoln's Melancholy*, 100–103.
10. Donald, *Lincoln*, 250–51.
11. *Chicago Tribune*, May 22, 1860; *The Buffalo Commercial*, May 23, 1860; *New-York Tribune*, May 25, 1860; *Richmond (IN) Weekly Palladium*, June 7, 1860; Arnold, *Life of Abraham Lincoln*, 169 (quote).
12. James A. Briggs to AL, May 25, 1860, AL Papers, DLC; AL to ML, Mar. 4, 1860, *CW*, 3:555.
13. ML to Hannah Shearer, Oct. 20, 1860, *L&L*, 66.
14. Fehrenbacher, *Recollected Words*, 27; Hay, *Inside Lincoln's White House*, 244; Randall, *Mary Lincoln*, 179–86; Reynolds, *Abe*, 502.
15. John T. Stuart (Interview), late-June 1865, *HI*, 63; Donald, *Lincoln*, 311–13; McDermott, *Mary Lincoln*, 63–64; Reynolds, *Abe*, 194 (quote), 203–4, 393–94.
16. ML to Alexander Williamson, July 5, 1866, *L&L*, 376; Brooks, *Lincoln Observed*, 83; Stimmel, *Personal Reminiscences of Abraham Lincoln*, 181 (quote); Epstein, *Lincoln's Men*, 76; French, *Witness to the Young Republic*, 375; Laas, "Elizabeth Blair Lee," 387–90; Reynolds, *Abe*, 407, 601–8, 617–18; Winkle, *Lincoln's Citadel*, 206.
17. ML to Mercy Ann Levering, Dec. 15, 1840, *L&L*, 21; ML to David Davis, Jan. 17, 1861, *L&L*, 71–72; Randall, *Mary Lincoln*, 243; Kenneth J. Winkle, "'An Unladylike Profession': Mary Lincoln's Preparation for Greatness," in Williams, *Mary Lincoln Enigma*, 82–111.
18. ML to Simon Cameron, Mar. 29, 1861, *L&L*, 83; Baker, *Mary Todd Lincoln*, 135, 197; Brownstein, *Lincoln's Other White House*, 216–17; Stahr, *Stanton*, 359, 422.
19. Fehrenbacher, *Recollected Words*, 275; Keckley, *Behind the Scenes*, 275.
20. ML to William H. Seward, Mar. 22, 1861, *L&L*, 81; ML to Simon Cameron, Mar. 29, 1861, *L&L*, 83; Sept. 12, 1861, *L&L*, 103; ML to Mary Brayman, June 17, 1861, *L&L*, 90; ML to Montgomery Meigs, Oct. 4, 1861, *L&L*, 107; ML to AL, Nov. 3, 1862, *L&L*, 140–41; ML to Edwin M. Stanton, Feb. 11, 1863, *L&L*, 146; Nov. 9, 1864, *L&L*, 182; Baker, "Biography as Social History," 212.
21. Reynolds, *Abe*, 606.

22. Baker, *Mary Todd Lincoln*, 200–207, 234–35; *L&L*, 165–66; Reynolds, *Abe*, 598–608.
23. ML to Hannah Shearer, Oct. 6, 1861, *L&L*, 108–9; ML to AL, Nov. 2, 1862, *L&L*, 139–40.
24. Keckley, *Behind the Scenes*, 56–57; ML to James Gordon Bennett, Oct. 4, 1862, *L&L*, 138.
25. *L&L*, 84; Baker, *Mary Todd Lincoln*, 187–92; Reynolds, *Abe*, 393, 611–17.
26. Baker, *Mary Todd Lincoln*, 189–91; Reynolds, *Abe*, 611–12.
27. ML to Ruth Harris, May 17, 1862, *L&L*, 125.
28. Baker, *Mary Todd Lincoln*, 196; Reynolds, *Abe*, 617.
29. Apr. 14, 1865, *Lincoln Log*; ML to Francis Bicknell Carpenter, Nov. 15, 1865, *L&L*, 284; Reynolds, *Abe*, 885–920.
30. ML to Francis Bicknell Carpenter, Nov. 15, 1865, *L&L*, 284–85.
31. Reynolds, *Abe*, 90–114; Thomas, *Abraham Lincoln*, 518–22.
32. ML to Charles Sumner, May 9, 1865, *L&L*, 228; Arnold, *Life of Abraham Lincoln*, 432–39; Hodes, *Mourning Lincoln*, 206–7; *L&L*, 223; Randall, *Lincoln's Sons*, 163–64.

15. Finding Forgotten Women

1. Tazewell County Circuit Court, Judge's Docket, May 1840–Apr. 1846, Tazewell County Courthouse, Pekin, IL; *Illinois State Register* (Springfield), June 7, 1844; Tazewell County (IL) Courthouse, National Register of Historic Places Inventory and Nomination Form, Aug. 8, 1985, National Park Service, U.S. Dept. of the Interior, Washington; *LPAL*.
2. May 15–16, 1832, *Lincoln Log*; AL, Muster Roll of Lincoln's Company, May 27, 1832, *CW*, 1:10–13; AL, Speech in the U.S. House of Representatives, July 27, 1848, *CW*, 1:509; 1860 U.S. Census; Isaac Perkins Gravestone, Stillman's Run Battlefield Memorial, Stillman Valley, IL; *Vandalia Whig and Illinois Intelligencer*, May 30, 1832; *Pekin (IL) Daily Times*, Aug. 7, 2013; *History of Tazewell County*, 205, 617; Clayton, *Illinois Fact Book*, 199; Jung, *The Black Hawk War of 1832*, 88–92; Olar, "The Life and Death of Major Isaac Perkins."
3. Illinois Statewide Marriage Index, Illinois State Archives, Springfield; Injunction, Aug. 21, 1845, *Dobbs v. Dobbs*, *LPAL*.
4. *Dobbs v. Dobbs*, case file, box 76, Tazewell County Circuit Court, Tazewell County Courthouse, Pekin, IL; *Dobbs v. Dobbs*, Decrees, Apr. 10, 1845, Apr. 16, 1845, Sept. 4, 1845, Sept. 5, 1845, Sept. 9, 1845, all in General Record D, 402–3, 496, 507, 523, 614; Decree, Apr. 14, 1846, General Record E, 64–5, all in Tazewell County Circuit Court, Tazewell County Courthouse, Pekin, IL; *LPAL*.

5. Jane Perkins, 1860 U.S. Census; *The Gardner (KS) Gazette*, July 26, 1907.
6. McDermott, "Dissolving the Bonds Matrimony," 71–97.

16. Polly Rogers and Her Husband's Lawyer

1. Marriage License, Sept. 25, 1835, Sangamon County Records, Illinois Regional Archives Depository, University of Illinois Springfield; Illinois Public Domain Land Tract Sales, Menard County, 68:29–202, passim, 69:23, Illinois State Archives, Springfield, IL; 1850 and 1860 U.S. Federal Censuses; Basch, "Invisible Women," 346–66; McDermott, "Dissolving the Bonds Matrimony," 91–93; *PAL*, 1:41n1.
2. Public Notice, Nov. 2, 1835, *Rogers v. Rogers*, *LPAL*; Illinois Statewide Marriage Index, Illinois State Archives, Springfield; *Laws of the State of Illinois* (1819), 35–37; Revised Code of Illinois Laws (1827), 180–83; *Rogers v. Rogers*, case study in *PAL*, 1:41–48; Basch, *Framing American Divorce*, 51; Cott, *Public Vows*, 47–53; McDermott, "Dissolving the Bonds of Matrimony," 91–97.
3. *Rogers v. Rogers*, *LPAL*: Duff, *A. Lincoln*, 36.
4. Revised *Code of Laws of Illinois* (1827), 180–81.
5. *Rogers v. Rogers*, *LPAL*.
6. Illinois Statewide Marriage Index, Illinois State Archives, Springfield; *Rogers v. Rogers*, *LPAL*; McDermott, *Jury in Lincoln's America*, 113–15.
7. McDermott, "Dissolving the Bonds of Matrimony," 94–96.

17. Melissa Goings Goes Missing

1. 1850 U.S. Federal Census; *People v. Goings*; East, "Melissa Goings," 79–83; *Peoria (IL) Journal Star*, May 15, 2015.
2. Dekle Sr., *Prairie Defender*, 133–40; Duff, *A. Lincoln*, 347–50; McDermott, *Jury in Lincoln's America*, 84–117.
3. Maryland Marriages, 1667–1899, *Ancestry.com*; 1840, 1850 U.S. Federal Census; Armstrong Goings Gravestone, Clay City Cemetery, Clay City, IL; Josephus Goings Gravestone, Minden Cemetery, Minden, NE; Benjamin Goings Gravestone, Elmore Cemetery, Flournoy, CA.
4. Testimony of James Brady, Apr. 24, 1857; Testimony of Josephus Goings, Apr. 21, 1857, *People v. Goings*, *LPAL*; East, "Melissa Goings," 81–82.
5. Inquest Jury Verdict, Apr. 21, 1857, *People v. Goings*, *LPAL*.
6. *People v. Goings*, *LPAL*.
7. Indictment, Oct. 8, 1857, *People v. Goings*, *LPAL*.
8. Order, Oct. 10, 1857, *People v. Goings*, *LPAL*.
9. *A Compilation of the Statutes of the State of Illinois*, 2 vols. (1856), 1:362; Oct. 4, 1858, *Lincoln Log*; *Illinois State Journal* (Springfield), Sept. 2, 1858; *People v. Goings*, *LPAL*; East, "Melissa Goings," 82; *CW*, 8:456.

10. Address of William L. Elwood, June 1921, Chancery Record Y, 336–43, Woodford County Circuit Court, Eureka, IL; East, "Melissa Goings," 83.
11. Hay, *Inside Lincoln's White House*, 64.
12. Reynolds, *Abe*, 152.
13. Davis, *Lincoln's Men*, 112.
14. 1860 U.S. Federal Census; Goings Burial Record, Benicia, CA.

18. The Law and the New Salem Women

1. Apr. 18, 1831, *Lincoln Log*; *Green v. Abell*, Menard County Circuit Court, Nov. 1845, *LPAL*; Abner Y. Ellis (Statement), Jan. 1866, *HL*, 171; George U. Miles to William Henry Herndon, Mar. 23, 1866, *HL*, 237; John Bennett to William Henry Herndon, Aug. 3, 1866, *HL*, 263; Johnson Gaines Greene (Interview), Oct. 5, 1866, *HI*, 366; Thomas, *Lincoln's New Salem*, 121, 127–28, 142; Thomas, *Lincoln's Old Friends*, 46, 79, 99–100, 111–12.
2. *Green v. Abell*, Menard County Circuit Court, Nov. 1845, *LPAL*; Nov. 3–6, 1845, *Lincoln Log*.
3. Hannah Armstrong (Interview), c. 1866, *HI*, 526; *People v. Armstrong*, *LPAL*; *PAL*, 4:1–48; Donald, *Lincoln*, 150–51; Duff, *A. Lincoln*, 350–59; Reynolds, *Abe*, 250–57; Thomas, *Abraham Lincoln*, 159–60; Thomas, *Lincoln's New Salem*, 142; Stowell, "Murder at a Methodist Camp Meeting," 219–34.
4. The women included in Neely's encyclopedia are Grace Bedell, Anna Ella Carroll, Mary Lincoln, Elizabeth Todd Grimsley, Emilie Todd Helm, Elizabeth Keckley, Nancy Lincoln, Sarah Johnston Lincoln, Mary Owens, Ann Rutledge, Mary Surratt, and Ida Tarbell. Neely, *Abraham Lincoln Encyclopedia*, 22–302, passim; Duff, *A. Lincoln*; Fraker, *Lincoln's Ladder*; Frank, *Lincoln as a Lawyer.*
5. Basch, *Framing American Divorce*; Basch, "Invisible Women," 346–66; Robert L. Griswold, "Law Sex, Cruelty, and Divorce in Victorian America, 1840–1900" in Hawes, *Family and Society in American*, 145–72.
6. AL to John Tillson, Feb. 15, 1850, *CW*, 2:73; AL Conducted Research for Stout, *LPAL*; AL to Joseph Gillespie, Mar. 29, 1850, *CW*, 8:592; *Matheny v. Welles et al.*, Mar. 1855; *Welles et al. v. Hofferkemp et al.*, Mar. 1855; *Welles et al. v. Welles et al.*, Mar. 1855; *Mahoney v. Welles et al.*, Mar. 1856; *Welles v. Welles*, Apr. 1857; *Thompson et al. v. Welles and Welles*, Apr. 1858, all in *LPAL*; *Welles et al. v. Welles et al.*, *Matheny v. Welles et al.*, *Welles et al. v. Hofferkemp et al.*, *PAL*, 3:44–64, 46n10, 49n20; AL Sold Land as Agent for Maria Bullock (1788–1861), *LPAL*; *Bullock v. Viney*, Apr. 1859, *LPAL*; *PAL*, 4:113–36; AL to Maria L. Bullock, Aug. 31, 1855, *CW*, 2:323; AL to Maria L. Bullock, Jan. 3, 1859, *CW*, 3:348.
7. Hannah Armstrong (Interview), c. 1866, *HI*, 526.

20. The Woman's President

1. Memorandum: Appointment of Gabriel R. Paul, Aug. 23, 1862, *CW*, 5:390–91; 1870 and 1880 U.S. Federal Censuses; Ohio, U.S. County Marriage Records, 1774–1993; *Courier-Journal* (Louisville), June 16, 1849; Eicher, *Civil War High Commands*, 149; Hoptak, "'Great in Heart and Mighty in Valor.'"
2. *CW*, 5:391n1; Eicher, *Civil War High Commands*, 149; Nofi, *Civil War Treasury*, 381.
3. AL to William H. Seward, Mar. 1861, *CW*, 8:426; Sarah Ellen Walworth, May 16, 1861, Recommendations for Office, Applications and Recommendations for Public Office, 1797–1901, National Archives, College Park, MD; Sarah Ellen Walworth to AL, Dec. 6, 1860, Jan. 7, 1864, Dec. 15, 1864, all in AL Papers, DLC; AL to William H. Seward, Mar. 1861, *CW*, 8:426, 426n1; Kashatus, *Abraham Lincoln*, 70 (quote); Mabee, "Sojourner Truth and President Lincoln," 521.
4. Livermore, *My Story of the War*, 575.
5. AL to Mary Motley, May 17, 1862, *CW*, 5:220–21.
6. *National Republican* (Washington), Feb. 10, 1864; Ida M. Tarbell, "Lincoln's Great Victory in 1864," *McClure's Magazine* 13 (July 1899): 269; Baker, *Mary Todd Lincoln*, 197–99; Epstein, *Lincoln's Men*, 76; Winkle, *Lincoln's Citadel*, 206.
7. AL to the Editor of *Sangamo Journal*, June 13, 1836, *CW*, 1:48; Address before the Young Men's Lyceum of Springfield, Illinois, Jan. 27, 1838, *CW*, 1:112; Temperance Address, Feb. 22, 1842, *CW*, 1:272; Remarks at Bloomington, IL, Nov. 21, 1860, *CW*, 4:143–44; Second Speech at Frederick, MD, Oct. 4, 1862, *CW*, 5:450; *Illinois State Journal* (Springfield), Jan. 1, 1857; Helen Ruth Reed, "A Prophecy Lincoln Made," *Boston Herald*, Feb. 9. 1930; Baker, "The Domestication of Politics," 622; Burton, *Age of Lincoln*, 111; Fehrenbacher, *Recollected Words*, 244; Kerber, *No Constitutional Right to Be Ladies*, 3–123.
8. AL to Mary Owens, Aug. 16, 1837, *CW*, 1:94–95; Fehrenbacher, *Recollected Words*, 111; Holzer, *Dear Mr. Lincoln*, 32–33; Hooper, *Lincoln's Generals' Wives*, 1–14; *L&L*, 137.
9. AL to Jessie Benton Frémont, Sept. 10. 1861, *CW*, 4:515; Sept. 12, 1861, *CW*, 4:519; Jessie Benton Frémont to AL, June 10, 1861; Sept. 12, 1861, both in AL Papers, DLC; *ANB*; Hooper, *Lincoln's General's Wives*, 16–78; Massey, *Bonnet Brigades*, 167; Nicolay, *Personal Traits*, 271–72 (quote); Reynolds, *Abe*, 389–94; Venet, *Neither Ballots nor Bullets*, 35; White, *Visits with Lincoln*, 1–22.
10. Mary Buckley to AL, October 1861, Lincoln Papers, DLC; 1860 U.S. Federal Census.

11. Herr, *Letters of Jessie Benton Frémont*, 549 (quote); Pryor, *Six Encounters with Lincoln*, 213–67; Winkle, *Lincoln's Citadel*, 112.
12. *Ladies' Home Journal*, 35 (Feb. 1918): 8; Schwartz, "Picturing Lincoln," 150–53, 166–69.

21. The Wants and Worries of Women

1. New York, U.S., Death Newspaper Extracts, 1801–1890 (Barber Collection); *Brooklyn (NY) Eagle*, Aug. 8, 1864.
2. Gravestones, Green-Wood Cemetery, Brooklyn, NY; Ann Liborius, New York, U.S. Death Newspaper Extracts, 1801–1890 (Barber Collection); *Brooklyn (NY) Eagle*, Jan. 29, 1866; Cornelia Liborius, Burial Record, Green-Wood Cemetery, Brooklyn, NY; *Brooklyn (NY) Eagle*, Nov. 17, 1882; 1850 and 1860 U.S. Federal Censuses; Faust, *This Republic of Suffering*, 61–101; Pryor, *Six Encounters with Lincoln*, Reynolds, *Abe*, 187–88.
3. AL to John F. Lee, Dec. 21, 1861, *CW*, 5:78; AL to Edward Bates, Apr. 20, 1863, *CW*, 6:180; AL to Edwin M. Stanton, Sept. 2, 1863, *CW*, 6:429; Sept. 7, 1863, *CW*, 6:436; Oct. 9, 1863, *CW*, 6:507; AL to William S. Rosecrans, Apr. 23, 1864, *CW*, 7:310–11; Hannah Armstrong to AL, May 19, 1864, AL Papers, DLC; AL to Gideon Welles, July 22, 1864, *CW*, 7:456; Faust, *This Republic of Suffering*, xi–xviii; Livermore, *My Story of the War*, 114–16; Massey, *Bonnet Brigades*, 69–70.
4. Livermore, *My Story of the War*, 574.
5. Sarah J. Hale to AL, Sept. 9, 1863, AL Papers, DLC; AL's Proclamation of Thanksgiving, Oct. 3, 1863, *CW*, 6:497; Donald, *Lincoln*, 471; Kaplan, "Manifest Domesticity," 592–93; Pleck, "The Making of the Domestic Occasion," 775–77; Reynolds, *Abe*, 726–29.
6. Jan. 16, 1864, *Lincoln Log*; *Evening Star* (Washington), Jan. 16, 1864; *National Republican* (Washington), Jan. 18, 1864.
7. *National Republican* (Washington), Jan. 18, 1864.
8. AL to Caleb B. Smith, May 31, 1861, *CW*, 4:391; ML to Caleb B. Smith, May 31, 1861, *L&L*, 87; AL to William P. Fessenden, July 21, 1864, *CW*, 7:454; *ANB*.
9. AL Memorandum: Advice to Adèle Douglas, Nov. 27, 1861, *CW*, 5:32.
10. Mary S. Duncan to AL, Nov. 2, 1861, RG 96, Entry 12, NARA.
11. AL to Seth Williams, Jan. 8, 1862, *CW*, 5:93, 93–94n1.
12. *CW*, 7:296n1.
13. AL to Whom It May Concern, Apr. 11, 1864, *CW*, 7:295–96.
14. Pryor, *Six Encounters with Lincoln*, 250–59; White, *Visits with Lincoln*, xiii.
15. AL Endorsement, Jan. 3, 1863, *CW*, 6:35; List of Army Promotions, c. July 1861, *CW*, 4:418; AL to Simon Cameron, Nov. 13, 1861, *CW*, 5:22; Pass for

Annie Wittenmeyer, July 25, 1862, *CW*, 8:54–55; AL to Edwin M. Stanton, Jan. 12, 1863, *CW*, 6:55; AL Endorsement, Mar. 19, 1863, *CW*, 6:128; AL to Hannah Armstrong, Sept. 18, 1863, *CW*, 6:462; Pass for Mrs. Samuel P. Hamilton, Feb. 14, 1864, *CW*, 7:184; Pass for Annie P. Shepherd, June 30, 1864, *CW*, 7:419–20; Pass for Mrs. Adams, Sept. 8, 1864, *CW*, 7:540; Pass for Mrs. Defoe, Sept. 26, 1864, *CW*, 8:24; Pass for Mrs. Read, Oct. 21, 1864, *CW*, 8:57; Pass for Mary A. Stevens, Nov. 14, 1864, *CW*, 8:108; Mary Buckley to AL, January 28, 1865, RG 94, Entry 519, NARA; Pass for Daughter of Judge Young, Feb. 18, 1865, *CW*, 8:307; Pass for Elizabeth Gaugan and Daughter, c. Feb. 1865, *CW*, 8:578; June 19, 1864, *Lincoln Log*.

16. Conroy, "Slavery's Mark on Lincoln's White House"; Keckley, *Behind the Scenes*, 58; Miller, *President's Kitchen Cabinet*, 83–97; Washington, *They Knew Lincoln*, 84–88.
17. Oct. 29, 1864, *Lincoln Log*; White, *Visits with Lincoln*, 120–21.
18. *National Anti-Slavery Standard* (New York), Dec. 17, 1864; *The Liberator* (Boston), Dec. 23, 1864; Donald, *Lincoln*, 541; Glymph, "'Invisible Disabilities,'" 237–39.
19. Cox, *Lincoln and Black Freedom*, 30–35; Mabee, "Sojourner Truth and President Lincoln," 519–29; Painter, *Sojourner Truth*, 203–7; Reynolds, *Abe*, 821–28; White, *House Built by Slaves*, xviii–xx, 145–47; White, *Visits with Lincoln*, 113–27.

22. Sanitary Fairs and the Ministrations of Angels

1. Mar. 18, 1864, *Lincoln Log*; *Evening Star* (Washington), Mar. 19, 1864; *National Republican* (Washington), Feb. 23, 1864; Mar. 18, 1864; *Washington Chronicle*, Mar. 19, 1864; Stereo Card, 1864, National Portrait Gallery, Smithsonian Institution, Washington; Kramer, "Lincoln at the Fair," 341–42; Robertson, "The Union's 'Other Army.'"
2. AL, Remarks at Closing of Sanitary Fair, Mar. 18, 1864, *CW*, 7:253–54.
3. Winkle, *Lincoln's Citadel*, 223–24.
4. Baker, "The Domestication of Politics," 636; Gallman, *Defining Duty in Civil War*, 188–222; Kristie Ross, "Arranging a Doll's House: Refined Women as Union Nurses," in Clinton, *Divided Houses*, 97–113; Winkle, *Lincoln's Citadel*, 223–24.
5. AL to Edward Everett, Nov. 20, 1863, *CW*, 7:24; Edward Everett to AL, Nov. 20, 1863; Jan. 30, 1864, both in AL Papers, DLC; Kashatus, *Abraham Lincoln*, 70; Reynolds, *Abe*, 836–84.
6. *Address of Hon. Edward Everett*, 59–60.
7. AL to Dorothea L. Dix, Feb. 19, 1862, Emory University, Atlanta; Feb. 7–19, 1862, *Lincoln Log*.

8. AL to Dorothea L. Dix, May 4, 1862, *CW*, 10:132; Holst, "One of the Best Women I Ever Knew," 12–17.
9. George Pomeroy was appointed second lieutenant of the Third Infantry on July 17, 1862. AL to Edwin M. Stanton, July 15, 1862, *CW*, 5:326–27, 627n1.
10. July 3, 1863, *Lincoln Log*; Boyden, *Echoes from Hospital and White House*, 246 (quote); Holst, "One of the Best Women I Ever Knew," 14–19.
11. 1870 U.S. Federal Census; Boyden, *Echoes from the Hospital and the White House*, 246–49; Foard, "Nurse Pomeroy," 52–57.
12. AL to Edwin M. Stanton, Oct. 15, 1863, *CW*, 6:516.
13. Order Concerning Mrs. Annie Wittenmyer, Oct. 20, 1864, *CW*, 8:54; AL to Emma Egbert, Jan. 1, 1865, *CW*, 8:204; AL to Edwin M. Stanton (regarding Hobart), Nov. 10, 1864, *CW*, 8:102–3; *CW*, 8:204–5n1 (regarding Egbert).
14. Mary Livermore to AL, Oct. 11, 1863, AL Papers, DLC; Jane Hoge to AL, Nov. 24, 1862; AL to Jane Hoge, Nov. 25, 1862, Jane Hoge and Mary Livermore to AL, Oct. 21, 1863, all in AL Papers, DLC; Hoge and Livermore in *ANB*.
15. AL to Ladies in Charge of Northwestern Fair, Oct. 26, 1863, *CW*, 6:539–40; *CW*, 6:30–31n1; AL to James H. Hoes, Dec. 17, 1863, *CW*, 7:75; Livermore, *My Story of the War*, 429–30, 563–65; *Chicago Tribune*, Nov. 17, 1863; *Illinois State Journal* (Springfield), Dec. 1863; Oct. 31, 1864; Hoge and Livermore, *ANB*.

    After the war, the Soldiers' Home gave Lincoln's Emancipation Proclamation to the Chicago Historical Society, where it was on display in October 1871 when the society was destroyed in the Great Chicago Fire. *CW*, 7:75n1.
16. Livermore, *ANB*; Livermore, *My Story of the War*, 129, 563–64; Giesburg, *Civil War Sisterhood*; Madway, "Purveying Patriotic Pageantry," 268–301; Newman, "All's Fair," 56–65; Thompson, "Sanitary Fairs of the Civil War," 51–67.
17. AL to Esther Stockton, Jan. 8, 1864, *CW*, 7:117.

23. A Lady Clerk and Abraham Lincoln

1. Massey, *Bonnet Brigades*, 113, 132–33; Burton, *Age of Lincoln*, 222; Schultz, *Women at the Front*, 62.
2. AL to Heads of Departments and Bureaus, Sept. 4, 1861, *CW*, 4:508, 509n1.
3. Mary Ann Curry to AL, Mar. 26, 1862; AL Endorsement on Envelope of Mary Ann Curry to AL, Mar. 26, 1862, both in RG 56, Entry 210, NARA.
4. For federal jobs: Jane Munsell to AL, Nov. 12, 1861, RG 56, Entry 210, NARA; AL to James F. Simmons, May 21, 1862, *CW*, 5:228; AL to Salmon

P. Chase, Aug. 18, 1863, *CW*, 6:397; AL to Unknown, Jan. 4, 1864, *CW*, 7:108; AL Endorsement for Miss Gilbert, May 21, 1864; *CW*, 7:355; AL to William Dennison, Feb. 6, 1865, *CW*, 8:261. For postmasters: Nomination of Caroline E. Bibighaus, Mar. 6, 1862, RG 46, Entry 550; Appointment of Bushnell, Feb. 28, 1865; Appointment of Caroline L. Cowan, Mar. 11, 1863, both in RG 59, Entry 791; Nomination of Mary Jane Frey, Feb. 1862, RG 46, Entry 791; Nomination of Louisa Jonas, June 13, 1864, RG 46, Entry 568, all in NARA; Blevins, "Women and Federal Officeholding in the Late Nineteenth Century."

5. AL to Montgomery Blair, July 24, 1863, *CW*, 6:346.
6. An article from the *St. Louis Republican*, reported in *The Rock Island (IL) Argus*, May 20, 1864; Sizer, *Political Work of Northern Women Writers*, 77–84.
7. AL to Montgomery Blair, Mar. 21, 1864, *CW*, 7:257–58; William Dugger Burial Record; Hannah Dugger Gravestone, both in Dugger Cemetery, Carlinville, IL; 1850 and 1860 U.S. Federal Censuses; Charles A. Walker, ed., *History of Macoupin County, Illinois*, 2 vols. (Chicago: S. J. Clark Publishing, 1911), 1:419; Illinois Civil War Muster and Descriptive Rolls, Illinois State Archives, Springfield; *Chicago Tribune*, Apr. 4, 1911.
8. *Register of Officers and Agents, Civil, Military, and Naval, in the Service of the United States* (1871), 47; 1870, U.S. Federal Census; Burial Records, Glenwood Cemetery, Washington; *Evening Star* (Washington), Apr. 5, 1886; *The Times-Picayune* (New Orleans), Apr. 23, 1886; *New York Times*, May 2, 1886; Schnell, "Two Lincolns," 4–5.
9. 1880, 1900, and 1910 U.S. Federal Censuses; *Official Register of the United States Containing a List of Officers and Employees in the Civil, Military, and Naval Service* (1897), 1:77; (1903), 1:75; (1905), 1:73; *The Critic* (Washington), May 29, 1886; *Washington Post*, Sept. 2, 1908; Apr. 6, 1911; *Inter Ocean* (Chicago), Apr. 4, 1911.
10. *Washington Post*, Apr. 6, 1911; *Inter Ocean* (Chicago), Apr. 4, 1911 (quote); *Register of Officers and Agents, Civil, Military, and Naval, in the Service of the United States* (1871), 47; 1870, 1880, 1900, and 1910 U.S. Federal Censuses; Burial Records, Glenwood Cemetery, Washington; *Evening Star* (Washington), Apr. 5, 1886; *Washington Post*, Sept. 2, 1908; Schnell, "Two Lincolns," 4–5.

24. Socks and Gratitude

1. AL to Susannah Weathers, Dec. 4, 1861, *CW*, 5:557; Susannah Weathers Burial Record, Mount Hope Cemetery, Rossville, IN; Jesse Weathers (husband) Gravestone, Smith Cemetery, Rensselaer, IN; 1860 U.S. Federal Census.

2. Dec. 4, 1861, *Lincoln Log*.
3. AL to Susannah Weathers, Dec. 4, 1861, *CW*, 5:57.
4. AL to Eliza A. Hamilton, Oct. 29, 1860, *CW*, 4:134, 134n1; Mary Hancock Colyer to AL, Mar. 22, 1861, Lincoln Papers, DLC; AL to Mary Hancock Colyer, Apr. 2, 1861, *CW*, 4:319; Orville Hickman Browning to AL, Aug. 11, 1862, AL Papers, DLC; Holzer, "'Tokens of Respect' and 'Heartfelt Thanks,'" 177–92.
5. Libbie S. Bailey to AL, Oct. 30, 1860, AL Papers, DLC.
6. AL to Eliza P. Gurney, Sept. 4, 1864, *CW*, 7:535; Eliza P. Gurney to AL, Oct. 8, 1864, AL Papers, DLC; Oct. 26, 1862, *Lincoln Log*; *ANB*.
7. AL to Mrs. M. J. Green, Sept. 22, 1860, *CW*, 4:118; AL to LuLu Waldron, Apr. 27, 1862, *CW*, 5:200, *CW*, 5:200n1.

25. The Widow and Oak Ridge Cemetery

1. Hill, "Transformation of the Lincoln Tomb," 39–56; *L&L*, 235.
2. Lincoln National Monument Association, Apr. 25, 1865, flyer, Alfred Whital Stern Collection of Lincolniana, DLC; ML to Hannah Shearer, Apr. 24, 1859, *L&L*, 55; Baker, *Mary Todd Lincoln*, 251–52; *L&L*, 10–11, 240–41; Randall, *Mary Lincoln*, 387–87.
3. The Mather Block was located on the site of the present Illinois State Capitol, a few blocks southwest of the Old State Capitol square. ML to Richard J. Oglesby, June 5, 1865, *L&L*, 241–42.
4. *Illinois State Journal* (Springfield), June 14, 1865; Arnold, *Life of Abraham Lincoln*, 435–36, 435n1; Fehrenbacher, *Recollected Words*, 431; *L&L*, 240, 241n9; Prichard, "'Home Is the Martyr,'" 14–42.
5. ML to Richard J. Oglesby, June 10, 1865, *L&L*, 244.
6. ML to Richard J. Oglesby, June 11, 1856; *Chicago Tribune*, June 16, 1865; *L&L*, 245.
7. Bach, "Acts of Remembrance," 25–28.
8. Lincoln National Monument Association, Apr. 25, 1865, flyer, Alfred Whital Stern Collection of Lincolniana, DLC; Bach, "Acts of Remembrance," 49.
9. AL, Annual Message to Congress, Dec. 1, 1862, *CW*, 5:537.

26. Vinnie Ream's Abraham Lincoln

1. Lemp, "Vinnie Ream and Abraham Lincoln," 24–29.
2. Cooper, *Vinnie Ream*, 1–3; Giesberg, *Army at Home*, 68–91; Massey, *Women in the Civil War*, 132–34.
3. Cooper, *Vinnie Ream*, 7; Dabakis, "Sculpting Lincoln," 84, 99n12; Hoxie, *Vinnie Ream*, 59 (quote).

4. Dabakis, "Sculpting Lincoln," 79–90; Lemp, "Vinnie Ream and Abraham Lincoln," 24; Hoxie, *Vinnie Ream*, 1.
5. *Daily Milwaukee News*, Aug. 14, 1866; Dec. 18, 1866; *Chicago Tribune*, Aug. 21, 1866; *Wilmington (NC) Daily Dispatch*, Aug. 18, 1866; *Brooklyn (NY) Eagle*, Dec. 27, 1866; *Courier-Journal* (Louisville), Aug. 17, 1866; *Glasgow (Scotland) Herald*, Apr. 10, 1868; *Brooklyn (NY) Union*, July 15, 1868; *New York Daily Herald*, Feb. 5, 1869; *Indianapolis News*, Aug. 10, 1870; *Pittsburgh Post*, June 18, 1870; Lemp, "Vinnie Ream," 25–29.
6. Hoxie, *Vinnie Ream*, 23 (quote); "Unveiling the Statue of the Late President Lincoln," flyer, Jan. 25, 1871, reprinted in Hoxie, *Vinnie Ream*, 17; *Evening Star* (Washington), Jan. 7, 1871.
7. *Evening Star* (Washington), Sept. 2, 1871; Dabakis, "Sculpting Lincoln," 90–92; Lemp, "Vinnie Ream," 24–29.
8. Address of Lyman Trumbull, Jan. 25, 1871, Hoxie, *Vinnie Ream*, 20.
9. Hoxie, *Vinnie Ream*, 59–61.
10. Tomso, "Lincoln's 'Unfathomable Sorrow,'" 1–12.
11. ML to Charles Sumner, Sept. 10, 1866, *L&L*, 387; ML to Alphonso Dunn, Mar. 18, 1867, Apr. 2, 1867, *L&L*, 418; Emerson, *Giant in the Shadows*, 280.
12. Jane Addams, Address at the Presentation Ceremony of the Monument to Lucretia Mott, Elizabeth Cady Stanton, and Susan B. Anthony, Feb. 15, 1921, *Jane Addams Digital Edition*, Ramapo College of New Jersey, Mahwah, http://digital.janeaddams.ramapo.edu/items/show/11064 (accessed Oct. 13, 2024).

27. Ida Tarbell's Lincoln

1. Tarbell, *All in a Day's Work*, 161–62; Brady, *Ida Tarbell*, 9, 31–37, 90–94; Rice, "Ida M. Tarbell," 57–72.
2. Tarbell, *All in a Day's Work*, 162–65
3. Tarbell, *All in a Day's Work*, 161–62.
4. Tarbell, *All in a Day's Work*, 164–67; Brady, *Ida Tarbell*, 95–102; Emerson, *Giant in the Shadows*, 276.
5. Ida Tarbell, "Abraham Lincoln," 6 (Jan. 1896): 214.
6. Tarbell, *All in a Day's Work*, 161–65; "The McClure's Life of Abraham Lincoln," *McClure's Magazine* 5 (Oct. 1895): 480; "Abraham Lincoln," *McClure's Magazine* 5 (Nov. 1895): 483–512.
7. *Chicago Tribune*, Nov. 1, 1895.
8. Nicolay, *ANB*.
9. "Miss Tarbell's Life of Lincoln," Letters and Comments, *McClure's Magazine* 6 (Jan. 1896): 206–8.

10. AL to John T. Stuart, Dec. 23, 1839, *CW*, 1:59; AL to John T. Stuart, Mar. 30, 1861, Tarbell, *Life of Lincoln*, 4:136; *CW*, 4:303; Emerson, *Giant in the Shadows*, 276.

    Tarbell's full series on the "The Early Life of Abraham Lincoln" ran in *McClure's Magazine* monthly from November 1895 through November 1896. Her second series on Lincoln's the later life appeared in *McClure's Magazine* from December 1898 through September 1899.
11. *Chicago Tribune*, Feb. 10, 1900; *New York Times*, Mar. 3, 1900; Thomas, *Portrait for Posterity*, 174–75.
12. *McClure's Magazine* 5 (Nov. 1895): 512 (quote); Thomas, *Portrait for Posterity*, 175.
13. "The McClure's Life of Abraham Lincoln," *McClure's* 5 (Oct. 1895): 480; Ida Tarbell, "Abraham Lincoln," 6 (Jan. 1896): 236–38; Thomas, *Portrait for Posterity*, 195–97.
14. Thomas, *Portrait for Posterity*, 201–2; Wick, "'He was a Friend of us Poor Men,'" 255–82.
15. Thomas, *Portrait for Posterity*, 196–97; Thomas, *Abraham Lincoln*, 527.

28. Harriet Monroe and the Literature of Lincoln

1. Harriet Monroe, "Nancy Hanks," *Century Magazine* 77 (Feb. 1909): 507.
2. John, *Best Years of the Century*, 261; Massa, "The Columbian Ode and 'Poetry, a Magazine of Verse,'" 51–69; Peterson, *Lincoln in American Memory*, 238–39; Pohlad, "Harriet Monroe's Abraham Lincoln," 25–26.
3. *New York Times*, Jan. 27, 1909; *Brooklyn (NY) Eagle*, Jan. 28, 1909; *Boston Globe*, Feb. 1, 1909; *The Paducah (KY) Sun*, Feb. 12, 1909; *Cincinnati Enquirer*, Feb. 13, 1909; Pohlad, "Harriet Monroe's Abraham Lincoln," 25–27.
4. Furey, "Poetry and the Rhetoric of Dissent," 671–86; Lynn, "Otherworldly Orbit of Jane Addams"; Williams, *Harriet Monroe*, 3–27.
5. Peterson, *Lincoln in American Memory*, 182–83.
6. Vachel Lindsay's poem "Lincoln Walks at Midnight" (1914); *Edgar Lee Master's Spoon River Anthology* (1915); Carl Sandburg's *Abraham Lincoln: The Prairie Years* (1926).
7. Harriet Monroe, "Comments and Reviews: Incarnations," *Poetry* 2 (June 1913): 103.
8. Harriet Monroe, "Comment: Vachel Lindsay," *Poetry* 24 (May 1924): 90–95 (quote); Edgar Lee Masters, "What Is Poetry," *Poetry* 6 (Sept. 1915): 306–8; Harriet Monroe, "Comment: Edgar Lee Masters," *Poetry* 24 (July 1924): 90–95; Edgar Lee Masters, "What Is Great Poetry," *Poetry* 26 (Sept. 1925): 349–51; Chandler, "The Spoon River Country," 249–329; Marc

Chénetier, "Vachel Lindsay's American Mythocracy and Some Unpublished Sources," in Hallwas, *Vision of This Land*, 45; Hartley, "Edgar Lee Masters," 56–83; Dennis Q. McInerny, "Vachel Lindsay: A Reappraisal," in Hallwas, *Vision of This Land*, 29–41.

9. Harriet Monroe, "Comment: Carl Sandburg," *Poetry* 24 (Sept. 1924): 320–26; Harriet Monroe, "Poets as Prosers," *Poetry* 28 (Sept. 1928): 328–38; Pohlad, "Harriet Monroe's Abraham Lincoln," 27–28.
10. Harriet Monroe, "Reviews: Abraham Lincoln, A Primer," *Poetry* 15 (Dec. 1919): 159–62.
11. Tarbell, *Life of Abraham Lincoln*; Schwartz, "Picturing Lincoln," 150; Schwartz, *Abraham Lincoln and the Forge of National Memory*, 178–80.

29. She Ruth

1. Randall, "Has the Lincoln Theme Been Exhausted," 270–94, 270n1.
2. Neely, "The Lincoln Theme since Randall's Call," 10–70.
3. Randall, "Has the Lincoln Theme Been Exhausted," 270.
4. Finding Aid, Ruth Painter Randall (1892–1971) Papers, Illinois History and Lincoln Collections, University of Illinois Library, Urbana, IL; Randall, *I Ruth*, 9–57.
5. Randall, *I Ruth*, 123–26, 164–67; James G. Randall, "Chase, Salmon Portland," *Dictionary of American Biography* (New York: Charles Scribner's Sons, 1930), 4:27–34; Young, "Randall's Lincoln, "1–13.
6. Randall, *I Ruth*, 123–26, 217–18.
7. Randall, *Mary Lincoln*, viii.
8. Roy P. Basler, "Paradoxical, 'Hellcatical' Mary Lincoln; Kinder Light on Much Maligned Woman," *Chicago Tribune*, Feb. 8, 1953.
9. Randall, *I Ruth*, 230–41.
10. *I Varina* (1962), *I Jessie* (1963), and *I Elizabeth* (1966).
11. *Chicago Tribune*, Jan. 23, 1971.

30. Mary and Sally and Me

1. Field, *In Pieces*, 381–86; *St. Louis Post-Dispatch*, book section, Sept. 16, 2018.
2. Hodes, *Mourning Lincoln*, 115, 276, 314.

Epilogue

1. Jane Addams, "Autobiographical Notes upon Twenty Years at Hull-House: A War Time Childhood," *American Magazine* 69 (Apr. 1910): 729; Schramm, *Lincoln in Illinois: Commemorating the Bicentennial of the Birth of Abraham Lincoln*, 3.

Appendix: The Women

1. Elizabeth Abell to AL, Jan. 22, 1861, RG 107, NARA; Oliver Abell to Abraham Lincoln, Apr. 1861, with AL Endorsement, AL, DLC; Memorandum: Appointment of Oliver G. Abell, c. Apr. 1, 1861, *CW*, 4:310, 310n1; Schnell, "Two Lincolns," 4; Thomas, *Lincoln's Old Friends*, 127.
2. Burial Record, La Harpe Cemetery, La Harpe, IL.
3. Affidavit of Ames, with AL Endorsement, July 6, 1864, RG 94, Entry 409, NARA.
4. *PAL*, 4:1–48.
5. Bailey to AL, Oct. 30, 1860, AL Papers, DLC.
6. Bedell to AL, Oct. 15, 1860, *CW*, 4:130n1.
7. York State Census; New York, U.S., Civil War Muster Roll Abstracts, 1861–1900; Edward Beren Gravestone, Gettysburg National Cemetery, Gettysburg, PA.
8. Nomination of Bibighaus, Mar. 6, 1862, RG 46, Entry 550, NARA; Bibighaus Gravestone, Mount Lebanon Cemetery, Lebanon, PA.
9. *Springfield State Journal-Register* (IL), Apr. 29, 2018.
10. Browning, *Diary*, 1:491, 2:70.
11. Browning Gravestones, Woodland Cemetery, Quincy, IL; Nelson, "Eliza Caldwell Browning," 28n30.
12. Buckley to AL, October 1861, Lincoln Papers, DLC; 1860 U.S. Federal Census.
13. *PAL*, 4:113–36.
14. AL Appointment of Bushnell, Feb. 28, 1865, RG 59, Entry 791, NARA.
15. Illinois Statewide Marriage Index, Illinois State Archives, Springfield; Harriet A. Chapman (Jesse W. Weik Interview), c. 1886–87, *HI*, 781–83.
16. *ANB*.
17. Mary Hancock Colyer to AL, Mar. 22, 1861, Lincoln Papers, DLC; 1860 U.S. Federal Census; *Boston Globe*, Nov. 5, 1872.
18. Appointment of Cowan, Mar. 11, 1863, RG 59, Entry 791, NARA; Cowan Gravestone, Greenwood Cemetery, Biddeford, ME; *Portland (ME) Evening Express*, Dec. 2, 1893.
19. *CW*, 1:259n1, 261n6.
20. *ANB*; Pryor, *Six Encounters with Lincoln*, 220–22.
21. AL to ML, Nov. 90, 1862, *CW*, 5:492; 1860 U.S. Federal Census; Washington, *They Knew Lincoln*, 81–88.
22. *ANB*.
23. *LPAL*.
24. *PAL*, 1:259–300, 260n5.

25. Duggar Burial Record, Glenwood Cemetery, Washington.
26. 1870 U.S. Federal Census; Gravestones, Arlington National Cemetery, Arlington, VA; *Washington Herald*, Oct. 8, 1906.
27. *ANB*.
28. Krause, *Now They Belong to the Ages*, 78–80.
29. *L&L*, 10; Gravestone, Charles Evans Cemetery, Reading, PA; Illinois Statewide Marriage Index, Illinois State Archives, Springfield.
30. AL to Emma Egbert, Jan. 1, 1865, *CW*, 8:204, 204–5n1; Egbert Family Gravestones, Grove Hill Cemetery, Oil City, PA; *Daily Evening Express* (Lancaster, PA), Dec. 13, 1864.
31. *St. Louis Post-Dispatch*, book section, Sept. 16, 2018.
32. *ANB*; White, *Visits with Lincoln*, 1–22.
33. Nomination of Mary Jane Frey, Feb. 1862, RG 46, Entry 791, NARA; *Register of Officers and Agents, Civil, Military, and Naval, in the Service of the United States* (1873), 1:870.
34. 1840 and 1850 U.S. Federal Censuses; Armstrong Goings Gravestone, Clay City Cemetery, Clay City, IL; Josephus Goings Gravestone, Minden Cemetery, Minden, NE; Benjamin Goings Gravestone, Elmore Cemetery, Flournoy, CA.
35. *LPAL*; 1850 U.S. Federal Census.
36. AL to Green, Sept. 22, 1860, *CW*, 4:118.
37. Burial Record, 1793–1867, Oakland Cemetery, Petersburg, IL; Thomas, *Lincoln's Old Friends*, 79, 99–101, 111–13.
38. Family Record Written by AL, c. 1851, *CW*, 2:94–95.
39. AL to John T. Stuart, Mar. 30, 1861, *CW*, 4:303; Elizabeth Grimsley to AL, Nov. 22, 1864, AL Papers, DLC; Neely, *Abraham Lincoln Encyclopedia*, 130–31.
40. Gurney to AL, Oct. 8, 1864, AL Papers, DLC; Oct. 26, 1862, *Lincoln Log*; *ANB*.
41. *ANB*.
42. AL to Hamilton, Oct. 29, 1860, *CW*, 4:134, 134n1; 1860 U.S. Federal Census; Death Certificate, Massachusetts Vital Records, 1840–1911, New England Historic Genealogical Society, Boston, MA.
43. Gravestone, City Cemetery, Charleston, IL; Neely, *Abraham Lincoln Encyclopedia*, 137.
44. Paul H. Verduin, "Brief Outline of the Joseph Hanks Family," in *HI*, 779–83.
45. *HI*, 780.
46. AL to Stephen G. Burbridge, Aug. 8, 1864, *CW*, 7: 484–85 (quote); Emilie Helm to Montgomery Blair, Jan. 30, 1865, AL Papers, DLC; Emilie Todd

Helm to Jesse W. Weik, c. 1887, *HI*, 694; Leonard, *All the Daring of the Soldier*, 89.

47. Stathis, "Ella Elvira Hobart Gibson," 1–37.
48. Hoge to AL, Nov. 24, 1862; AL to Hoge, Nov. 25, 1862, both in AL Papers, DLC; *ANB*.
49. Matilda Ivers to AL, Sept. 1863, RG 56, Entry 210, NARA; *Hutchinson's Washington and Georgetown Directory* (1863), 118.
50. Nomination of Jonas, June 13, 1864, RG 46, Entry 568; Appointment of Jonas as Deputy Postmaster at Quincy, Illinois, June 28, 1864, RG 59, Entry 791, both in NARA; Gravestone, Dispersed of Judas Cemetery, New Orleans, LA; Markens, *Lincoln and the Jews*, 17–22.
51. *ANB*; Keckley, *Behind the Scenes*; Reynolds, *Abe*, 601–2.
52. Juliette Kinzie to AL, Nov. 16, 1863; June 16, 1864, both in AL Papers, DLC; Keating, *World of Juliette Kinzie*, 151–74; *ANB*.
53. 1850 Federal U.S. Census.
54. Arnold, *Life of Abraham Lincoln*, 439–40; *ANB*.
55. *McClure's Magazine* 5 (Nov. 1895): 499.
56. ML to Sarah Lincoln, Dec. 19, 1867, *L&L*, 465, 465n7.
57. Jane Hoge and Mary Livermore to AL, Oct. 21, 1863, AL Papers, DLC; *ANB*; Livermore, *My Story of the War*.
58. *ANB*.
59. Family Record Written by Abraham Lincoln, c. 1851, *CW*, 2:94–95; Dennis Hanks to AL, Apr. 5, 1864, AL Papers, DLC; Matilda Johnston Moore (Interview), Sept. 8, 1865, *HI*, 110, 764; Illinois Statewide Marriage Index, Illinois State Archives, Springfield; Elizabeth Hanks Gravestone, Old City Cemetery, Charleston, IL.
60. AL to Mary Motley, May 17, 1862, *CW*, 5:220–21, 221n1; Appointment of John Lothrop Motley as Minister to Austria, Aug. 10, 1861, RG 59, Entry 33, NARA; 1850 U.S. Federal Census; Dorset, England, Marriage and Banns, 1813–1921; Dorset, England, Deaths and Burials, 1813–2001; *Boston Globe*, Oct. 6, 1915.
61. Mary Owens Vineyard to William Henry Herndon: May 1, 1866, May 23, 1866, *HI*, 248, 255–56; Vineyard Gravestones, Pleasant Ridge Cemetery, Weston, MO; 1850 U.S. Federal Census; *Platt County Conservator* (Platt City, MO), Jan. 10, 1863; Neely, *Abraham Lincoln Encyclopedia*, 230; Thomas, *Lincoln's Old Friends*, 97–98.
62. AL Appointment of Gabriel R. Paul, Aug. 23, 1862, *CW*, 5:390–91; 1870 and 1880 U.S. Federal Censuses; Ohio, U.S. County Marriage Records, 1774–1993.

63. Holst, "One of the Best Women I Ever Knew," 12–14.
64. Gravestone, Oak Ridge Cemetery, Springfield, IL; *Illinois State Journal* (Springfield), Dec. 14, 1963; "Marion Dolores Pratt," *American Archivist* 27 (Apr. 1, 1964): 290–91.
65. Randall, *I Ruth*; *Chicago Tribune*, Jan. 23, 1971.
66. *ANB*.
67. Marriage License, Sept. 25, 1835, Sangamon County Records, Illinois Regional Archives Depository, University of Illinois Springfield; 1850 and 1860 U.S. Federal Censuses; McDermott, "Dissolving the Bonds Matrimony," 91–93. Illinois State Archives, Springfield; *PAL*, 1:41n1.
68. Gravestone, Old Concord Cemetery, Petersburg, IL; Thomas, *Abraham Lincoln*, 125–26.
69. *Shelby v. Shelby*, 1841; *Shelby v Freeman and Freeman*, 1858, both in Sangamon County, Illinois, *LPAL*; 1850 U.S. Federal Census; U.S. Federal Mortality Scheduled, 1850–1885; Hart, "Springfield's African Americans," 40n15.
70. List of Army Promotions, c. July 1861, *CW*, 4:418, 418n1; Bobbitt, *With Dearest Love to All*, 46–47; Eicher, *Civil War High Commands*, 491.
71. Krause, *Now They Belong to the Ages*, 54–57.
72. *HI*, 781; Neely, *Abraham Lincoln Encyclopedia*, 137, 188.
73. *CW*, 1:259n1, 261n6.
74. AL to William P. Fessenden, July 21, 1864, *CW*, 7:454, 454n1; Burial Record, Congressional Cemetery, Washington, DC.
75. Emma A. Stark to AL, Aug. 13, 1858, AL Papers, DLC; Bill of Complaint, July 7, 1858, *Stark v. Stark*, *LPAL*; First Debate with Stephen A. Douglas at Ottawa, Illinois, Aug. 21, 1858, *CW*, 3:1.
76. Gravestone, Allegheny Cemetery, Pittsburgh, PA; 1860 Federal U.S. Census; *Pittsburgh Daily Commercial*, Jan. 27, 1864, *CW*, 7:117n1.
77. *CW*, 1:159n3; ML to Mary Harlan Lincoln, Mar. 22, 1869, *L&L*, 505; Bettie Brown Gravestone, Oak Ridge Cemetery, Springfield, IL; *L&L*, 59, 59n5.
78. *ANB*.
79. *ANB*.
80. AL to LuLu Waldron, Apr. 27, 1862, *CW*, 5:200, *CW*, 5:200n1.
81. Krause, *Now They Belong to the Ages*, 58–60.
82. Gravestone, Oak Ridge Cemetery, Springfield, IL.
83. AL to William H. Seward, [Mar. 1861], *CW*, 8:426; Sarah Ellen Walworth, May 16, 1861, Recommendations for Office, Applications and Recommendations for Public Office, 1797–1901, National Archives, College Park, MD; Walworth to AL, Dec. 6, 1860; Jan 7, 1864; Dec. 15, 1864, all in

AL Papers, DLC; AL to William H. Seward, [Mar. 1861], *CW*, 8:426, 426n1; Sarah Walworth Gravestone, Greenridge Cemetery, Saratoga Springs, NY; Ogilvie, *Biographical Dictionary of Women in Science*, 2:1344–45.

84. *CW*, 7:296n1; Kleber, *Encyclopedia of Louisville*, 921; Ramage, *Kentucky Rising*, 167–68.
85. AL to Weathers, Dec. 4, 1861, *CW*, 5:57.
86. *PAL*, 3:46, 46n10, 49n20.
87. *CW*, 8:55n1; *ANB*; "Mrs. Annie Wittenmyer," *Annals of Iowa* 4 (Jan. 1900): 77–88.

BIBLIOGRAPHY

A Note on Sources: This collection of essays is grounded by hundreds of Lincoln biographies and articles I have read and studied over three decades of work as a Lincoln scholar. My perspective on Abraham Lincoln is all my own, and I disagree with some prevailing interpretations, particularly those that malign Mary Lincoln without nuance. However, *all* of the major Lincoln biographies and the leading biographers, many whom I have been privileged to know, have informed my understanding of Lincoln's life and the era in which he lived. I know I stand on the shoulders of Lincoln giants. However, for simplicity's sake, I have limited citation across the chapters to a relatively small number of Lincoln biographies, relying most heavily on three full-length biographies from three eras of Lincoln historiography: Benjamin Thomas's *Abraham Lincoln* (1952), David Donald's *Lincoln* (1995), and David Reynolds's *Abe* (2020). These three scholars asked slightly different questions rooted in the historical interests of the times in which they worked. The bibliography below is a complete list of cited works as well as books and articles I deem most instructive for understanding Abraham Lincoln and women. Citation of primary sources in footnotes is limited to Abraham Lincoln's letters and incoming correspondence, Mary Lincoln's letters, newspapers, and a few other select sources.

Adams, James N., comp. *Illinois Place Names*. Springfield: Illinois State Historical Society, 1989.

Address of Hon. Edward Everett at the Consecration of the National Cemetery at Gettysburg, 19th November 1863. Boston: Little, Brown & Co., 1864.

Anderegg, Michael A. *Lincoln and Shakespeare*. Lawrence: University of Kansas Press, 2015.

Angle, Paul M. *"Here I Have Lived": A History of Lincoln's Springfield*, 1935; rpt. Chicago: Abraham Lincoln Book Shop, 1971.

Arnold, Isaac N. *The Life of Abraham Lincoln*. Chicago: A. C. McClurg, 1885.

Attie, Jeanie. *Patriotic Toil: Northern Women and the American Civil War.* Ithaca, NY: Cornell University Press, 1998.

Bach, Jennifer L. "Acts of Remembrance: Mary Todd Lincoln and Her Husband's Memory." *Journal of the Abraham Lincoln Association* 25 (Summer 2004): 25–49.

Baker, Jean H. *Mary Todd Lincoln: A Biography*. 2nd ed. New York: Norton, 2008.

Baker, Jean H. "Mary Todd Lincoln: Biography as Social History." *The Register of the Kentucky Historical Society* 86 (Summer 1988): 203–15.

Baker, Jean H. "Mary Todd Lincoln: Managing Home, Husband, and Children." *Journal of the Abraham Lincoln Association* 11 (1990): 1–12.

Baker, Paula. "The Domestication of Politics: Women and American Political Society, 1780–1920." *American Historical Review* 89 (June 1984): 620–47.

Banner, Lois W. "Biography as History." *American Historical Review* 114 (June 2009): 579–86.

Barker, Harry Ellsworth, comp. *Abraham Lincoln and Mary Owen*. Springfield, IL: Barker's Art Store, 1922.

Barnes, Teresa. "History and Ordinary Womanhood." *Historical Reflections* 38 (Summer 2012): 98–108.

Barringer, William E. *Lincoln's Vandalia: A Pioneer Portrait*. New Brunswick, NJ: Rutgers University Press, 1949.

Bartlett, William E. *There I Grew Up: Remembering Abraham Lincoln's Indiana Youth*. Indianapolis: Indiana Historical Society, 2008.

Barton, William E. *The Lineage of Abraham Lincoln*. Indianapolis: Bobbs-Merrill, 1929.

Barton, William E. *The Women Lincoln Loved*. Indianapolis: Bobbs-Merrill, 1927.

Basch, Norma. *Framing American Divorce, From the Revolutionary Generation to the Victorians*. Berkeley: University Press of California, 1989.

Basch, Norma. "Invisible Women: The Legal Fiction of Marital Unity in Nineteenth Century America." *Feminist Studies* 5 (Summer 1979): 346–66.

Basler, Roy P. "Lincoln, Blacks, and Women." In *The Public and the Private Lincoln: Contemporary Perspectives*, edited by Cullom Davis et al., 38–53. Carbondale: Southern Illinois University Press, 1979.

Benner, Martha L., Cullom Davis, Daniel W. Stowell, Susan Krause, John A. Lupton, Stacy Pratt McDermott, Christopher A. Schnell, and Dennis E. Suttles, eds. *The Law Practice of Abraham Lincoln*. Urbana: University of Illinois Press, 2000; online, 2008. (*LPAL*).

Berry, Stephen. *House of Abraham: Lincoln and the Todds, A Family Divided by War.* New York: Houghton-Mifflin, 2007.

Billings, Roger, and Frank Williams Jr., eds. *Abraham Lincoln, Esq.: The Legal Career of America's Greatest President*. Lexington: University of Kentucky Press, 2010.

Blevins, Cameron. "Women and Federal Officeholding in the Late Nineteenth Century." *Current Research in Digital History* 2 (Aug. 23, 2019) https://crdh.rrchnm.org/essays/v02-08-women-and-federal-officeholding/ (accessed Oct. 9, 2024).

Bobbitt, Mary Reed, ed. *With Dearest Love to All: The Life and Letters of Lady Jebb*. Berkeley: University of California Press, 1960.

Borden, Louise A. *Lincoln and Me*. New York: Scholastic, 2001.

Boritt, Gabor. *The Gettysburg Gospel: The Lincoln Speech That Nobody Knows*. New York: Simon & Schuster, 2006.

Boyden, Anna L. *Echoes from Hospital and White House: A Record of Mrs. Rebecca R. Pomeroy's Experience in War-Times*. Boston: D. Lothrop, 1884.

Brady, Kathleen. *Ida Tarbell: Portrait of a Muckraker*. Pittsburgh: University of Pittsburgh Press, 1989.

Briggs, Harold E., and Ernestine B. Briggs. *Nancy Hanks Lincoln: A Frontier Portrait*. New York: Bookman, 1952.

Brooks, Noah. *Abraham Lincoln and the Downfall of American Slavery*. 1888; rpt., New York: G. P. Putnam & Sons, 1908.

Brooks, Noah. *Lincoln Observed: The Civil War Dispatches of Noah Brooks*. Edited by Michael Burlingame. Baltimore: Johns Hopkins University Press, 1998.

Browning, Orville Hickman. *The Diary of Orville Hickman Browning*. Edited by Theodore Calvin Pease and James G. Randall. 2 vols. Springfield: Illinois State Historical Society, 1925.

Brownstein, Elizabeth. *Lincoln's Other White House: The Untold Story of the Man and His Presidency*. New York: John Wiley, 2005.

Burlingame, Michael, ed. *An Oral History of Abraham Lincoln: John G. Nicolay's Interviews and Essays*. Carbondale: Southern Illinois University, 1996.

Burton, Orville Vernon. *The Age of Lincoln*. New York: Hill & Wang, 2006.

Cahill, Daniel. *Harriet Monroe*. New York: Twayne Publishers, 1973.

Cashin, Joan E. "American Women and the American Civil War." *Journal of Military History* 81 (January 2017): 199–204.

Chandler, Josephine Craven. "The Spoon River Country." *Journal of the Illinois State Historical Society* 14 (Oct. 1921–Jan. 1922): 249–329.

Clinton, Catherine. "Abraham Lincoln: The Family That Made Him, the Family He Made." In *Our Lincoln: New Perspectives on Lincoln and His World*, edited by Eric Foner, 249–66. New York: Norton, 2008.

Clinton, Catherine. *Mrs. Lincoln: A Life*. New York: Harper, 2009.

Clinton, Catherine. "Wife Versus Widow: Clashing Perspectives on Mary Lincoln's Legacy." *Journal of the Abraham Lincoln Association* 28 (Winter 2007): 1–19.

Clinton, Catherine, and Nina Silber, eds. *Battle Scars: Essays on Gender and the Civil War*. New York: Oxford University Press, 2006.

Clinton, Catherine, and Nina Silber, eds. *Divided Houses: Gender and the Civil War*. New York: Oxford University Press, 1992.

Coleman, Charles H. *Abraham Lincoln and Coles County, Illinois*. New Brunswick, NJ: Scarecrow Press, 1955.

Coleman, Charles H. "Sarah Bush Lincoln, the Mother Who Survived Him." In "Historical Essays," special issue of *Eastern Illinois University Bulletin* (May 1962).

Conkling, Alice, and E. H. Merryman. "A Story of the Early Days in Springfield, and a Poem," *Journal of the Illinois State Historical Society* 16 (Apr.–July 1923): 144–46.

Conroy, James B. *Lincoln's White House: The People's House in Wartime*. Lanham, MD: Rowman & Littlefield, 2016.

Conroy, James B. "Slavery's Mark on Lincoln's White House." White House Historical Association Blog, https://www.whitehousehistory.org/slaverys-mark-on-lincolns-white-house (accessed Oct. 9, 2024).

Cooper, Edward S. *Vinnie Ream: An American Sculptor*. Chicago: Academy Chicago Publishers, 2004.

Cott, Nancy F. *Public Vows: A History of Marriage and the Nation*. Cambridge, MA: Harvard University Press, 2000.

Cox, LaWanda. *Lincoln and Black Freedom: A Study in Presidential Leadership*. Columbia: University of South Carolina Press, 1994.

Dabakis, Melissa. "Sculpting Lincoln: Vinnie Ream, Sarah Fisher Ames, and the Equal Rights Movement." *American Art* 22 (Spring 2008): 78–101.

Davis, William C. *Lincoln's Men: How President Lincoln Became Father to an Army and a Nation*. New York: Free Press, 1999.

Dekle, George R., Sr. *Abraham Lincoln's Most Famous Case: The Almanac Trial*. Santa Barbara, CA: Praeger, 2014.

Dekle, George R., Sr. *Prairie Defender: The Murder Trials of Abraham Lincoln*. Carbondale: Southern Illinois University Press, 2017.

Dirck, Brian R. *Lincoln in Indiana*. Carbondale: Southern Illinois University Press, 2017.

Donald, David. *Lincoln*. New York: Simon & Schuster, 1995.

Donald, David. *Lincoln at Home: Two Glimpses of Abraham Lincoln's Family Life*. New York: Simon & Schuster, 2000.

Duff, John J. *A. Lincoln: Prairie Lawyer*. New York: Bramhall House, 1960.

Duncan, Kunigunde, and D. E. Nichols. *Mentor Graham: The Man Who Taught Lincoln*. Chicago: University of Chicago Press, 1944.

Dye, Nancy Schrom, and Daniel Blake Smith. "Mother Love and Infant Death, 1750–1920." *Journal of American History* 73 (Sept. 1986): 329–53.

East, Ernest E., and James T. Hickey. "The Melissa Goings Murder Case." *Journal of the Illinois State Historical Society* 46 (Spring 1953): 79–83.

Eggleston, Larry G. *Women in the Civil War: Extraordinary Stories of Soldiers, Spies, Nurses, Doctors, Crusaders, and Others*. Jefferson, NC: McFarland, 2003.

Eicher, John H., and David J. Eicher. *Civil War High Commands*. Stanford, CA: Stanford University Press, 2001.

Emerson, Jason. *Giant in the Shadows: The Life of Robert T. Lincoln*. Carbondale: Southern Illinois University Press, 2012.

Emerson, Jason. *The Madness of Mary Lincoln* (Carbondale: Southern Illinois University Press, 2012.

Emerson, Jason. *Mary Lincoln for the Ages*. Carbondale: Southern Illinois University Press, 2019.

Emerson, Jason. *Mary Lincoln's Insanity Case: A Documentary History*. Urbana: University of Illinois Press, 2015.

Epstein, Daniel Mark. *Lincoln's Men: The President and His Private Secretaries*. New York: Smithsonian, 2010.

Epstein, Daniel Mark. *The Lincolns: Portrait of a Marriage*. New York: Ballentine Books, 2008.

Etcheson, Nicole. *The Emerging Midwest: Upland Southerners and the Political Culture of the Old Northwest, 1787–1861*. Bloomington: Indiana University Press, 1996.

Etcheson, Nicole. "Manliness and the Political Culture of the Old Northwest, 1790–1860." *Journal of the Early Republic* 15 (Spring 1995): 59–77.

Evans, Mary. *Born for Liberty: A History of Women in America*. New York: Free Press, 1989.

Fahs, Alice. "The Feminized Civil War: Gender, Northern Popular Literature, and the Memory of the War, 1861–1900." *Journal of American History* 85 (Mar. 1999): 1461–94.

Faust, Drew Gilpin. *This Republic of Suffering: Death and the American Civil War*. New York: Vintage Books, 2008.

Fehrenbacher, Don E. *Prelude to Greatness: Lincoln in the 1850s*. Stanford, CA: Stanford University Press, 1962.

Fehrenbacher, Don E., and Virginia Fehrenbacher. *The Recollected Words of Abraham Lincoln*. Stanford, CA: Stanford University Press, 1996.

Fenster, Julie. *The Case of Abraham Lincoln: A Story of Adultery, Murder, and the Making of a Great President*. New York: Palgrave Macmillan, 2007.

Ferguson, Andrew. *Land of Lincoln: Adventures in Abe's America*. New York: Atlantic Monthly Press, 2007.

Field, Sally. *In Pieces*. New York: Grand Central Publishing, 2018.

Fleischner, Jennifer. *Mrs. Lincoln and Mrs. Keckley: The Remarkable Story of the Friendship between a First Lady and a Former Slave*. New York: Broadway Books, 2003.

Foard, Chris. "Nurse Pomeroy: Comforter-in-Chief to the Lincoln Family." *Military Images* 37 (Autumn 2019): 52–57.

Fornieri, Joseph R., and Sara Vaughn Gabbard, eds. *Lincoln's America, 1809–1865*. Carbondale: Southern Illinois University Press, 2008.

Fraker, Guy C. *Lincoln's Ladder to the Presidency: The Eighth Judicial Circuit*. Carbondale: Southern Illinois University Press, 2012.

Frank, John P. *Lincoln as a Lawyer*. Urbana: University of Illinois Press, 1961.

French, Benjamin Brown. *Witness to the Young Republic: A Yankee's Journal, 1828–1879*, ed. Donald B. Cole and John J. McDonough. Hanover, NH: University Press of New England, 1989.

Furey, Hester L. "Poetry and the Rhetoric of Dissent in Turn-of-the-Century Chicago." *Modern Fiction Studies* 38 (Autumn 1992): 671–86.

Furguson, Ernest B. *Freedom Rising: Washington in the Civil War*. New York: Knopf, 2004.

Gallman, J. Matthew. *Defining Duty in Civil War: Personal Choice, Popular Culture, and the Union Home Front*. Chapel Hill: University of North Carolina Press, 2015.

Gannett, Lewis. "The Ann Rutledge Story: Case Closed?" *Journal of the Abraham Lincoln Association* 31 (Summer 2010): 21–60.

Gates, Henry Louis, Jr. *Colored People*. New York: Alfred A. Knopf, 1994.

Giesberg, Judith Ann. *Army at Home: Women and the Civil War on the Northern Homefront*. Chapel Hill: University of North Carolina Press, 2009.

Giesberg, Judith Ann. *Civil War Sisterhood: The U.S. Sanitary Commission and Women's Politics in Transition*. Boston: Northeastern University Press, 2000.

Gilder, Richard Watson. *Lincoln the Leader*. Boston: Houghton & Mifflin, 1909.

Glymph, Thavolia. "'Invisible Disabilities': Black Women in War and in Freedom." *Proceedings of the American Philosophical Society* 160 (Sept. 2016): 237–46.

Green, Harvey. *The Light of the Hearth: An Intimate View of the Lives of Women in Victorian America*. New York: Pantheon, 1983.

Greenbie, Sydney, and Marjorie Barstow Greenbie. *Anna Ella Carroll and Abraham Lincoln: A Biography*. Tampa, FL: University of Tampa Press, 1952.

Guelzo, Allen C. "'Public Sentiment Is Everything': Abraham Lincoln and the Power of Public Opinion." In *Lincoln and Liberty: Wisdom for the Age*, edited by Lucas E. Morel, 171–90. Lexington: University Press of Kentucky, 2014.

Hall, Richard H. *Women on the Civil War Battlefront*. Lawrence: University Press of Kansas, 2006.

Hallwas, John E., and Dennis J. Reader, eds. *The Vision of This Land: Studies of Vachel Lindsay, Edgar Lee Masters, and Carl Sandburg*. Macomb: Western Illinois University, 1979.

Harris, William C. *Lincoln's Rise to the Presidency*. Lawrence: University of Kansas Press, 2007.

Harrison, Lowell Hayes. *Lincoln of Kentucky*. Lexington: University Press of Kentucky, 2000.

Hart, Richard E. "Springfield's African Americans as a Part of the Lincoln Community." *Journal of the Abraham Lincoln Association* 20 (Winter 1999): 35–54.

Hartley, Lois. "Edgar Lee Masters: Biographer and Historian." *Journal of the Illinois State Historical Society* 54 (Spring 1961): 56–83.

Hawes, Joseph M., and Elizabeth I. Nybakken, eds. *Family and Society in American History*. Urbana: University of Illinois Press, 2001.

Hay, John. *Inside Lincoln's White House: The Civil War Diary of John Hay*. Edited by Michael Burlingame and John R. Turner Ettlinger. Carbondale: Southern Illinois University Press, 1999.

Haymond, William S. *An Illustrated History of the State of Indiana*. Indianapolis: S. L. Morrow, 1879.

Hearn, Chester G. *Lincoln and McClellan at War*. Baton Rouge: Louisiana State University Press, 2012.

Herndon, William H., and Jesse William Weik. *Herndon's Lincoln: The True Story of a Great Life*. 3 vols. Chicago: Belford, Clarke & Co., 1889.

Herr, Pamela, and Mary Lee Spence, eds. *The Letters of Jessie Benton Frémont*. Urbana: University of Illinois Press, 1993.

Hill, Nancy. "The Transformation of the Lincoln Tomb." *Journal of the Abraham Lincoln Association* 27 (Winter 2006): 39–56.

History of Tazewell County, Illinois. Chicago: Charles C. Chapman, 1879.

Hodes, Martha. *Mourning Lincoln*. New Haven, CT: Yale University Press, 2016.

Hodes, Martha. *My Hijacking: A Personal History of Forgetting and Remembering*. New York: Harper, 2023.

Hofstadter, Richard. "Abraham Lincoln and the Self-Made Myth." In *The American Political Tradition and the Men Who Made It*, 93–136. New York: Vintage, 1948.

Holst, Erika. "'One of the Best Women I Ever Knew': Abraham Lincoln and Rebecca Pomeroy." *Journal of the Abraham Lincoln Association* 31 (Summer 2010): 12–20.

Holzer, Harold. *Dear Mr. Lincoln: Letters to the President*. Carbondale: Southern Illinois University Press, 2006.

Holzer, Harold. "'Tokens of Respect' and 'Heartfelt Thanks': How Abraham Lincoln Coped with Presidential Gifts." *Illinois Historical Journal* 77 (Autumn 1984): 177–92.

Hooper, Candice Shy. *Lincoln's Generals' Wives: Four Women Who Influenced the Civil War, for Better and for Worse*. Kent, OH: Kent State University Press, 2016.

Hoptak, John. "'Great in Heart and Mighty in Valor': General Gabriel Paul and His Mortal Wounding at Gettysburg." *The Blog of the Gettysburg National Military Park*, July 10, 2016, https://npsgnmp.wordpress.com/2014/07/10/great-in-heart-and-mighty-in-valor-general-gabriel-paul-and-his-mortal-wounding-at-gettysburg/ (accessed Oct. 9, 2024).

Horrocks, Thomas A. *Lincoln's Campaign Biographies*. Carbondale: Southern Illinois University Press, 2014.

Humphrey, Mary E. "Springfield of the Lincolns." *Abraham Lincoln Association Papers*. Springfield, IL: Abraham Lincoln Association, 1930.

Hunter, Douglas. "Book Breaking and Book Mending." *Slate*, July 15, 2018.

Hurt, James. *Writing Illinois: The Prairie, Lincoln, and Chicago*. Urbana: University of Illinois Press, 1992.

Irvine, Cyndy. "Mary Lincoln and Her Visit to Wisconsin's Wild Region." *Wisconsin Magazine of History* 95 (Summer 2012): 2–11.

John, Arthur. *The Best Years of the Century: Richard Watson Gilder, Scribner's Monthly, and the Century Magazine*. Urbana: University of Illinois Press, 1981.

Jung, Patrick J. *The Black Hawk War of 1832*. Norman: University of Oklahoma Press, 2007.

Kaplan, Amy. "Manifest Domesticity." *American Literature* 70 (Sept. 1998): 581–606.

Karsten, Peter. *Heart versus Head: Judge-Made Law in Nineteenth-Century America*. Chapel Hill: University of North Carolina Press, 1997.

Kashatus, William C. *Abraham Lincoln, the Quakers, and the Civil War: "A Trial of Principle and Faith."* Santa Barbara, CA: Praeger, 2014.

Keating, Ann Durkin. *The World of Juliette Kinzie: Chicago before the Fire*. Chicago: University of Chicago Press, 2019.

Keckley, Elizabeth. *Behind the Scenes: Thirty Years a Slave, and Four Years in the White House*. New York: G. W. Carleton, 1868.

Kerber, Linda K. *No Constitutional Right to Be Ladies: Women and the Obligations of Citizenship*. New York: Hill & Wang, 1998.

Kessler-Harris, Alice. *Women Have Always Worked: A Concise History*. Urbana: University of Illinois Press, 2018.

King, C. J. *Four Marys and a Jessie: The Story of the Lincoln Women*. Manchester, VT: Friends of Hildene, 2015.

Kirkpatrick, Melanie. *Lady Editor: Sarah Josepha Hale and the Making of the Modern American Woman*. New York: Encounter, 2021.

Kleber, John E., ed. *Encyclopedia of Louisville*. Louisville: University Press of Kentucky.

Kramer, Sidney. "Lincoln at the Fair." *Abraham Lincoln Quarterly* 3 (Sept. 1945): 341–42.

Krause, Susan. "Abraham Lincoln and Joshua Speed, Attorney and Client." *Illinois Historical Journal* 89 (Spring 1996): 35–37.

Krause, Susan, Kelley A. Boston, and Daniel W. Stowell. *Now They Belong to the Ages: Abraham Lincoln and His Contemporaries in Oak Ridge Cemetery*. Springfield: Illinois Historic Preservation Agency, 2005.

Krueger, Lillian. "Mary Todd Lincoln Summers in Wisconsin." *Journal of the Illinois State Historical Society* 34 (June 1941): 249–53.

Laas, Virginia Jeans. "Elizabeth Blair Lee: Union Counterpart of Mary Boykin Chestnut." *Journal of Southern History* 50 (Aug. 1984): 387–90.

Lemp, Joan A. "Vinnie Ream and *Abraham Lincoln*." *Woman's Art Journal* 6 (Autumn 1985–Winter 1986): 24–29.

Leonard, Elizabeth D. *All the Daring of a Soldier: Women of the Civil War Armies*. New York: W. W. Norton, 1999.

Lincoln Log, The. Based on Earl Schenck Miers, ed. *Lincoln Day by Day, A Chronology, 1809–1865*, 3 vols. Washington: Lincoln Sesquicentennial Commission, 1960; revised and enhanced digital edition Springfield, IL: Abraham Lincoln Presidential Library and Museum, https://thelincolnlog.org/ (accessed Oct. 9, 2024).

Lindsay, Vachel. *Collected Poems*. New York: Macmillan, 1925.

Livermore, Mary. *My Story of the War: A Woman's Narrative of Four Years' Personal Experience*. Hartford, CT: A. D. Worthington, 1889.

Louden, Irvine. *Death in Childbirth: An International Study of Maternal Care and Maternal Mortality, 1800–1950*. New York: Oxford University Press, 1992.

Lunden, Jennifer. *American Breakdown: Our Ailing Nation, My Body's Revolt, and the Nineteenth-Century Woman Who Brought Me Back to Life*. New York: Harper Wave, 2023.

Lynn, Stacy. "The Otherworldly Orbit of Jane Addams." *Jane Addams Papers Project Blog*, Sept. 15, 2020, https://janeaddams.ramapo.edu/2020/09/the-otherworldly-orbit-of-jane-addams/ (accessed Oct. 9, 2024).

Lystra, Karen. *Searching the Heart: Women, Men and Romantic Love in Nineteenth Century America*. New York: Oxford University Press, 1989.

Mabee, Carleton. "Sojourner Truth and President Lincoln." *New England Quarterly* 61 (December 1988): 519–29.

Madway, Lorraine. "Purveying Patriotic Pageantry: The Civil War Sanitary Fairs in New York." *New York History* 93 (Fall 1912): 268–301.

Mahoney, Timothy. *Provincial Lives: Middle-Class Experience in the Antebellum Midwest*. New York: Cambridge University Press, 1999.

Markens, Isaac. *Lincoln and the Jews*. New York: Isaac Markens, 1909.

Marvel, William. *Lincoln's Autocrat: The Life of Edwin Stanton*. Chapel Hill: University of North Carolina Press, 2015.

Massa, Ann. "'The Columbian Ode' and 'Poetry, a Magazine of Verse': Harriet Monroe's Entrepreneurial Triumphs." *Journal of American Studies* 20 (Apr. 1986): 51–69.

Massey, Mary Elizabeth. *Bonnet Brigades*. New York: Knopf, 1966.

Massey, Mary Elizabeth. *Women in the Civil War*. Lincoln: University of Nebraska Press, 1994.

Mast, Erin Carlson. "Mary Lincoln's Séance at Soldiers' Home." President Lincoln's Cottage *Brave Ideas Blog*, Oct. 30, 2009, https://www.lincolncottage.org/mary-lincolns-seance-at-the-soldiers-home/#:~:text=Scholars%20maintain%20Lincoln%20attended%20seances,of%20an%20English%20duke%2C%20caused (accessed, Oct. 9, 2024).

Matthews, Jean. "Race, Sex, and the Dimensions of Liberty in Antebellum America." *Journal of the Early Republic* 6 (Autumn 1986): 275–91.

Maxwell, William Quentin. *Lincoln's Fifth Wheel: The Political History of the United States Sanitary Commission*. New York: Longmans, Green, 1956.

McClure, Alexander K. *Abe Lincoln's Yarns and Stories*. Chicago: Education & Co., 1901.

McCurry, Stephanie. "Enemy Women and the Laws of War in the American Civil War." *Law and History Review* 35 (Aug. 2017): 667–710.

McDermott, Stacy Pratt. "'An Outrageous Proceeding': An Analysis of a Northern Lynching and the Enforcement of Anti-lynching Legislation in Illinois." *Journal of Negro History* 84 (Winter 1999): 61–78.

McDermott, Stacy Pratt. "Dissolving the Bonds of Matrimony: Women and Divorce in Sangamon County, Illinois, 1837–1861." In *In Tender Consideration: Women, Families, and the Law in Abraham Lincoln's Illinois*, edited by Daniel W. Stowell, 71–103. Urbana: University of Illinois Press, 2002.

McDermott, Stacy Pratt. *The Jury in Lincoln's America*. Athens: Ohio University Press, 2012.

McDermott, Stacy Pratt. "Law in an Illinois Corner: The Impact of the Law on an Antebellum Family." In *In Tender Consideration: Women, Families, and the Law in Abraham Lincoln's Illinois*, edited by Daniel W. Stowell, 161–81. Urbana: University of Illinois Press, 2002.

McDermott, Stacy Pratt. *Mary Lincoln: Southern Girl Northern Woman*. New York: Routledge, 2015.

McGregor, Deborah Kuhn. *From Midwives to Medicine: The Birth of American Gynecology*. New Brunswick, NJ: Rutgers University Press, 1998.

McPherson, James M. *Battle Cry Freedom: The Civil War Era*. New York: Oxford University Press, 1988.

Meyer, Douglas K. *Making the Heartland Quilt: A Geographical History of Settlement and Migration in Early-Nineteenth-Century Illinois*. Carbondale: Southern Illinois University Press, 2000.

Miller, Adrian. *The President's Kitchen Cabinet: The Story of the African Americans Who Have Fed Our First Families from the Washingtons to the Obamas*. Chapel Hill: University of North Carolina Press, 2017.

Monroe, Harriet. *A Poet's Life: Seventy Years in a Changing World*. New York: Macmillan, 1938.

Moore, Frank. *Women of the War: Their Heroism and Self-Sacrifice: True Stories of Brave Women in the Civil War*. Hartford, CT: S. S. Scranton, 1867.

Nash, Robert J. "Scholarly Personal Narrative As a Way to Connect the Academy to the World." *Counterpoints* 463 (2015): 39–52.

Nash, Robert J., and DeMethra LaSha Bradley. *Me-Search and Re-Search: A Guide to Writing Scholarly Personal Narrative Manuscripts.* Charlotte, NC: Information Age Publishing, 2011.

Neely, Mark E., Jr. *The Abraham Lincoln Encyclopedia.* New York: McGraw-Hill, 1982.

Neely, Mark E., Jr., "The Lincoln Theme since Randall's Call: The Promises and Perils of Professionalism." *Papers of the Abraham Lincoln Association* 1 (1979): 10–70.

Neem, Johann N. *Democracy's Schools: The Rise of Public Education in America.* Baltimore: Johns Hopkins University Press, 2017.

Nelson, Iris A. "Eliza Caldwell Browning: Lincoln's Loyal Confidante." *Journal of Illinois History* 9 (Spring 2006): 23–42.

Newman, Richard S. "All's Fair: Philadelphia and the Sanitary Fair Movement during the Civil War." *Pennsylvania Legacies* 13 (June 2013): 56–65.

Nicolay, Helen. *Personal Traits of Abraham Lincoln.* New York: Century, 1912.

Nicolay, John G., and John Hay, *Abraham Lincoln: A History.* 10 vols. New York: Century Co., 1890.

Nicolay, John G., and John Hay. *The Complete Works of Abraham Lincoln.* 12 vols. 1894; new, enlarged ed. New York: Francis D. Tandy Co., 1905.

Nofi, Albert A. *A Civil War Treasury.* New York: Da Capo Press, 1995.

Olar, Jared. "The Life and Death of Major Isaac Perkins." *Pekin History Blog,* June 8, 2016, https://fromthehistoryroom.wordpress.com/2016/06/08/the-life-and-death-of-major-isaac-perkins/ (accessed, Oct. 9, 2024).

Ogilvie, Marilyn, and Joy Harvey, eds. *The Biographical Dictionary of Women in Science: Pioneering Lives from Ancient Times to the Mid-20th Century.* 2 vols. New York: Routledge, 2000.

Packard, Jerrold M. *The Lincolns in the White House: Four Years That Shattered a Family.* New York: St. Martin's, 2005.

Painter, Nell Irvin. *Sojourner Truth: A Life, A Symbol.* New York: W. W. Norton & Co., 1996.

Peterson, Merrill D. *Lincoln in American Memory.* New York: Oxford University Press, 1995.

Pleck, Elizabeth. "The Making of the Domestic Occasion: The History of Thanksgiving in the United States." *Journal of Social History* 32 (Summer 1999): 773–89.

Pohlad, Mark B. "Harriet Monroe's Abraham Lincoln." *Journal of the Abraham Lincoln Association* 37 (Summer 2016): 16–41.

Pratt, Harry E. *The Personal Finances of Abraham Lincoln.* Springfield, IL: Abraham Lincoln Association, 1943.

Prichard, Jeremy. "'Home Is the Martyr': The Burial of Abraham Lincoln and the Fate of Illinois's Capitol." *Journal of the Abraham Lincoln Association* 38 (Winter 2017): 14–42.

Pryor, Elizabeth Brown. *Clara Barton, Professional Angel*. Philadelphia: University of Pennsylvania Press, 1987.

Pryor, Elizabeth Brown. *Six Encounters with Lincoln: A President Confronts Democracy and Its Demons*. New York: Viking, 2017.

Quitt, Martin H. "New Year's Day 1841: A Puzzling Triptych." *Journal of the Abraham Lincoln Association* 39 (Winter 2018): 1–25.

Radford, Victoria, ed. *Meeting Mr. Lincoln: Firsthand Recollections of Abraham Lincoln by People, Great and Small, Who Met the President*. Chicago: Ivan R. Dee, 1998.

Ramage, James A., and Andrea S. Watkins. *Kentucky Rising: Democracy, Slavery, and Culture from the Early Republic to the Civil War*. Louisville: University Press of Kentucky, 2011.

Randall, James G. "Has the Lincoln Theme Been Exhausted." *American Historical Review* 41 (Jan. 1936): 270–94.

Randall, James G. *Lincoln the President*. 4 vols. New York: Dodd, Mead, 1945–55.

Randall, Ruth Painter. *The Courtship of Mr. Lincoln*. Boston: Little, Brown, 1957.

Randall, Ruth Painter. *I Ruth*. Boston: Little, Brown, 1968.

Randall, Ruth Painter. *Lincoln's Sons*. Boston: Little, Brown & Co., 1955.

Randall, Ruth Painter. *Mary Lincoln: Biography of a Marriage*. Boston: Little, Brown, 1953.

Raymond, James C. "I-Dropping and Androgyny: The Authorial I in Scholarly Writing." *College Composition and Communication* (Dec. 1993): 478–83.

Reynolds, David S. *Abe: Abraham Lincoln and His Times*. New York: Penguin, 2020.

Rice, Judith A. "Ida M. Tarbell: A Progressive Look at Lincoln." *Journal of the Abraham Lincoln Association* 19 (Winter 1998): 57–72.

Robertson, Elizabeth. "The Union's 'Other Army': The Women of the United States Sanitary Commission." The Gilder Lehrman Institute of American History, New York, n.d.

Rosa, Rafael. "Abraham Lincoln and Women: A Psychohistorical Analysis." PhD diss., Drew University, 2017.

Ross, Rodney A. "Mary Todd Lincoln, Patient at Bellevue Place, Batavia." *Journal of the Illinois State Historical Society* 63 (Spring 1970): 5–34.

Rozinek, Erika. "Trembling for the Nation: Illinois Women and the Election of 1860." *Journal of Illinois History* 5 (Winter 2002): 309–24.

Ryan, Mary P. *Mysteries of Sex: Tracing Women and Men through American History*. Chapel Hill: University of North Carolina Press, 2006.

Sachs, Honor. *Home Rule: Households, Manhood, and National Expansion on the Eighteenth-Century Kentucky Frontier*. New Haven, CT: Yale University Press, 2015.

Saunders, George. *Lincoln in the Bardo*. New York: Random House, 2017.

Schnell, Christopher. "Two Lincolns and a 'Treasury Girl.'" *Lincoln Editor* 9 (Jan.–Mar. 2009): 4–5.

Schramm, Ron, and Richard E. Hart. *Lincoln in Illinois: Commemorating the Bicentennial of the Birth of Abraham Lincoln*. Springfield, IL: The Abraham Lincoln Association, 2009.

Schroeter, Joan G. "Julia Butler Newberry and Mary Todd Lincoln: Two 'Merry' Widows." *Journal of the Illinois State Historical Society* 95 (Autumn 2002): 264–74.

Schultz, Jane E. *Women at the Front: Hospital Workers in Civil War America*. Chapel Hill: University of North Carolina Press, 2004.

Schwartz, Barry. *Abraham Lincoln and the Forge of National Memory*. Chicago: University of Chicago Press, 2000.

Schwartz, Barry. "Ann Rutledge in American Memory: Social Change and the Erosion of a Romantic Drama." *Journal of the Abraham Lincoln Association* 26 (Jan. 2005): 1–27.

Schwartz, Barry. "Picturing Lincoln." In *Picturing History: American Painting, 1770–1930*, edited by William Ayres, 135–55. New York: Rizzoli International Publications, 1993.

Shenk, Joshua Wolf. *Lincoln's Melancholy: How Depression Challenged a President and Fueled His Greatness*. Boston: Houghton Mifflin, 2005.

Sibley, Katherine A. S. ed. *Southern First Ladies: Culture and Place in White House History*. Lawrence: University of Kansas Press, 2020.

Silber, Nina. *Daughters of the Union: Northern Women Fight the Civil War*. Cambridge, MA: Harvard University Press, 2005.

Silber, Nina. *Gender and Sectional Conflict*. Chapel Hill: University of North Carolina Press, 2008.

Simon, John Y. "Abraham Lincoln and Ann Rutledge." *Journal of the Abraham Lincoln Association* 11 (1990): 13–33.

Sizer, Lyde Cullen. *The Political Work of Northern Women Writers and the Civil War, 1850–1872*. Chapel Hill: University of North Carolina Press, 2000.

Smith, Michael Thomas. "Abraham Lincoln, Manhood, and Nineteenth-Century American Political Culture." In *The Distracted and Anarchical People: New Answers for Old Questions about the Civil War–Era North*, edited by Andrew W. Slap, 29–41. New York: Fordham University Press, 2013.

Snyder, Charles M. *The Lady and the President: The Letters of Dorothea Dix and Millard Fillmore*. Lexington: University of Kentucky Press, 1975.

Speech of Henry Clay, in Defence of the American System, against the British Colonial System. Washington: Gales and Seaton, 1832.

Stahr, Walter. *Stanton: Lincoln's War Secretary*. New York: Simon & Schuster, 2017.

Stathis, Stephen W., and Daniel Canfield Strizek. "Ella Elvira Hobart Gibson: Nineteenth-Century Teacher, Lecturer, Author, Poet, Feminist, Spiritualist, Free Thinker, and America's First Woman Military Chaplain." *Journal of Church and State* 58 (Winter 2016): 1–37.

Stillé, Charles J. *History of the United States Sanitary Commission, Being the General Report of Its Work during the War of the Rebellion*. New York: Hurd & Houghton, 1868.

Stimmel, Smith. *Personal Reminiscences of Abraham Lincoln*. Minneapolis: William H. M. Adams, 1928.

Stowell, Daniel W. "Murder at a Methodist Camp Meeting: The Origins of Abraham Lincoln's Most Famous Trial." *Journal of the Illinois State Historical Society* 101 (Fall–Winter, 2008): 219–34.

Stowell, Daniel W., Susan Krause, John A. Lupton, Stacy Pratt McDermott, Christopher A. Schnell, Dennis E. Suttles, Kelley B. Clausing, and R. Dan Monroe, eds. *Papers of Abraham Lincoln: Legal Documents and Cases*. 4 vols. Charlottesville: University of Virginia Press, 2008.

Stroble, Paul E., Jr. *High on the Okaw's Western Bank: Lincoln and Vandalia*. Urbana: University of Illinois Press, 1992.

Strozier, Charles B. *Your Friend Forever, A. Lincoln: The Enduring Friendship of Abraham Lincoln and Joshua Speed*. New York: Columbia University Press, 2016.

Swedlund, Alan C. *Shadows in the Valley: A Cultural History of Illness, Death, and Loss in New England, 1840–1916*. Amherst: University of Massachusetts Press, 2010.

Szefel, Lisa. *The Gospel of Beauty in the Progressive Era: Reforming American Verse and Values*. New York: Palgrave Macmillan, 2011.

Tarbell, Ida M. *In the Footsteps of the Lincolns*. New York: Harper, 1924.

Tarbell, Ida M. *The Life of Abraham Lincoln*. 2 vols. New York: Doubleday & McClure, 1900.

Temple, Wayne C. *Abraham Lincoln: From Skeptic to Prophet*. Mahomet, IL: Mayhaven Publishing, 1995.

Temple, Wayne C. *By Square & Compass: Saga of the Lincoln Home.* Mahomet, IL: Mayhaven, 2002.

Thomas, Benjamin P. *Abraham Lincoln: A Biography.* New York: Knopf, 1952; rev. ed. Carbondale: Southern Illinois University Press, 2008.

Thomas, Benjamin P. *Lincoln's New Salem.* 1934; rev. ed. Carbondale: Southern Illinois University Press, 1987.

Thomas, Benjamin P. *Portrait for Posterity: Abraham Lincoln and His Biographers.* New Brunswick, NJ: Rutgers University Press, 1947.

Thomas, Dale. *Lincoln's Old Friends of Menard County, Illinois.* Charleston, SC: History Press, 2012.

Thompson, William Y. "Sanitary Fairs of the Civil War." *Civil War History* 4 (March 1958): 51–67.

Tomso, Gregory. "Lincoln's 'Unfathomable Sorrow': Vinnie Ream, Sculptural Realism, and the Cultural Work of Sympathy in Nineteenth-Century America." *European Journal of American Studies* 6, no. 2 (2011): 1–12.

Tubbs, Anna Malaika. *The Three Mothers: How the Mothers of Martin Luther King, Jr., Malcolm X, and James Baldwin, Shaped a Nation.* New York: Flat Iron Books, 2021.

Varon, Elizabeth R. "Tippecanoe and the Ladies, Too: White Women and Party Politics in Antebellum Virginia." *Journal of American History* 82 (Sept. 1995): 494–521.

Venet, Wendy Hamand. *Neither Ballots nor Bullets: Women Abolitionists and the Civil War.* Charlottesville: University Press of Virginia, 1991.

Venet, Wendy Hamand. *A Strong-Minded Woman: The Life of Mary Livermore.* Amherst: University of Massachusetts Press, 2005.

Vidal, Gore. *Lincoln.* New York: Random House, 1984.

Walvin, James. *Manliness and Morality: Middle-Class Masculinity in Britain and America, 1800–1940.* Manchester, UK: Manchester University Press, 1991.

Warren, Louis Austin. *Lincoln's Parentage and Childhood: A History of the Kentucky Lincolns Supported by Documentary Evidence.* New York: Century Co., 1926.

Warren, Louis Austin. "The Woman in Lincoln's Life with Special Emphasis on Her Cultural Attainments." *Filson Club Historical Quarterly* 20 (July 1946): 207–19.

Washington, John E. *They Knew Lincoln.* Edited by Kate Masur. New York: Oxford University Press, 2018.

White, Barbara A. *Visits with Lincoln: Abolitionists Meet the President in the White House.* Lanham, MD: Lexington Books, 2011.

White, Jonathan W. *A House Built by Slaves: African American Visitors to the Lincoln White House*. New York: Rowman & Littlefield, 2022.

White, Ronald C. *The Eloquent President: A Portrait of Lincoln through His Words*. New York: Random House, 2005.

Whites, LeeAnn, and Alecia P. Long, eds. *Occupied Women: Gender, Military Occupation, and the American Civil War*. Baton Rouge: Louisiana State University Press, 2009.

Wittenmyer, Annie. *Under the Guns: A Woman's Reminiscences of the Civil War*. Boston: E. B. Stillings, 1895.

Wick, Robert G. "'He was a Friend of Us Poor Men': Ida M. Tarbell and Abraham Lincoln's View of Democracy." *Indiana Magazine of History* 114 (Dec. 2018): 255–82.

Williams, Ellen. *Harriet Monroe and the Poetry Renaissance: The First Ten Years of Poetry, 1912–1922*. Urbana: University of Illinois Press, 1977.

Williams, Frank J., and Michael Burkhimer, eds. *The Mary Lincoln Enigma: Historians on America's Most Controversial First Lady*. Carbondale: Southern Illinois University Press, 2012.

Wilson, Douglas A. *Honor's Voice: The Transformation of Abraham Lincoln*. New York: Knopf, 1998.

Wilson, Douglas A. "William H. Herndon and Mary Todd Lincoln." *Journal of the Abraham Lincoln Association* 22 (Summer 2001): 1–26.

Wilson, Douglas A., and Rodney O. Davis, eds. *Herndon's Informants, Letters, Interviews and Statements about Abraham Lincoln*. Urbana: University of Illinois Press, 1998.

Winkle, Kenneth J. "Abraham Lincoln: Self-Made Man." *Journal of the Abraham Lincoln Association* 21 (Summer 2000): 1–16.

Winkle, Kenneth J. *Abraham and Mary Lincoln*. Carbondale: Southern Illinois University Press, 2011.

Winkle, Kenneth J. *Lincoln's Citadel: The Civil War in Washington*. New York: Norton, 2013.

Winkle, Kenneth J. *The Young Eagle: The Rise of Abraham Lincoln*. Dallas: Taylor Trade Publishing, 2001.

Winkler, Donald. *Lincoln's Ladies: The Women in the Life of the Sixteenth President*. Nashville: Cumberland House, 2004.

Woloch, Nancy. *Women and the American Experience*. 5th ed. New York: McGraw Hill, 2011.

Wormeley, Katherine. *The United States Sanitary Commission: A Sketch of Its Purposes and Work*. Boston: Little, Brown, 1863.

Wyllie, Irvin G. *The Self-Made Man in America*. New Brunswick, NJ: Rutgers University Press, 1954.

Young, James Harvey. Randall's Lincoln: An Academic Scholar's Biography." *Journal of the Abraham Lincoln Association* 19 (Summer 1998): 1–13.

Zall, Paul M. *Lincoln on Lincoln*. Lexington: University of Kentucky Press, 1999.

Zboray, Ronald J., and Mary Saracino Zboray. "Whig Women, Politics, and Culture in the Campaign of 1840: Three Perspectives from Massachusetts." *Journal of the Early Republic* 17 (Summer 1997): 277–315

Ziparo, Jessica. *This Grand Experiment: When Women Entered the Federal Workforce in Civil War–Era Washington, D.C.* Chapel Hill: University of North Carolina Press, 2017.

INDEX

Italicized page numbers indicate figures.

STACY LYNN edited Abraham Lincoln's papers for nearly twenty-five years. She is the author or editor of four books, including a biography of Mary Lincoln. She is currently associate editor of the Jane Addams Papers.

Illinois Lives
Memoirs from the Prairie State

Memoirs—the personal, evocative, true stories we tell—have the power to educate, enlighten, and entertain. In its continuous and longstanding goal to amplify diverse voices, for more than fifty years SIU Press has published hundreds of memoirs and autobiographies. The Illinois Lives series contains those that remain in print, offering readers a collection of compelling narratives that capture the richness of lived experiences in the Prairie State.

Books in Illinois Lives: Memoirs from the Prairie State

Wings Over Illinois
Arthur E. Abney

The Boy of Battle Ford and the Man
W. S. Blackman
SHAWNEE CLASSICS

Growing Up with Southern Illinois, 1820–1861: From the Memoirs of Daniel Harmon Brush
Daniel Harmon Brush, edited by Milo Milton Quaife
SHAWNEE CLASSICS

Foothold on a Hillside: Memoirs of a Southern Illinoisan
Charles Caraway
SHAWNEE BOOKS

Growing Up in a Land Called Egypt: A Southern Illinois Family Biography
Cleo Caraway
SHAWNEE BOOKS

The Gentleman from Illinois: Stories from Forty Years of Elective Public Service
Alan J. Dixon

It's Good to Be Black
Ruby Berkley Goodwin

The Personal Memoirs of Julia Dent Grant: (Mrs. Ulysses S. Grant)
Julia Dent Grant, edited by John Y. Simon
WORLD OF ULYSSES S. GRANT

Chicago Heights: Little Joe College, the Outfit, and the Fall of Sam Giancana
Charles Hager and David T. Miller

A Nickel's Worth of Skim Milk: A Boy's View of the Great Depression
Robert J. Hastings
SHAWNEE BOOKS

A Penny's Worth of Minced Ham: Another Look at the Great Depression
Robert J. Hastings
SHAWNEE BOOKS

Always of Home: A Southern Illinois Childhood
Edgar Allen Imhoff
SHAWNEE BOOKS

Reminiscences of a Soldier's Wife: An Autobiography
Mrs. John A. Logan
SHAWNEE CLASSICS

Loving Lincoln: A Personal History of the Women Who Shaped Lincoln's Life and Legacy
Stacy Lynn

A Decisive Decade: An Insider's View of the Chicago Civil Rights Movement during the 1960s
Robert B. McKersie

Tell Us a Story: An African American Family in the Heartland
Shirley Portwood

Nobody Calls Just to Say Hello: Reflections on Twenty-Two Years in the Illinois Senate
Philip J. Rock and Ed Wojcicki

A Woman's Story of Pioneer Illinois
Christiana Holmes Tillson, edited by Milo Milton Quaife
SHAWNEE CLASSICS

Autobiography of Silas Thompson Trowbridge M.D.
Silas Thompson Trowbridge
SHAWNEE CLASSICS

The Maverick and the Machine: Governor Dan Walker Tells His Story
Dan Walker

Son of Southern Illinois: Glenn Poshard's Life in Politics and Education
Carl Walworth and Glenn Poshard

Woman from Spillertown: A Memoir of Agnes Burns Wieck
David Thoreau Wieck

Army Life of an Illinois Soldier: Including a Day-by-Day Record of Sherman's March to the Sea
Charles W. Wills
SHAWNEE CLASSICS